Touching the Ancient One

A True Story of
Tragedy and Reunion

Rupert Pratt

Touching the Ancient One: A True Story of Tragedy and Reunion

Cover photo taken by Rupert Pratt in 1998 from Kesugi Ridge. In the background is the Susitna River Valley, near Gold Creek, Alaska.

Published by Wheatmark®
610 East Delano Street, Suite 104
Tucson, Arizona 85705 U.S.A.
www.wheatmark.com

Publisher's Cataloging-In-Publication Data
(Prepared by The Donohue Group, Inc.)

Pratt, Rupert.
  Touching the ancient one : a true story of tragedy and reunion / by Rupert Pratt.

    p. : ill.; cm.
  Includes bibliographical references.
  ISBN: 1-58736-581-2

1. Pratt, Rupert. 2. Survival after airplane accidents, shipwrecks, etc.—Alaska. 3. Aircraft accident victims—United States—Biography. 4. United States. Army Air Forces—Biography. 5. Airplanes, Military—Accidents—Alaska. 6. Aircraft accidents—Alaska. I. Title.

TL553.7 .P73 2006
613.6/9/0973 2005937107

I dedicate this book to the memory of those men whose lives were cut short on Alaska's Kesugi Ridge:

Earl Betscher
Edward Burge
James Hill
Edward Knapp
Richard Knickerbocker
Donald McDonough
Edmund McMahon
Alvi Raymer
Jacob Siplivy
William Ronald West-Watson

In tribute to those whose quick action saved lives:

Nick Botner
Cliff Hudson
Carl Russell
Don Sheldon

In salute to my fellow survivors:

Edward Fox
Eli LaDuke
Huey Montgomery
Edward Olson
Bobby Sallis

And to my family:

Millie Pratt, Gregory Pratt, Jonathan Pratt, Boriana Pratt, Elizabeth Milla Pratt, and Nathan Rupert Pratt

for bringing joy to my life.

Contents

Part Two
1996–2005

Acknowlegments

My thanks to all who played a part in producing this book, but first to Millie for more than fifty years of love and support, and lately for her excellent editing skills. Thanks to son Greg, whose gift got all this started, and for following through as a thoughtful and efficient proofreader. To son Jon, who recently chose to experience the Alaska wilderness with me. Also, special thanks to longtime friends Tom and Nancy DeVito for their reading, suggesting, and purposeful prodding.

Thanks to my fellow crash survivors, Ed Fox, Eli LaDuke (now deceased), Huey Montgomery (now deceased), Ed Olson, and Bobby Sallis, not only for their enduring friendship, but for their willingness to revive long-ago and painful memories.

Nick Botner, Cliff Hudson, and Dr. Carl Russell played essential parts in the rescue of six traumatized airmen in 1954. More recently, they have provided lost pieces of the puzzle. I also honor Don Sheldon (now deceased) for his major role in our rescue. I shall be forever grateful to these men.

Families have willingly contributed records, photographs, and memories. I'm grateful to them and to our entire reunion family. We are bound together by a tragic event of long ago, and more recently by the friendships and joys we've shared.

Introduction

On February 5, 1954, I was a passenger on a United States Air Force C-47 that crashed on a mountain ridge in interior Alaska. The accident was reported extensively at the time, and the story regained attention in 1996 when the survivors gathered for a reunion; interest was heightened because the families of the men who lost their lives were also invited. *People* magazine and several newspapers around the country comprehensively reported details of the reunion. However, accompanying narratives about the crash left me dissatisfied because of my firsthand knowledge. Furthermore, other accounts written over the years have omitted important information or just plain got it wrong.

I wanted my family, present members and those yet unborn, to have a true, detailed account. Call it egotism if you wish; I prefer to call it a sense of history. A modest booklet would be sufficient, I had thought.

I started writing soon after the first reunion in 1996. Not long into the project, I realized that my relatives would want to know more than the bare facts. They would want to know personal details, my thoughts, and ultimately the effect the incident had on my life. Moreover, I believed they would appreciate my trying to convey the spirit of the time and place. The modest booklet would have to be a little larger.

Even before the reunion year had ended, my thoughts centered on others who had been touched by the tragedy. Survivors, families, rescuers, and friends were, and continue to be, a part of my life. In addition, I considered the men who had died. They had become more to me than names on faded newsprint. I made two big decisions. The first was that I had to bring them all into the story. And second, the story had to come into the present. The project immediately took a colossal leap from a family history booklet to a full-fledged book.

I have divided the book into two parts, since it does deal with two different time periods. *Part One* contains the story of the crash and rescue, along with personal elements. *Part Two* details how the 1996 reunion came about and the relationships resulting from that. For the survivors, who had not seen one another for forty-two years, and for our families, the reunion was a significant event; the fact that we invited relatives of men who had died in the crash heightened emotions. The willingness and desire of those families to take part changed the complexion of the group in a positive way. There were other reunions beyond 1996 and there were trips back to Alaska and to the crash site on Kesugi Ridge. I have included those events.

I'm satisfied that I've given an accurate account of the accident. My memories are vivid, and I've used other primary sources to supplement my recollections. I've relied heavily on the memories of my fellow survivors and on the accident report, which contains our statements. That report also holds statements of other witnesses, rescue participants, and the official findings of the Air Force Board of Inquiry.

Another important and reliable source of information I credit to my mother, Glenna Morrison. She saved every letter I wrote to her while I was in the service. The letters, in addition to supplying personal details, also brought to mind related events I might otherwise have forgotten.

Writing the book (or "memoirs," if you wish) has been beneficial for me. Being forced to examine my feelings has been a cleansing process. For years, I shoved thoughts of the crash to the back of my mind, telling the story to only a few close friends. Back in 1954, I had a "suck up my gut and get on with it" attitude, a point of view not discouraged in the armed forces of that day. I have since come to understand that such tragedies have far-reaching effects on many lives. I'm convinced that some change—dare I call it growth—in my life can be traced directly to the events that took place during my two years in Alaska.

For the most part, the book is written as a first-person account. Nevertheless, in several places I have used other literary techniques to bring certain information to the story. Some people have been given fictitious names to prevent possible embarrassment. Where that is the case, the name is enclosed within quotes on the first use.

Throughout, I've been liberal with dialogue. Exact words from five decades ago do not easily spring to mind. Nevertheless, I do recall the essence of conversations. In some places, I've used dialogue between parties where I was not present. Those conversations are based on what the participants have told me. In some instances, they are a part of the historical record.

This book, though complete, doesn't mean that the story is finished. Bonds formed during the past nine years will be long-lasting, extending to several generations of the families involved. That is my hope—and my expectation.

Part One

1953–1957

Chapter One

Mountains are conspicuous in my story. Mountains and hills have been, even from my youth, my strongest symbols of life. I attribute such a viewpoint to my Appalachian upbringing. The hill behind our house was our pastureland. Twice a day I climbed it to bring the cows down for milking. Even now, I remember the rough outcroppings, the steep paths, the brier patches—and balancing those obstacles, the cool and shady oak and hickory groves that were a refuge against the often brutal summer heat. Those physical characteristics and others, along with the lessons they taught, have their symbolic counterparts in my life journey.

Salt Rock, West Virginia,[1] my growing up place, is hemmed in against the Guyandotte River by several hills, none tall enough to be called a "mountain." I knew them all intimately. An experience I had on one became a benchmark for me. The Johnnie Porter Hill rises somewhat above the others. Its northern base lies at a stream bordering what was my grandfather's property. The hill was mostly pastureland, alternating with wooded areas. No one lived on the hill, but there was an apple orchard on top.

Salt Rock Methodist Church had a men's Bible study group with half a dozen members of varying ages. At age fifteen, I was the youngest of the group and undoubtedly not its most devout member, having been a somewhat reluctant recruit. One night it was suggested that instead of meeting in a home or at church, we go to the top of Johnnie Porter Hill. That spelled adventure—more relevant to a fifteen-year-old than any spiritual growth that might result.

It was a night in early November, cool, but without wind. There was a cloudless sky with more stars than I had ever seen—before or since. The Milky Way stretched from horizon to horizon like a highway for God. We passed the night in the apple orchard, and under the guidance of the older men, sang hymns, prayed, read our Bibles by flashlight, and talked. God seemed close to me. The feeling lingered as we came down a frost-covered path next morning. That mountain memory is etched on my heart.

There have been other mountains, some touched only briefly, some observed from afar. One, however, has been especially significant for me—almost as much as the hills of my youth, and in some ways more so. Such a connection didn't happen overnight, and it didn't happen in isolation. It has its roots in a tragedy that occurred many years ago.

On October 10, 1953, I took an early morning bus from Salt Rock to Huntington where I boarded a train that would carry me across the United States to Oakland, California. Tucked into my handbag were my Air Force orders, safe from loss but handy enough to be produced on request. As with all written military orders, the wording was cryptic:

> Ea of the fol named amn is rel fr asgmt p/1 stu this orgn; TDY sta 1205th ASU, Ft Wadsworth Station Island NY; asgd & WP 2353d PerP Sq, 2349th PerP Gr (OR) (ConAC) Parks AFB Calif o/a 21 Sep 53 RUAT Comdr not earlier than 0001 & NLT 2400 15 Oct 53 for subq asgmt.
> A/3C EDWARD J. KNAPP AF13471380
> A/3C DONALD R MCDONOUGH AF13471365
> A/3C RUPERT C. PRATT AF15500802

In brief, three of us had been released from duty at Fort Wadsworth on Staten Island, given a three-week leave, and ordered to report to Parks Air Force Base for processing. It wasn't clearly stated, but we had been told that the "subq asgmt" was the Territory of Alaska, exact destination unknown. I knew that a couple hundred miles north of Huntington, near Pittsburg, Ed Knapp and Don McDonough were also preparing to leave. They would have duplicates of the orders I carried, and would, as I had, be saying their farewells to parents, relatives, and friends.

That four-day cross-country train trip to California was an exhilarating experience for me. Until joining the Air Force, I had been no farther from home than Springfield, Ohio, and then only once. Military time totaling five months had been entirely in the Northeast, and not too far removed from the towering walls of hardwood forests I had always known. West of Cincinnati the land changed drastically, but it didn't take me long to accept the novelty of a world where the sun rose and set on a far horizon.

My knowledge of the West came from a mix of college texts and Zane Grey stories. I was able, without much difficulty, to synchronize those viewpoints with reality. West of the Mississippi River, our train closely followed the routes of the Union Pacific and Central Pacific, the first lines to link the East and West Coasts. Even with my newfound appreciation for the plains, I felt more at home in the Rockies and the Sierra Nevada Mountains, especially the latter. Steep switchbacks and dark tunnels constantly surprised me during the half day it took the train to crawl up to the summit. We descended the less severe west side, and by the time we had reached the Sacramento Valley, I had become tired enough to want the trip to be over.

As absorbing as the scenery was during the trip, I had also been romanticizing about my eventual destination. At Fort Wadsworth, Knapp, McDonough, and I had received condolences for having drawn Alaskan duty. I politely listened to horror stories of living conditions there. Secretly, I was delighted. I had long been fascinated with "America's last frontier." Jack London's novels of the North had captivated me with descriptions of vast unpopulated wilderness, high mountains, wolf packs, and dogsled trails.

An airman from Ohio, near Ironton, was also in my car. We sat together, engaged each other in conversation, and agreed to stay together all the way to Parks. We arrived in Oakland on Wednesday, October 14, and boarded the ferry to San Francisco. The wind on the bay was cold; I wished I had heavier clothing. The weather had been warm until then, so we had worn our khaki uniforms.

We told the San Francisco taxi driver to take us to a "good but cheap hotel." We weren't due at Parks until the next day. In our shared room, we took showers, washing away the travel grime. Tired as we were, we knew it would likely be our only opportunity to see the city, so we dug our dress blues out of our duffel bags and went downtown. Our hotel was located high on one of the hills; we found the downhill cable car ride exciting.

There were many military personnel on the streets that night, from all branches. The Korean War had ended in July, less than four months after my enlistment, but the Cold War raged on and America was sending men and women to many parts of the world. San Francisco was one of the largest areas of embarkation. Businesses catered to military personnel, but in many ways took advantage of them. Every few steps we were accosted by someone with something to sell. I succumbed to one pitch: I had a photograph taken to have mailed to my mother. An "oil painting," it was called. I don't remember what I paid, but I recall the purchase being a rather serious jolt to my meager net worth. My mother eventually received it and was pleased.

Before going back to the hotel, we ate in a "fancy" restaurant, which was to be my last civilian meal for several weeks. The next morning, we located the bus station and traveled to Parks, about thirty miles away. Parks AFB[2] was a rather unpleasant interlude. It was large, with thousands of residents, permanent and transient. I never saw my traveling companion again. I think he was going to the Pacific area. We were on travel alert and couldn't leave the base. The average wait before shipment overseas was one to two weeks.

It remained cool, and swirling winds kicked up dust that stung our eyes. After a few days, as if to compensate, it started to rain. The dirt streets became muddy, and walking boards were placed alongside the low wooden buildings. There wasn't much to do. Each barracks had a sergeant-in-charge who was also a transient. Our sergeant would hold roll call in the morning and we would spend an hour policing the area, picking up cigarette butts and stray pieces of paper. After that, it was back to the barracks until mealtime. I spent most of my time reading, or writing letters. Most men didn't know exactly where they were going. When I was asked, I simply said, "Alaska." That was the destination of everyone in our barracks, and in several of the surrounding barracks. Our NCO[3] speculated that our group was going to Ladd Air Force Base at Fairbanks.

Ed Knapp and Don McDonough had also arrived, flying from western Pennsylvania. We were in different barracks, but saw one another every day. There were two other familiar faces from basic training days; I think both men were going to Japan.

In the BX[4] one day, I wandered into the jewelry section. I had been thinking about sending a gift to Millie Mereness. Not that it was a special occasion—I just wanted to send her something. I picked out a watch and spent most of the rest of my money. I rationalized that there wasn't anywhere else to spend it anyway. I put the watch in the mail the following morning.

My relationship with Millie needs explanation. We had met on the weekend of June 20. I was still in basic training at Sampson Air Force Base[5] in Geneva, New York, and had been invited home with roommates Thomas DeVito, Jr. and Walter Magdalenski, both from Schenectady, New York. It was the last weekend before we were to ship out to tech school. The war was winding down and the misery of basic was about to end, events enhancing our moods. Hobbie Easthom, another airman from the Huntington area, went with us. Walt had arranged for dates for us on Saturday night. He'd had some trouble finding someone for me, but had finally lined up the younger sister of one of the other girls. Her name was Mildred Mereness. I knew the date was just a one-time happening, so I gave it little thought.

We made the four-hour trip Saturday morning with a friend of Tom's father. I stayed at Tom's home. His parents, Tom, Sr. and Natalie, were welcoming and gracious. After an early dinner, we joined Walt and Hobbie and set off to meet the girls at the Mereness residence. Marion Mereness was Tom's date. Hobbie had been paired up with the cute and chatty Nancy Ross. Walt would be with Tootsie Versoci, whom he had dated before.

Walt made the introductions. Millie was a slender blue-eyed blonde, and lovely, I thought. She carried herself with dignity. I sensed right away that she was different from other girls I knew.

Millie and I rode with Walt and Tootsie. We went to a double feature movie at the Mohawk Drive-in Theater on Central Avenue. The time passed quickly as Millie and I talked. I soon realized that she was intelligent, with a depth of personality that intrigued me. Our backgrounds made for interesting conversation. Sometime during the evening, it came as a shock when she offhandedly told me she would be entering high school in the fall.

"How old *are* you?" I managed to ask.

"Fifteen."

I had recently turned twenty, with three years of college behind me, and I had assumed she was at least an upperclassman in high school. My capacity for jumping to conclusions had led me to imagine there might be something extraordinary happening. Now, to learn I was dating a child was highly disconcerting. *What was Walt thinking?* Why hadn't he told me? His head was close to Tootsie's in the front seat. I fought down the urge to punch him in the back.

The evening ended soon after a stop at a drive-in restaurant for milkshakes. We took Millie home first. While Tootsie and Walt waited in the car, I went onto the front porch with her. I felt awkward and confused. I'd had a good time, but I knew I wouldn't see her again. Even if that were possible, our age difference was too great an obstacle.

Yet, when the instant of parting came, I said, "Do you have paper and pencil?"

She opened the small purse she was carrying and produced both. I wrote my Sampson address on the paper and handed it to her.

"Should you want to write to me," I said. "I won't be there much longer, but they'll forward my mail."

She took it without saying anything, but I saw her glance back at me through the curtains on the front door as she closed it.

Basic training at Sampson ended, members of Flight 2547[6] said goodbye, and, for the most part, went their separate ways to tech schools. Walt went to Texas. I don't remember where Hobbie went. Seven of us—Ed Knapp, Tom DeVito, David Dill, Sam Caudle, Richard Boshart, John Kasha—and I went to New Jersey to attend Petroleum Analysis School. Airmen from other flights were also included, bringing our total to sixteen.[7] We were first sent to Fort Lee, Virginia, where it was soon discovered there had been a mistake; the real petroleum school was in Bayonne, New Jersey. After a week at Fort Lee, they sent us back north. Our living quarters were at Fort Wadsworth,[8] a U.S. Army post on Staten Island, across the bay from New York City. We commuted daily by military bus to Bayonne.

Tom invited me home with him on our second weekend after school started. He had dated Nancy Ross the weekend before and thought I might want to double date with them. Millie had been writing to me, long and interesting letters. I hesitated only briefly before accepting the invitation, and the pattern for the summer was set. Our weekends were full, and our dates were memorable events that sustained Tom and me throughout the week.

As early as my second date with Millie, I knew I was in trouble. In spite of myself, I had fallen in love. Her age was a big issue for me, however.

The weeks passed and we went to Schenectady almost every weekend. We took the train most of the time, but toward the end of our schooling, Tom's father let him take his Buick, which we parked outside the post. One weekend, my mother, Glenna Morrison, and my stepfather, Dawson, came to visit, making the long trip on a Trailways bus through Virginia and Pennsylvania. That was the only weekend I didn't see Millie.

The glamour of New York City drew us, too. We would often take the ferry over in the evenings to attend shows, ball games, or movies. Most of those activities were at reduced prices, or outright free to military personnel. How we kept up with our demanding schoolwork is a mystery. Several men didn't, and washed out.

School ended in September and we were granted leaves before shipping out; Tom to England along with Richard Boshart and Andy Breza, and me to Alaska with Ed Knapp and Don McDonough. We were all to put our newly acquired skills to work in "new petroleum laboratories" the Air Force had "just opened." I decided to go to Schenectady one last time before heading home. There were unresolved issues.

I had told Millie how I felt about her and that I wanted to marry her someday, hedging with, "but you're young and I'll be away two years, possibly more, depending on where I go after my Alaska duty. So—we probably shouldn't get too involved at this point."

During our last hours together, I repeated that pitiful rhetoric several times, secretly hoping that maybe we could push beyond it to a higher level of commitment.

"I love you, too," she finally conceded, "and it's possible we'll marry someday—but I *do* have three years of high school left."

I saw the wisdom in her argument and took the best deal I could negotiate—an uneasy agreement that we wouldn't forget each other— that we would hold open the issue of our love and deal with it later.

"I'll write as often as I can," she promised.

She did write often. I received several letters while on leave in Salt Rock. A couple more caught up with me at Parks. They were upbeat and full of promise. I missed her a great deal. I was excited about Alaska, but had the dismal feeling it might be two years before I saw Millie again. Much could happen in that time. Giving her the watch made me feel a little better.

On October 20, we received new orders indicating that our destination was indeed Ladd Air Force Base.[9] On Thursday, October 22, Air Force buses took us to the harbor in San Francisco, where we boarded the *USS Jackson*. The following morning, we sailed under the Golden Gate Bridge to begin our voyage north.

On October 29, six days after sailing, Knapp, McDonough, and I stumbled up from the depths of the *Jackson*. I stood transfixed at the rail. Tall, snow-covered mountains rose right out of the harbor into the early morning sky. Seward[10] lay strung out along the shore, looking insignificant compared to the splendor around it. I could see roads and other signs of civilization partway up the peaks. An automobile rolled along one of the streets. Lights twinkled and smoke curled up from dozens of low buildings. A bitterly cold wind whipped my trouser legs, reassuring me that I really was in Alaska.

Chapter Two

"Fatigues and fatigue jackets," the tech sergeant told our group as we gathered our belongings in the cramped sleeping quarters. "And long johns and sweaters, too. If you're smart, you'll dig out your scarves to cover your ears. Dammit, it's cold out there!"

His was the voice of authority. He had drawn Alaska duty for the third time.

We were anchored several hundred feet from shore, but a series of wooden snow-covered docks connected the boat to the mainland. It took several hours for all thirteen hundred of us to disembark and lug our gear up to the trains. Several locals watched from interested, but not unsympathetic faces. Before going ashore, we had been divided into groups according to destination. Three large Air Force bases would swallow most of the troops: Elmendorf[11] at Anchorage, Ladd at Fairbanks, and Eielson, a SAC[12] base thirty miles southeast of Fairbanks. A handful of Army men were going to Fort Richardson, near Anchorage. Alaska was peppered with far-flung outposts, most in the process of becoming part of the emerging DEW Line Command.[13] Many airmen were headed for those lonely spots by way of Elmendorf and Ladd.

Several trains waited. It was early afternoon before ours was finally loaded and ready to move. The passenger cars weren't equipped for comfort; many seats had been removed. McDonough looked around the interior and rolled his eyes. In the absence of overhead bins, we threw our luggage on the floor. There were about twenty of us in the car. Near the front was a large wood-burning stove that made the interior quite warm. A stack of firewood and kindling lay on the floor behind the stove. Two airmen were quickly assigned to keep the fire going.

After a while, our train moved slowly out of town and along the bay before turning up through a gap in the mountains. The windows fogged as we climbed higher. I was able to glimpse snow-laden trees lining the sides of the tracks. The number of trees diminished as we climbed higher. Sparse vegetation covered the high valleys. Rugged windblown mountain peaks surrounded us like hovering giant sentinels. Snow devils spiraled up from the mounds beside the tracks. I found a window seat and kept clearing a pane in order to look out.

We traveled through beauty difficult to describe, on into the night, which came early. The tech sergeant who had advised us about our apparel and who was ranking NCO in our car, opened C-ration boxes and heated some cans on top of the stove. C-rations, barely palatable in normal situations, now actually tasted good. Except for some crackers and fruit, we hadn't eaten since breakfast on the ship.

I was tired, and after eating, tried to sleep in my seat, without much success. Eventually, I found a bare spot on the floor big enough to stretch out. With my head on my handbag, I settled down for the night. The train lurched and squeaked, but I did manage to doze off. I awoke numerous times during the night, once when I heard someone say, "Anchorage." I got up and looked out a window, but couldn't see anything. Our coach was bumped a few times, and I judged we were dropping cars off on a siding. When we got underway again, the ride was smoother. Once, while stirring to change my position on the floor, I realized that the only sounds were the steady click-clack of the wheels on the rails and the rhythmic snoring of tired men.

Daylight brought still more astonishing scenery. We were in the Alaska Range, we were informed. Then we dropped down out of the mountains, and the tracks hugged lower forested slopes. The tech sergeant brought out C-rations again. Not being very hungry that time, I ate sparingly. I was tired, though. Sleeping on a hard floor allowed little rest.

The three of us had more time to talk on the last leg of our journey. Mostly, we speculated about what the "new lab" would be like. We envisioned a spacious interior filled with all the latest equipment. We got along well together, having compatible tastes and personalities.

We had begun to share personal, and often intimate, details of our lives. Knapp's parents were Joseph and Mary Knapp of Juniata, Pennsylvania. He had attended Juniata Elementary School and graduated from Dunbar Township High School in 1952. He told us about delivering *The Evening Standard*, the local Uniontown newspaper. Following graduation, he had worked at a concrete block plant at Little Summit, operated by his brother-in-law, Harry Williams. We agreed it was strange that I had also worked one summer at a building block plant belonging to one of my relatives.

An avid sports fan, Knapp followed every Steelers and Penguins game. During basic training, he had been our flag bearer, able to make the flag snap smartly when the flight came to attention. One of his most admirable attributes was his close attention to even the smallest detail, thereby setting a good example for McDonough and me. Knapp and I had grown closer in tech school, and we'd been pleased that we were going to be together in Alaska.

I hadn't known McDonough, who was from North Braddock, Pennsylvania, until tech school, since he had been in another flight. The only child of Ella Mae Sparrow had a manner of calm acceptance; he seemed unruffled by common annoyances, yet passionate about many things. His humor was dry, and just the medicine I often needed.

About noon, we passed through Nenana,[14] a little village along the Tanana River.[15] I could see many Native Americans on the streets near the tracks. It was Jack London's Alaska, I told myself. I pressed my face to the frosted glass so I wouldn't miss anything. We didn't stop, but moved slowly on along the frozen river, and then back up onto snow-covered ridges. It was cold outside, about ten below, someone said. Even so, it looked peaceful. Unlike in Seward the day before, there seemed to be no wind. Smoke from the occasional cabin curled straight up and then spread out, hanging in the air.

Almost exactly twenty-four hours after leaving Seward, we eased our way into Fairbanks.[16] The railroad paralleled the Chena River,[17] which ran through the town. I was somewhat surprised, having expected a village of moderate size. Instead, the city spread out for at least a mile, with mixed commercial and residential structures in great evidence. Near a metal bridge and to the left of the tracks was a large building that looked like a hospital. The city's business district was on the right. Modern buildings, one several stories high, dominated the area close to the river. However, my frontier expectations were appeased by several log structures nestled between other buildings in nearly every block.

Ladd was adjacent to the town, and at two o'clock we pulled in on a siding there. Blue trucks and buses were lined up along the tracks. Blue parka-clad figures, with faces indistinct within fur-encircled hoods, waited for us.

We emerged, carrying our duffel bags and handbags, the only two items we had been allowed since leaving Parks. I turned up the collar of my fatigue jacket against the cold. The four layers of clothing I was wearing seemed inadequate. I was suddenly despondent. I had been fine while traveling and seeing new things. Now, at the end of the journey, I didn't see much to be thrilled about. No high mountains were visible. The snow wasn't deep, but engulfed everything around the bleak station. It crunched under our feet like broken glass. Knapp and McDonough shot me looks only a few notches above despair.

We shivered while we waited for our names to be called. Gradually, we were separated into groups that I supposed were going to different parts of the base. As our group piled gear into waiting trucks, I told myself that two years wasn't really that long. At least I wasn't going to war—an assurance I hadn't had when I enlisted.

Nevertheless, for the first time, I had reason to question my decision. My mother had believed the war was near its end and that I should try to delay induction until I finished college. That meant serving in the Army, but for two years instead of four. In the early fifties, entering the military was almost a certainty for a healthy young man. It was either enlist or be drafted. However, being a college student was a way to delay that date with Uncle Sam. I entered Marshall College in January 1951. I wasn't trying to avoid service, but I took advantage of the rules to prolong induction. Deferral was automatic if the student passed a government test and continued to have passing grades. On graduation day, the deferral debt would become due, with the student expected to serve his time. Therefore, my options had been clear; either then or later, I'd be in the Army—or in the service of my choice.

By January 1953, through carrying extra credit and attending summer school, I had completed nearly three years toward a degree. I'd had two draft calls for which I had obtained deferrals and was awaiting a third call. I was getting tired of the process; it was a weight hanging over my head.

For more than two years, I had been watching close friends enter the military. Paul Swanson, Bill Hutchinson, Manford Hutchinson, and Jerry Adkins were in uniform. Ed Harbour was in Korea. His older brother, Wink, had served his time there and had returned. Marion Nida and Larry Gill were about to be drafted. Larry Lewis, a fellow football player at Barboursville High, had died early in the war. Carl Owens, from Tyler Creek, had come home wounded. Numerous other acquaintances had been drafted or had joined. A part of me just wanted to go and get it over with.

The military draft wasn't my only concern at that time. There was "Rose." My feelings for Rose dominated a major portion of my thinking, being a source of joy and pain, in somewhat equal proportions. I had watched her from afar for a long time before getting up nerve to approach. When I finally did overcome my timidity, I discovered, to my delight, that she had similar feelings toward me. The romance grew, then flourished over a period of several months. Eventually, though, when I approached the subject of my service responsibilities, she became rather distant with me.

No matter what angle I tried to approach it from, she appeared unwilling to enter a discussion. I reacted with anger and told her that we shouldn't see each other for a while. My push was answered with her shove, and we broke up. On reflection, it wasn't fair to burden her with the problem, especially when I was so indecisive about it myself. After our breakup, she remained constantly in my thoughts.

Early in the spring semester, my third draft notice arrived, and I decided to end the suspense. The Air Force, despite a longer enlistment period, was my first choice. Going to flight school was definitely on my mind. But the decision wasn't easy, since my mother and Dawson preferred I wait and do the shorter Army time. They were sure the war would soon be over; Eisenhower had promised. The 1952 election was the only one I recall in which Mother crossed party lines and voted Republican.

One day in late winter, with my dog, Spike, I climbed the hill behind my house. It was the hill I had climbed thousands of times in my life to bring down cows from the high pasture, to pick berries, to gather nuts, or just to be alone. It was my place for serious thinking, even during early childhood. That particular day was warm, and the trees seemed to be bursting with the promise of spring, although I knew there were still several weeks of cool weather to go. We climbed to the top, and I sat under a familiar honey locust tree. It was from there, during World War II, that I had watched squadrons of bombers overhead, so close that I could see the tail gunners moving around. Now, from my vantage point, I could see the tops of other hills receding in every direction, like brown cones with their bases touching. They were old hills, I had learned at Marshall, older even than the mountains of the American West. Things were open and unbounded up there, and the view was a far one. I spent an hour or more sitting under that tree, and when I was ready to go down, I had things fairly well sorted out.

In early March, I went with Ronnie Ray and Cline Bates to the recruiting station in Huntington and joined the United States Air Force. Except for the disappointment of eventually learning that my eyesight would disqualify me for flight school, I hadn't regretted enlisting. Now, though, beside the dismal railroad tracks at Ladd, I wondered what I had let myself in for.

We boarded the buses. McDonough and Knapp sat across the aisle from me. Their faces seemed to mirror my feelings. Ten minutes later, after passing an oil drum yard, a fuel tank farm, and meandering along what seemed like deserted back roads, we reached an area of high activity. Huge hangars sat near a runway with rows of fighter jets in front. Other large buildings were nearby, appearing to be headquarters, barracks, and mess halls. I spotted a movie theatre and a library. It was the heart of Ladd, I suspected. I began to feel better. We left that area, followed a concrete road around the ends of two runways, and entered a gravel-covered side road that was frozen so hard it would have felt like a paved highway had it not been for the gravel pelting the underside of the bus. We were soon unloading in front of a gray Quonset hut among other similar Quonset huts. It was mid-afternoon, and already darkness was settling on the landscape.

"Drop your gear inside and report to the quartermaster building right across the road there!" a master sergeant shouted. "You need to pick up Arctic clothing and your linens!"

The hut contained a dozen bunks with a rolled up mattress on each. Tall gray metal lockers lined the curved walls behind the bunks. I picked out a bed near the door and put my bags on it. McDonough and Knapp took the ones in line with mine, away from the door. An oil stove in the center dominated the room. The far end had another door and an enclosed room. I learned a few minutes later that our hut was just one of three backed up against a raised platform on which a large dayroom had been constructed. All three of the huts shared the dayroom. The flat side of the dayroom faced the main road and served as a common entrance.

The sign on the quartermaster building said it was the 5001st Supply Squadron. There were about thirty of us. Other squadrons on the base had absorbed the rest of the train passengers.

I shouted out my sizes when the clerk finally got to me. He laid out numerous articles on the counter. The winter gear consisted of heavy, bulky clothing: sweaters, pants, long johns, a pile hat, two pairs of new boots still in boxes, and a new pair of arctic mittens. I opened the boot boxes. There was a rubber pair that the clerk said was for in-between weather. The other box contained a pair of white felt "bunny boots," the kind everyone except new arrivals was wearing. My number twelves looked enormous. The rest of the clothing, except for a few items, wasn't new. In fact, some of it looked threadbare. The clerk laid a brown parka in front of me. Its fabric was similar to khaki and it had no fur around the hood. I had already learned that the fur filtered out ice crystals as breath was drawn inside. The majority of base inhabitants seemed to have blue parkas. The only advantage of the brown ones that I could see was their length. They reached almost to the knees.

"Can I have a blue parka?" I asked.

"You're POL,"[18] the clerk replied matter-of-factly, though not unkindly. "POL gets the brown!"

"Yeah, POL—you can tell by the smell!" someone in line chanted.

I felt my ears stinging. A corporal behind me nudged my elbow. "It's not an insult," he said, and then added, "Unless it comes from someone who's not POL! We'll be driving gas and oil rigs. Blue parkas are too expensive for our line of work." I wanted to say I was there to work in a petroleum lab but decided silence might be the better choice.

The chow hall was a good quarter-mile from our barracks. At dinner that evening, I mentioned the lab to some other men at my table. I was hoping to get information. They seemed to have no knowledge about it.

That evening, tired as I was, I wrote a letter to my mother. I tried to be upbeat.

Dear Mother,

Well, a long and tiring trip has finally come to an end and maybe now I can settle down for a while. I know you've been anxious to hear from me. I'm fine. We got here this afternoon about 2:00.

We boarded the USS *President Jackson* last Thursday morning and left Friday morning. We got in Seward, Alaska, Wednesday night. Altogether, I was on the ship about one week. We ran into a rough storm Monday, and had rough sailing the rest of the way. Everybody got pretty sick, including me, but I managed to keep my food down, which a lot of the fellows can't say. It's a miserable life aboard a crowded troop ship. There were 1300 of us and there was hardly any room to turn around. I pulled KP the whole trip, but I didn't mind that because it made the time go faster, and I didn't have much time to think about being seasick. We left Seward yesterday by troop train and got here today. Oh, I almost forgot to tell you where I'm at. I'm at Ladd AFB at Fairbanks, Alaska.

There's not really too much I can say for Alaska. It's just about what I thought it would be. It's wild, cold, and beautiful. You've never seen mountains until you've seen these. Mt. McKinley is not too far from here. Really, I believe I'm going to like it here just fine. The base is pretty nice. We can buy anything we want, just like at home. I don't know about my job yet, because I haven't been here long enough.

. . . it was fifteen below today at 4:00.[19]

Chapter Three

Later in the evening of our first day at Ladd, Tech Sergeant Leslie Hoover, new top sergeant for POL, discretely took McDonough, Knapp, and me into a corner of the dayroom. He was a quiet man, mild in speech and manner, which didn't keep him from being direct.

"You men have been telling everybody you're going to be working in a petroleum laboratory. I don't know where you got that idea. If you look at your orders again, you'll see there's no mention of a lab. In fact, there's no petroleum lab here." His tone was apologetic without being condescending. "We're all assigned to flightline refueling—or to fuel storage. Sorry you had to learn about it this way. Somebody slipped up if they told you different."

McDonough and I sat in the dayroom for some time. I vented my anger at those up the chain of command who had sent us there under "false pretenses." McDonough was angry, too, I could tell, although he was less vocal about it. Knapp went quietly back into the hut. I could see him through the door as he continued to unpack his bags. Eventually we joined him.

Knapp's method of dealing with adversity seemed to be quietly thinking things through. I sat back and waited for his judgment in the matter, knowing it would soon come. McDonough, too, seemed to be waiting, lying on his bunk with his hands behind his head. Knapp had been rolling and meticulously lining up socks in the tray of his footlocker. Finally, he closed the lid and sat on it.

"We can fight this," he said. When, after a few seconds, we hadn't commented on his announcement, he continued. "First, we have to find out why they sent us here."

McDonough broke his period of silence. "Maybe it's the same kind of thinking that sent us to Virginia instead of Staten Island!"

"No disrespect to Sergeant Hoover, but he's new here, too," Knapp said. "Maybe Ladd's opening a lab. Maybe they sent us here knowing that and just wanted to get us in place."

"Who do we ask?" McDonough said.

"POL commander. He'd know for sure. We'll go see him tomorrow."

For the next few hours, we clung to the strand of hope that Knapp had woven, but the truth wasn't long in coming. There was no lab or plans for one. POL was simply shorthanded and needed every able body available. It was nothing personal, our commander told us the next day at the POL office. It was just the reality of "keeping aircraft in the Alaskan skies." Of course, that explanation wasn't something we were ready to accept. We felt as if we'd been shanghaied. We agreed that we wouldn't let matters rest.

All new group arrivals had to attend several days of orientation. Buses transported us to various facilities that played key roles in keeping a large base operational. Those educational tours alternated with lectures in the spacious central base theatre. Topics included arctic living and the special conditions we might face. One particular subject impressed me. We were promised a court-martial should we be caught running outside when the temperature was minus 25 degrees or lower. The linings of our lungs would undoubtedly freeze under those circumstances, we were told.

After orientation, McDonough, Knapp, and I were assigned to the base gas station, servicing civilian vehicles. We grumbled a little among ourselves, but did our work. The sergeant-in-charge was short and somewhat rotund, looking to be pushing forty. The other men called him "Pops," so we did, too. There was generally personnel confusion at the busy station but with minor damage, since everyone just went ahead and did what they knew had to be done.

We left Pops' station after a week, when we were assigned to the bulk storage area, the "on-the-flightline" source of fuel. We ran the gas station for military vehicles and filled rigs that serviced non-jet aircraft. In our care were several storage tanks filled with two grades of aviation gasoline. A railroad siding ran alongside the tanks. Every day or so, tanker cars of fuel were dropped off for us to unload. We also stored and dispensed diesel oil. We had been assigned to the area because we weren't trained to drive refueling rigs.

We quickly mastered all the jobs on the site. None was difficult, just messy. The fuel and oils we handled quickly saturated our boots, turning them brown. Our clothing smelled of gasoline and diesel fuel. No coin-operated laundry was available to wash our parkas. To get them cleaned took at least three days in the base laundry, but we needed our parkas every day. Temperatures stood at the zero range and often well below. I went to the quartermaster.

"I want to go to church on Sundays," I explained to the corporal at the desk. "I need boots and a parka for work and another outfit for other times."

"No," he said firmly. "I know it's a problem with you guys, but we have orders. One set of arctic gear for each airman. When what you're wearing gets real bad, we'll give you another one—but only one at a time!" Then he added, "And never *blue* parkas!"

We rode base buses back and forth, wearing our smelly clothing. I imagined that people avoided sitting next to me.

Staff Sergeant James Crawford was in charge. Sergeant Crawford was different from the military authority we were used to. We had expected the no-nonsense, little recourse handling we had experienced throughout basic and tech school. Instead, Crawford, slow-talking and reflective, greeted us as equals and even asked our opinions. He was in his early thirties, I judged.

On our first day, Crawford supplied each of us with our own coffee mug from his large assortment.

"This sure isn't home," he said, his extended arms indicating the twelve-by-twelve flightline shack. "But I try to keep it as homey as I can."

His wife had just arrived from the States and had rented a cabin for them in Fairbanks. She was blonde and pretty. She usually dropped him off in the morning and drove off in the two-tone, late model Chevrolet he had driven up the challenging Alcan Highway. We looked forward to her brief visits, although we didn't mention that fact to Crawford. He occasionally brought the car alone, parked it behind the shack, and ran an extension cord out to plug into his engine's head bolt heater.[20]

Eight men worked at the site, although we were never all there at the same time. The new arrivals, Knapp, McDonough, and I, three civilians, an airman first class, and Crawford made up the workforce. Two of the civilians took turns working the less hectic night shift.

As we settled into a routine, I began to look for outside interests. Staff Sergeant Dale Watson, coach of the squadron basketball team, approached me about trying out. Mostly they played other squadrons, but also had some games against the University of Fairbanks, he said. It seemed a good fit, since I was interested in sports. It turned out they needed a center badly, and my six-foot-two-inch frame, though not extraordinary, was adequate to land me the position. Practice began right away, and was to run three or four times a week in the evening hours.

Life at Ladd wasn't all work, and I wasn't unhappy. I was interested in learning what it was like to live in the Far North. I explored the base, not just the populated areas, but the full perimeter, riding one of the buses or hitching a ride. A few areas were off limits, of course. Birch Hill, north of the runways, contained many fuel tanks. One day, Crawford took me up there. It was isolated except for an Army ski patrol we ran into on one of the back roads.

Knapp, McDonough, and I went into Fairbanks on one of our days off. We rode a base bus to the main gate and walked from there. A large sign outside the gate announced that it was "America's Farthest North Air Force Base."

It was a cold day and the town was enshrouded in "ice fog."[21] We explored several shops and stores, many of them log structures, before stopping at a bar for sandwiches and beer. Later, we enjoyed a movie in a theater inside the Chena Building, a tall silver-colored structure near the river.

Before going back to the base, I purchased a record player for thirty-five dollars. All three of us had brought 45 rpm phonograph records with us; Knapp added some more to his collection that day. His favorite was "In the Mission at St. Augustine," which he played repeatedly.

I wanted to buy a flight jacket, but didn't have enough money. The blue-gray waist-length jackets were popular, but expensive.

Buying one would set me back half a month's pay. They were non-military, but accepted in the Alaska Command as proper dress with either military or civilian clothing. It was the best solution to the dirty brown parka problem, even though they weren't as warm as parkas. I resolved to save money for the purchase.

Our quick consensus about Fairbanks was that it still had a frontier town feel. We had seen bearded men who looked as if they had just returned from their gold diggings. Some wore side arms. Someone had told me there were fifteen thousand people and forty bars within the city limits. From what we had seen, the bar figure didn't seem exaggerated. None of us had an interest in frequenting barrooms, so we agreed we'd seen enough of the town for the time being. When warm weather arrived, we'd get out into the surrounding countryside, providing we were still there.

One thing we noticed that day was the ratio of men to women. About half the girls and women we saw were Native American, most wearing beautiful fur parkas and other articles of clothing indicative of their heritage. We were later told that there were five men to every woman in the Ladd/Fairbanks environment, and most of those were married to servicemen. Romance, should we decide to pursue it, might present a challenge.

Basketball went well. We played our first game against the officers of one of the flight squadrons and I managed to survive against their six-four center. I was having fun, even though the petroleum laboratory debacle still weighed on my mind.

McDonough and Knapp also seemed to be adjusting to Ladd. I had noticed that they shared a common commitment. Good Catholics

5001 Supply Squadron, Ladd AFB, November 1953

to the core, and despite the parka problems we had, they attended Mass every Sunday, ordering their lives so that nothing interfered with their attendance. If one of them was more devout, I guess it was Knapp. He'd shower and shave, comb his brown hair until every strand was exactly in place, then brush and check his uniform before leaving the Quonset hut for the chapel on the edge of our squadron area.

McDonough's heart was just as pure, I'm sure, but there was a more relaxed quality to his preparation. His thick black hair seldom needed combing, and he didn't seem to be in a hurry. His dress was as casual as the military allowed. He was inclined to leave things lying around and would sometimes rush back to get a hat or some other essential part of his wardrobe. Nevertheless, I don't remember him missing church while we were in the 5001st Supply.

I hadn't been going to church—a recent change. My early years had been centered on the little Methodist church at Salt Rock, and my mother had modeled faith. As a boy, I saw it at work in many ways, but most often in small things. Once, I lost the plastic eyepiece of a telescope given to me by my Aunt Gaynelle. It had fallen off several times and Mother had reminded me to be careful with it. I was across the road, searching frantically among the leaves under an apple tree when she called to me.

"Lost it again, didn't you?"

"It's somewhere under this tree. It has to be!"

She was standing in the kitchen doorway, a good hundred feet away.

"I'll pray about it," she said.

I continued searching, feeling more frustrated by the minute. Her voice was calm.

"Back up a few feet. Now turn to your left." I did as she said. "Now take a couple of steps. Look down."

There lay the eyepiece, inches from my shoes. Had she seen it drop? I don't know. In any event, that kind of thing couldn't help but make an impression on my young mind, and probably went a long way toward strengthening my own faith. College, and exposure to the "scientific attitude" had failed to damage it, although I did become more inclined to question. When something in my inherited belief system didn't seem to fit reality, it became subject to close examination. That bothered Mother.

"But that goes against what the Bible says," she said on more than one occasion.

My usual rebuttal would start with, "That's what you *think* the Bible says."

At that point, I'd get a queasy feeling in my stomach. I was up against not only her unshakable beliefs, but also a formidable wall of Salt Rock's saints, present and departed. Nevertheless, I would plunge ahead.

"Maybe this is what it means," and I'd lay out my ideas.

She would always listen. Sometimes she would even make minor concessions, but generally my voice was like a toy arrow against a castle wall. It would have been much easier on both of us if I could have accepted her more fundamental line of thought.

If I had been asked about the state of my faith during my adjustment time at Ladd, I would have pronounced it strong. However, young military personnel don't normally speak of such things, and I wasn't giving a lot of attention to spiritual matters at the time, anyway. I didn't feel the need for church fellowship, even though I had made a promise to Mother. It was a long way from Salt Rock to Fairbanks, and accountability seemed just as distant.

Crawford said to me one day, "Pratt, you're a farm boy, so you must have some experience in carpentry."

"Some," I admitted.

"Well—this shack just isn't big enough for all of us. I'm going to get some lumber and I want you and Knapp and McDonough to put on an addition. I want the building more than doubled in size. Can you do it?"

"Sure," I said, without giving Knapp or McDonough time to answer. I welcomed the chance to do something different.

"The three of you will be excused from your other duties while you're building it. You can start right now and figure out what lumber we need."

Crawford didn't waste any time getting materials, and we were soon hard at work putting in a cinderblock foundation, laying down a subfloor, and starting the framing. The weather was turning colder and it was difficult to work outside for long stretches. It was hard to take measurements or handle a hammer and saw while wearing big arctic mittens.

On November 23, I wrote in a letter to my mother:

> I have been doing just about every kind of work. I'm a carpenter now. The sarge gave me a hammer and some lumber and told me to build a new shack. I fixed the foundation and got the subfloor on today. It will probably take a week or so to finish it.[22]

In the meantime, we had learned from an officer in the squadron that there actually *was* a petroleum laboratory at Elmendorf AFB. Together, we went to see our POL commander. He explained again that Ladd was extremely shorthanded. We told him we felt betrayed, having been trained in petroleum analysis and promised the chance to use that training. He was understanding of our position, but held out little hope. He did promise to talk to Capt. Wilson, our squadron commander, about the feasibility of getting us transferred.

"As a matter of fact," he said, "you'd be better off staying here and changing your MOS[23] from Petroleum Analysis to POL. You'll advance in rank faster. It's hard to get promotions if you're working outside your MOS."

We left his office feeling as if we hadn't made much headway.

The building project was coming along well, and we plunged into it with even more vigor while we waited for an answer. Crawford pooh-poohed our efforts toward a transfer.

"What more could you want than what you've got right here?" he asked, handing me a cup of steaming coffee.

I didn't answer.

Then, one afternoon in late November, Crawford stuck his head out the door as McDonough and I were pounding boards onto the side of the new addition.

"Just got a call from the CO's office. You three fellows are to get back there as soon as you can and pick up new orders. You're being shipped out to Elmendorf. Leaving tonight!" Then his face took on a pained expression. "Who the hell's gonna finish this shack?"

"It's almost done, anyway," Knapp said. "You'll make out just fine."

None of our trio really gave a hoot about the shack at that point. We hurried up to the main road and caught the next bus back to the 5001st. We grinned and punched one another every chance we got. McDonough kept chuckling aloud.

The clerk handed us our orders. McDonough's countenance fell.

"This isn't a transfer! They're sending us TDY[24] for one to three months!"

Capt. Wilson came out of his office door just at that moment. He must have heard our complaints. We weren't trying to hide them.

"That's the best we could do," he said. "The petroleum lab is on Elmendorf, but it's run by the Army. They use their own personnel and have a civilian director. We had to do some fast-talking to get you in there for even a short time. I can't give you much hope that you'll stay longer than three months, if even that. The only hope I *can* give you is that sometimes things change. By the way—you'll be living with the Army at Fort Richardson during your stay there."

We packed our duffel bags and handbags, stowed the rest of our belongings in our footlockers, and carried them across the road to the quartermaster's for storage. I hated to leave my record player behind, but had no choice. I tried one last time with the corporal, who by then knew me quite well.

"How about trading these brown parkas for blue ones?"

"Not a chance!"

"Maybe new clean bunny boots?"

"Have a good trip!"

Our airplane, a C-124 Globemaster[25] transport, was due to take off at 8 PM. We stood inside the terminal window, looking out at the monster. Some of our refueling rig drivers referred to them as "bumblebees." It took a full five thousand gallon rig to fill one.

It was my first flight. I hadn't had a chance to be around airplanes since second or third grade. During World War II, Dawson had taken a job at the Naval Ordinance plant in South Charleston, and we had lived there and at Spring Hill for two years. At nearby Charleston, there was a "seaplane base" located on the banks of the Kanawha River, near the business district. I'd often sit on a grassy knoll watching the activities while my mother shopped. When I thought no one was watching, I'd go down onto the docks where I could touch the single-engine floatplanes. Once, I had one foot on a pontoon before I was stopped by a burly, though smiling, aviator. He then helped me stand on a strut and look into the cockpit. That was a thrill I never forgot, and one that no doubt caused me to be even more enamored by airplanes.

Despite that infatuation, I had chosen to take the train from West Virginia to California so I could see the West up close. The flight to Anchorage was a thrill for me. I hadn't abandoned my dream of learning to fly, but it had been seriously curtailed. My friend Paul Swanson from Salt Rock had recently finished cadet training and was flying jets. I was envious and still nursing disappointment that my eyes weren't strong enough to qualify me for pilot training.

Paul had consoled me with, "There are ways to learn to fly without the Air Force teaching you."

About twenty of us boarded the C-124. We sat in bucket seats along both sides. Our bags had already been lashed onto the deck toward the front. We took off on time. I was surprised at the amount of vibration as we lifted off the runway and got into the air. It seemed to me that the aircraft struggled to gain altitude. Then we leveled off and got up to cruising speed. It was a smooth ride all the way to Anchorage. We landed at Elmendorf about nine-thirty.

Chapter Four

An Army vehicle came to the air terminal at Elmendorf to pick us up. The driver stood near the ramp as we exited the C-124, calling out our names until we heard and acknowledged. Although there would have been room for two of us in the cab, he motioned us all into the back. It was a cold ride, even though the temperature was higher than it had been in Fairbanks. There was an abundance of snow on the ground.

The truck left the base and followed a four-lane road for several miles before entering the main gate at Fort Richardson. A few minutes later, we pulled alongside a green Quonset hut. The driver left as soon as we had our gear out of the back.

A soldier stepped out of another hut and approached us.

"I'm Corporal 'Compton,'" he said. "Welcome to Fort Rich. This is the Quartermaster Depot Company. You men are to bunk in this building during your stay. Report to Capt. 'Reardon' in the morning for further orders."

"Do you work in the lab?" McDonough asked.

"Yes, I do. There are two of us at present, not including the director. You caught us at a good time. We're shorthanded."

"And where's the lab?" Knapp inquired.

"At Elmendorf. You must have come right by it. You'll see it tomorrow."

I would have liked to ask more questions, but Compton seemed to be in a hurry. We dragged our gear into the hut. Three bunks were unoccupied, with sheets and brown Army blankets folded neatly on the mattresses. Obviously, they had anticipated our arrival.

"Hey—the Air Force is here!" someone said from a corner of the hut. "We've been looking for you."

"You all spies, or what?" another asked.

"Fact is," I said, "we're here to find out how the Army gets such superior food and lodging!"

The laughter was good-natured. It was a common point of agreement that the Army had the worst food of all the services. The Navy had the best, I was convinced. During tech school in Bayonne, we had eaten the noon meal at a Navy cooking school. Lodging was another matter. The Air Force seemed to go out of the way to find the most run-down and dilapidated buildings to house personnel. I looked around the interior of the hut. Painted in varying shades of green, it was pleasant, quite different from the Quonset hut that had been our home at Ladd.

We had gotten used to the Army, having attended their school at Bayonne and having lived at Fort Wadsworth on Staten Island. We were used to ribbing and knew how to give it back. We could spit-polish with the best. The only time the Army had given us something we didn't handle well had been before tech school. When the Air Force sent us to Fort Lee by mistake, we had arrived during a severe heat wave. There a week, we were required to dress in class A uniform for every meal, ties and all. In addition, we stood reveille and retreat every day, sweating in the stifling heat, the wind stinging our faces with sand. We were overjoyed to leave Fort Lee. In general, though, the Army didn't intimidate us.

A tall, lanky soldier held out his hand.

"Name's 'Midkiff.' I'm from West Virginia. Where you from?"

"Would you believe West Virginia?"

"No—whereabouts?"

"A little place called Salt Rock."

His eyes opened wide.

"I'm from Chapmansville.[26] I go through Salt Rock every time I go to Huntington."

"And I've been through Chapmansville every time I've been to Logan."

I had found a friend. Midkiff would eventually give me a tour of Fort Richardson. However, it was Private First Class George Hyek who came to greet us the following morning. His pleasant face and friendly manner was welcome.

"You'll like it here. It's interesting work. 'Collingsworth,' the director, is okay to work for after you get to know him. They said you'd be here a month."

"One to three," Knapp corrected.

Hyek smiled.

"Well—with the Army, it seldom turns out the way it's planned. You could end up spending your whole tour here."

Capt. Reardon was "regular Army." We were guests, he said, but were expected to live by Army rules, stand inspection, and assume other duties. We weren't privileged. We'd travel to Elmendorf each day with the other soldiers assigned to the lab. We saluted sharply and backed out of his office, somewhat subdued.

Hyek and Compton were waiting in the cab of the truck with the engine running. Knapp got in with them. McDonough and I got in the back. The fifteen-minute ride was again a cold one. We'd take turns in the cab, we were assured.

The lab was a large building, somewhat isolated from other base buildings. Short scrubby pines surrounded it. One end had a garage at a lower level. We parked inside and took the interior stairs to the upper level.

Hyek introduced us to Collingsworth. He was heavyset, mid-to-late forties, and intense. He invited us to sit, and immediately started grilling us about our training. His questions were direct and personal. The three of us squirmed, answered as best we could, then relaxed a little when the questions stopped. He then outlined the expectations he had of us. The list was long.

It had been three months since we'd seen a lab. I found myself having to hit the books on some of the tests. They weren't as demanding as some we had encountered in school, but they were exacting, nevertheless.

The lab itself was a large room, about forty-by-forty, with tables and sinks in the center and along two sides. Another side was reserved for storage of untested fuel samples, mostly in jerry cans, but sometimes in smaller containers. The stockroom was toward the front of the building and backed up against Collingsworth's office. High shelves around all four sides of the stockroom were filled with flasks, glass and rubber tubing, and other lab materials.

There were many samples on the waiting list, mostly aviation gasoline, but with a smaller quantity of jet fuel. The samples came from all over Alaska. Some were even from Canada. Every time there was a problem with an aircraft that in any way involved fuel, a sample had to be tested. Every aircraft that crashed had its fuel, if any could be recovered, sent to our lab to be checked for impurities that might have led to the crash. We were surprised by the number of aircraft accidents, and mentioned it to Collingsworth.

"Alaska is a harsh place," he said. "It kills engines—especially aircraft engines."

We settled into a routine, working five and a half days a week with every fifth night spent "tending furnace." Surrounded by buildings using oil, our petroleum lab was heated by coal. Every three hours, twenty-four hours a day, clinkers had to be dragged out of the big furnace and coal added. We were threatened with court-martial if we let the fire go out. Cold would come quickly into the drafty building, and there were many things that would freeze in the lab. In addition, the furnace couldn't be reached from inside the building. We had to put on parkas and go out the front and around to the side in order to enter the lower-level furnace room. We could sleep during the night if we wanted, but had to set an alarm for furnace tending. There was a mattress on one of the shelves in the storage room and a radio next to it. Various furnace tenders had donated books and magazines to the cause, so reading matter was extensive. Furnace tenders got the next day off.

My first shift as furnace tender was nearly a disaster. At the end of our workday, I drove the others to Fort Richardson, ate, and returned to the lab. The furnace was to be stoked at eight, eleven, two, and five o'clock, and after that I would drive back to Fort Richardson and leave the truck in front of my barracks for the others to pick up.

The eight o'clock tending went well. Hyek had shown me how to drag clinkers out and the proper amount of coal to insert. Besides, I had tended it all day with no problems.

By ten o'clock, I was tired of reading and decided to sleep awhile. I set the old mechanical alarm clock for eleven o'clock and lay down on the mattress. I dropped off to sleep quickly.

I'm not sure if it was the minor key music from the radio or the temperature that awakened me, but I bolted upright, knowing something was wrong. I turned on the light. The clock said three-ten. The alarm had failed to go off. I picked it up. I had forgotten to wind the alarm key. Angry with myself, I quickly put on my boots and parka and hurried to the furnace.

There was no flame, but the center of the furnace contained a few coals that were still glowing. Frantically, I raked at the gray clinkers, getting them out and into a big bucket we had for that purpose. The bucket was soon overflowing and I took it out to the clinker pile several yards from the building. I repeated the process dozens of times. The pile of hot coals left was only a few inches wide. I tried to decide if I should put some coal on the embers or if I should spread the hot coals out first before putting new coal in. I decided on the former. After a few minutes, when there was no flame and only a little smoke was ascending from the pile, I realized I had choked it with too much coal. I worked for an hour raking coal aside, fanning what was left of the embers, throwing in wood, papers, and whatever I could find that looked like it would burn, and then added coal. It didn't look as if it was going to work. A harsh wind was stripping heat from the building at an alarming rate, and I feared the lab was getting dangerously cold.

In an act of desperation, I ran upstairs and grabbed a jerry can with a jet fuel sample. Pouring a little into a flask, I hurried back to the furnace room. I threw the fuel inside the furnace quickly, aiming for the pile of coal and jumped back. It caught with a "woof" sound accompanied by a flash of light. I kept piling in coal as the fire built until it was roaring. It was five o'clock by then and I prayed the heat would climb back quickly. By eight o'clock, when the others arrived, it should be normal temperature. I worried about it all day, but no one said anything that evening, so presumably any variance in temperature had gone unnoticed.

We enjoyed our work, even though there was no forgetting that we were part of the military. It was, however, a better situation than we'd had at Ladd. We didn't have to pull KP, although we did have a military inspection every Saturday morning. After that, we were free for the weekend. The three of us took the post bus to Anchorage one Saturday afternoon. Anchorage was much larger than Fairbanks. We walked around the streets taking in the sights, ate at a restaurant, and gawked at the women. We returned to the barracks that evening feeling as if we'd seen enough for a while, much the same emotion we'd had after our outing in Fairbanks.

About mid-December, we received notice that our TDY duty had been extended to a second month. We were safe, at least until early January.

Before Christmas, the whole company moved into three-story buildings adjacent to the Quonset huts we'd been living in. We had considerably more room and more controlled heating conditions. The mess hall and latrines were in the same building, allowing us to move around without having to put on our heavy clothing. I went to the post movie theatre often, sometimes with my coworkers and sometimes with Midkiff. I did my Christmas shopping in the Fort Richardson PX and left nearly a month's pay there. I sent gifts to several of my relatives, and one to Millie.

Millie was still writing several times a week. There had been a break in our mail delivery after we moved to Anchorage from Fairbanks, and one day I received a packet with seven or eight letters. I was also writing occasionally to "Eve," a girl I had met at Marshall. She had taught me to dance.

I corresponded with several people, mostly other young men who were in the service, just out, or waiting to enter. I wrote somewhat regularly to Paul Swanson, Ed Harbour, Jerry Adkins, and Marion Nida. All were still in the service. Larry Gill had just been drafted, my mother told me, but I didn't have his address yet. They were all friends I'd known all my life.

Tom DeVito was now in England, but hadn't been near a lab. We wrote often. I also wrote to Tom's parents and several members of my family. In those days before cheap phone calls and email, letter writing was an art more universally practiced.

Rose hadn't written, but I would have been surprised if she had. We had gone out once while I was home on leave. I had left for basic training without a proper goodbye, and that had bothered me. It was important for us to remain friends, I believed. The truth was that I had divided feelings about the two young women.

My love for Millie was a new and exciting experience, but because of the way we had left it, there was a feeling of uncertainty. Rose was the familiar; I didn't want to let go.

I had borrowed my Uncle Cline's car that Friday night. We dined at a Huntington restaurant, attended a football game, and were on our way back to her apartment. At first our conversation centered on our families, my military experiences, and her work.

Then, out of the blue, she asked, "Did you love me?"

We hadn't mentioned love before in that context and I hesitated a moment.

"Yes—I believe I did," I finally said.

I waited for her reaction, a part of me expecting her to reciprocate in some fashion, another part hoping she wouldn't.

Finally, she said, "And now?"

"Rose—I've met someone—"

"I thought you might have," she said quickly. "You're not the same."

I could see she was hurt.

I spent several minutes telling her about Millie. I soon sensed, however, that she would rather not hear what I was saying.

"I'm sorry," I said.

We'd had little to say the last few minutes of the ride. I hated to leave things that way.

"You can write to me, you know," I said.

Her dark eyes sparkled. "To what purpose?"

I wanted to plead for friendship, if for nothing else, but her question seemed rhetorical and I remained silent. I left her that evening fearing that my thoughtless, though honest revelation had created an unbridgeable gulf between us. Three months later, I still felt the loss.

I had been eyeing the mountains close to Fort Rich. Knapp, McDonough, and Hyek were game for climbing one of the closer ones. We were all off the day before Christmas, and we decided to leave before first light since we didn't know how long it would take. It was still dark when we left the mess hall, but it wasn't snowing, so we decided to try it. We carried canteens and put a few Baby Ruth candy bars and crackers in our pockets.

Our climb started easily, but gradually became steeper. We were on the western edge of the Chugach Mountain Range and although the mountain we chose wasn't as high as some farther east, it was challenge enough to give us a feeling of accomplishment. The snow was deep, two or three feet in places. However, many areas were windblown, allowing us to skirt the deeper stuff, for the most part. It took us about three hours to reach the top. We had hoped to see animals, but a white rabbit was all that crossed our path.

From the barren top we could see many surrounding mountains, although visibility wasn't good enough to see Anchorage, or even much of Cook Inlet. We took one another's photographs in various poses. The walk down was easier, but it was already dark when we got back to the barracks.[27]

I felt exhilarated that evening. The outing was the best experience I'd had since coming to Alaska. I'd been aware of the vast expanse of wilderness in the territory, but I hadn't really experienced it until that day. *Alaska really was different.* It was living up to my expectations.

The four of us decided to have a private party in the lab a few days before the New Year. One of us had to be there to take care of the furnace anyway, so we thought it would be a good time to loosen up. We bought beer and stocked up on some snacks from the PX. The night was spent eating, talking, drinking beer, and finally sleeping a little. We genuinely enjoyed one another's company.

George Hyek and Don McDonough, December 1953
Photo supplied by George Hyek

George Hyek and Ed Knapp, December 1953
Photo supplied by George Hyek

Time passed quickly after that. We received another extension on our TDYs, so we were guaranteed to stay until early February. Maybe Hyek was right. Maybe we'd be there for a full two years.

It wasn't to be. Just before the end of January, we got word from Capt. Reardon that orders were about to be cut for us to return to Fairbanks. They needed us badly, he said. He was sympathetic.

"We want you back here. We're shorthanded too. I'll work to bring you back."

"We'd appreciate it, sir," I said.

"How would you feel about transferring to the Army?" he asked. "That might be possible."

We talked about the proposal that evening. We hadn't known that such a thing was even feasible. We liked serving in the Air Force, even though we had complained a lot at Fairbanks, and to some extent at Elmendorf and Fort Richardson. Some of our complaints were justified, but some of them were typical servicemen's discontent. Complaint seemed to be a constant in all the services. Actually, switching from Air Force to Army would be a major move—one we wouldn't undertake without a lot of soul-searching.

In the late afternoon on February 3, Reardon called me into his office. I had tended furnace the night before and had the day off. He held three sets of orders in his hand.

"You're to get on a flight to Fairbanks on Friday the 5th," he said. "I'm putting you in charge of notifying the others and arranging for your flight. I want you to make those arrangements right away."

The others hadn't returned from the lab, so I had no vehicle available. I could have gone to the motor pool and checked one out, but elected to wait for the lab personnel. They were late, and by then I thought it best not to drive back to Elmendorf, but to go to air transport early the following day instead.

What happened then was unusual, in my experience. I delivered the orders to McDonough and Knapp. Even though we'd had known they were coming, it was still a blow and we spent a lot of Wednesday evening talking about our options, which seemed few. We went to work the following morning as usual, but with some melancholy, knowing it was to be our last day. I got busy running tests and tried not to think about it. They let us go a little early that afternoon because we had to pack. It was past four o'clock when we arrived at Fort Richardson.

I went into the mailroom, which was adjacent to company head-quarters. Capt. Reardon happened to be coming out the door as I was leaving the mailroom.

"You get all squared away with air transport about your flight to Fairbanks?" he asked.

I felt my knees go weak as I realized I'd forgotten to make arrange-ments. It had been nearly twenty-four hours since he'd given me the order to take care of it. It hadn't crossed my mind all day.

"Sir," I managed to say. "I haven't yet made those arrangements."

"What! And why not?"

"I forgot, sir."

"Dammit, soldier!" he said loud enough for anyone within a hundred feet to hear. "I'm not accustomed to having my orders disobeyed."

His face was red.

"Yes, sir. I'm sorry, sir."

"Sorry doesn't help! Do you have a vehicle?"

"Yes, sir—I can get one, sir."

"Well, I want you men on that plane. Today is the deadline for tomorrow's flight. Get your butt over to Elmendorf and make those reservations within the hour—and report to me as soon as you get back to let me know you've done so!"

I just barely made it before the office closed. I could tell Reardon was still fuming as I reported that we were scheduled for a morning flight, but he didn't berate me further.

In fact, before I left his office he said, "We'd still like to have you back here."

I've thought a lot about that incident. Obedience was something ingrained in me as a youngster and reinforced in my youth. I was conscientious and took my duties seriously. Moreover, I had a healthy fear of military authority. I'd never before failed to carry out a direct order. It was counter to my personality. As it turned out, it would have been infinitely better had I not made that deadline.

Chapter Five

February 5, 1954: I tell about it here, relating what I experienced. The experiences of others I also include, as told to me and/or substantiated by military records. In addition, other anecdotal material has surfaced, some only recently. At the time, I was unaware of these peripheral, though related happenings. I include them because they add perspective.

In the pre-dawn, Maudie Betscher was out of bed to see her husband off. She was six weeks pregnant and had been deathly sick every day. Today was no exception. With twenty-two-month-old Keith still sleeping, they kept their voices down.

Lt. Earl "Bob" Betscher was about to leave for Elmendorf to prepare for the day's flight. He'd been outside to start the car. Maudie shivered because of the cold he'd brought back inside the trailer. When he was ready to go, she smiled at the jaunty angle of his battered flight cap.

"Be careful, Bob," she whispered.

He smiled his broadest smile that said without words, "I will."

"Where to today?"

"Fairbanks. Flying a Beaver into Ladd with one or two passengers. Should be back early, though. You?"

"I thought I might take Keith and go visit Ann Cunningham—provided I feel better."

For several days, she had wanted to make a trip into town. Living in Mountain View, Alaska, had a certain ambiance attached to it, but sometimes she needed to visit the broader world.

"See you tonight," he said.[28]

Lt. Colonel William Ronald West-Watson of the British Royal Air Force, assigned to the British Joint Military Services in Washington, D.C., was hopeful that in just a few hours he would *finally* arrive at his destination. Capt. Jack Dempsey, U.S. Army, was driving him from Fort Richardson to the Elmendorf air terminal. West-Watson used the time to reflect on the past four days.

His flight from Washington to the West Coast, beginning on February 1, with an overnight stay in Chicago, had been interesting, if not enjoyable. His airplane had been scheduled to land in Seattle to catch a connecting flight to Anchorage, but because of Seattle fog had been forced to land in Portland, Oregon. Soon after landing, he had jotted a note to his wife Jill that stated, "Yellowstone Park and the Rockies with a goodly coat of snow looked simply wonderful in the brilliant sunshine."

Then things weren't so wonderful. Airplanes could take off from Seattle but couldn't land there. As it turned out, he had to stay overnight in Portland and then take a train to Seattle. As a result, he hadn't arrived in Anchorage until February 3, a day later than had been scheduled.

Col. Erling Fugelso, an army surgeon at Fort Richardson, had given him working space in his own office to study detailed plans of the medical field test that West-Watson was to observe at Ladd Air Force Base. The assignment, as part of the joint military "Operation North Star," was just one of the kinds of duties he performed in his capacity as a military medical doctor.

West-Watson considered it a special kindness that Col. Fugelso had invited him to his home, where he had enjoyed a good home-cooked dinner. Now, as Capt. Dempsey parked the car at the air terminal, West-Watson pulled out his pocket watch to check the time. Ten o'clock. Right on schedule.[29]

The weather wasn't as bitter cold as it had been, but the wind had a definite bite. George Hyek had volunteered to drive McDonough, Knapp, and me from Fort Richardson to the air terminal. We were to be there at 9:45 AM sharp.

The cab of the truck could hold three; I huddled in back with our luggage during the fifteen-minute ride. For three months, we'd taken turns riding in the back, to and from the petroleum laboratory at Elmendorf. On the last ride, it just happened to be my turn. I had never gotten used to it. The truck's canvas top was drafty. I pulled my parka hood up tighter. My big fur-backed mittens, hanging at the ends of my arms, were as graceful as logs, but they kept my hands warm.

We pulled up to the terminal and I hopped out, glad the airy ride was over. Dawn had broken and the low-lying Arctic sun periodically appeared from behind scattered clouds. Hyek helped us carry our gear into the small terminal. We presented our orders to the corporal at the counter.

"Pile your duffel bags on the wagon," he said.

"How long?" I asked.

"It's going to be a while."

"What kind of aircraft?" Knapp inquired.

"Gooney Bird . . . maybe."

After saying goodbye to Hyek and assuring him we'd be back, we took seats in green metal and plastic chairs lining the outside wall. Although we were early, several other men were already waiting in the smoke-filled room. A husky, dark-haired Airman First Class sitting across from us smiled good-naturedly.

McDonough and I chatted, speculating about our work situation back at Ladd. We worried that our old positions might have been filled in our absence. We weren't crazy about the jobs, but we were familiar with the routine and personnel.

"I wonder if Crawford got the addition on the shack done yet?" McDonough said.

Eventually, he took out a book he had bought at the PX. Knapp was quiet, but that wasn't unusual. He was paying attention, though. He went to talk to the corporal after a few minutes.

When he came back, he said, "Looks like we're going to travel in style today on a C-47."

More service personnel trickled in, piling their duffel bags on top of ours. The room buzzed. A British colonel was in earnest conversation with an Army Airborne captain.

As time passed and our departure didn't seem imminent, I took my own paperback book out of my handbag and settled down for the wait. It took only a few minutes for me to realize it wasn't the atmosphere for reading, so I put the book away. It seemed that almost everyone was smoking, and as I had discovered in my four months in Alaska, the tendency was to overheat the inside, as if to compensate for outside extremes. I took my parka off; I noticed others were shedding outer garments, as well.

The corporal Knapp had spoken with was the same one to whom I'd presented our orders the day before. The memory was painful because of the tongue-lashing I'd received from Capt. Reardon.

The morning briefing at the 5039th Air Transport Squadron had a surprise for Lt. Betscher. He was going to Fairbanks, all right, not in a Beaver[30] as originally scheduled, but in a C-47 with multiple passengers.

Betscher had mixed emotions. He liked flying heavier aircraft. He was current under all existing directives and had nearly two hundred hours in C-47s, which was about 20 percent of his total flying hours. He was proud of his record and confident in his ability. His commander, Capt. Ford, had commented that Betscher had "an acute sense of responsibility toward his job." However, he'd been looking forward to getting back early, but that might not be possible, since the aircraft he was to pilot was late coming from somewhere in the island chain.

Betscher was introduced to Col. Edward Burge, who was to fly second seat. Betscher knew Burge was new to the command. He was a native of Florida and loved the outdoors, he'd been told. Burge was an experienced pilot, probably more experienced than himself.

"Shouldn't Col. Burge be commander, since he outranks me?" Betscher asked.

"Yes, he does outrank you," Capt. Harris, Operations Officer, replied. "He's also logged nearly three thousand flying hours—but he hasn't been route-checked. As you know, you can't command a flight in Alaska unless you've been checked out on it. Therefore, for this flight, you're commander."

"They're late," Betscher said.

"Eight-nine-five's on the way in. We'll start loading baggage as soon as the wheels stop rolling. At last count, you have thirteen passengers. Corporal Knickerbocker is your crew chief."[31]

Eventually, we were called to board the airplane. It wasn't far down the flightline, so we walked, carrying our handbags. Our duffel bags had already been loaded on the C-47. The door was open and a boyish blond corporal, dressed in fatigues, came down the steps. He added a couple of parachutes to the pile of chutes under the fuselage.

The pilot joined our group and motioned us into a circle close to the steps.

"I'm Lt. Betscher," he said. Then nodding toward the corporal, added, "This is Corporal Knickerbocker, our crew chief. Major Burge, our copilot, is already on board."

Lt. Betscher introduced Col. West-Watson. Then he turned to the captain who had been talking to West-Watson in the terminal.

"This is Capt. Hill. He's Army Airborne," Betscher said. "As you can see, we have chutes here for you to wear on this flight. If you're accustomed to flying on larger aircraft, you may not be used to this, but our C-47 comes in just under the size limit that mandates passengers to wear them. Capt. Hill will brief you on their use. You'll have to wear them over your parkas."

Capt. Hill wasn't a large man, but he exuded self-confidence. His voice compelled my attention as he quickly and efficiently gave us instructions for getting into the parachutes.

As we were cinching up, he added, "You'll probably never have to use a parachute—but in the unlikely event you do, just grab your

D-ring—like this." I watched him carefully. "Then throw it away!" he said, extending his arm in an exaggerated motion.

As we lined up at the steps to enter, there was some laughter. One airman was pointing to the sign inside the door. "STOP! Look me over. Alaska has been rough on me," it said.

McDonough and Knapp were first on. I wanted to sit with them but was slower getting my chute straps adjusted. As it happened, I was the fifth or sixth passenger to board.

It felt good to get inside, out of the wind. The cargo deck was on a steep angle, the C-47 being a tail-wheel airplane.[32] We had to climb uphill to get to our seats. The pile of duffel bags was lashed down in front, mostly along the right side and covered with plastic netting. The seats were of canvas webbing hanging along the sides facing center. We took seats in pretty much the same order we had entered the aircraft. Mine was about sixth from the front and fifth from the rear door. I could see Knapp and McDonough up front. Knapp had the first seat and McDonough had the second.

As I settled in, I counted the men. There were thirteen passengers and three crewmembers, sixteen altogether. It seemed crowded. Our bulky clothing and the parachutes on our backs added to the congestion. Most of us were on the left side, but two men were taking seats in the back on the right.

The majority of passengers were Air Force, but a few were Army. Col. West-Watson sat in the radio operator's seat near the forward bulkhead. Knickerbocker was busy inspecting tiedown ropes on the baggage and giving some last-minute adjustments to parachute harnesses. I noticed he wasn't wearing a parachute.

I lowered myself into my seat and twisted sideways to get my seat belt buckled. The man to my left was doing the same. His handbag had "McMahon" stenciled on the side. Our arms bumped.

"Close quarters," I said.

"Sure is, but it's not such a long flight," McMahon said.

Eventually, the passengers were all seated and strapped in. Knickerbocker pulled the steps up and closed the door. The left engine fired, but failed to catch. When it fired again, white smoke blew backward over the wing. There was a lot of vibration, then the engine smoothed out. I glanced out the square window at black soot streaks on the trailing edge of the wing below me.

My one previous flight hadn't made me a veteran flyer. The November trip from Ladd to Elmendorf had been at night and the C-124 was so large that much of the sense of flying was lost. Now, as the other engine started, I knew this was going to be *real* flying, the way I had always imagined it. After a few minutes of revving up, we moved out to the runway. We lifted off after what seemed to me to be a short run.

I tried to see things below. I caught a glimpse of Anchorage's tall buildings. It was a little past noon and even though lengthening days were becoming noticeable, I knew that in just a few hours darkness would again come to Anchorage, and even sooner to Fairbanks, our destination.

We climbed through scattered clouds. From my position, I could see out the right-side windows. I spotted the Chugach Mountains to the right of our flight path and wondered which of the peaks was the one we had climbed on Christmas Eve. Then, it was solid white outside. Eventually, we broke through the clouds and the sun shone brightly through the windows. I swallowed several times to clear my ears as we leveled off and settled down to cruising speed.

The interior had warmed considerably. I took my reading glasses out of my pocket. The flight would take more than two hours, so I decided to settle in with the paperback I had tried to read in the terminal.

As I read, I was vaguely conscious of movement around me. People were changing positions. After some time had passed, I began to get sleepy. It had gotten even warmer. I looked at my watch. We'd been in flight for half an hour. We were still above the clouds. The sound of the engines was hypnotic and the ride was smooth.

Chapter Six

The cockpit door was open. I could see the copilot from where I was sitting. A series of routine procedures were, no doubt, being performed. Official records would later establish what some of those procedures were.[33]

The flight had been routine, with no unusual weather expected. We had taken off at 12:35 PM, climbed out of the Cook Inlet area, and set a course almost due north. The anticipated flight path would take us up the Susitna River Valley. We would then climb to higher elevations over the Alaska Range, passing over Summit and Healey. Near Nenana, we would drop to five thousand feet and turn northeast toward Fairbanks. Radar outposts lined the entire route. Talkeetna, at the junction of three rivers, was one of the first major checkpoints. Summit, on the Chilitna River, would follow.

At 1:04 PM, a Talkeetna radio check took place, with the pilots reporting an altitude of eleven thousand feet, ground speed of one hundred seventy-four knots, and an estimated 1:26 PM arrival over Summit.

Talkeetna gave them an updated weather report.

"At twelve-thirty: ten thousand overcast, thirty miles visibility, wind six knots. Summit has three thousand overcast, visibility fifteen miles in light rain, wind at sixteen knots."

They would have been able to see the ground on occasion. The Alaska Railroad parallels the south-flowing Susitna River. The daily passenger train from Anchorage to Fairbanks was in the vicinity at the time and perhaps visible to the pilots. It isn't known whether they knew that light rime was starting to form on the surface of the airplane.

Cliff Hudson, in his little Aeronica Chief, had just landed at the Talkeetna town airstrip after making a delivery in the Talkeetna Mountains. He had wanted to return in time to meet the passenger train from Anchorage. Hudson's struggling airfreight business needed all the customers it could get, and unexpected business sometimes arrived by rail. Unfortunately, the train had already come and gone. Before settling into his landing pattern, he had spotted the blue and gold cars five miles to the north, stretched out like a snake along the river. He was a patient man; there would be other trains.

Hudson was a man of many talents. Growing up on a farm in Granger, Washington, had given him a good start in self-sufficiency. In 1948, after a hitch in the United States Army and an adventure in Mexico, he followed his older brother, Glen, to Talkeetna. Glen had been there since 1937, when he had started an air service business. Cliff went to work for the Alaska Railroad, first as a section hand, then in the roundhouse, and later as a crane operator in the power plant.

It wasn't long before he decided Alaska without wings was difficult, so he went to Seattle with a friend and bought a Sky Ranger, his first of many airplanes.

Then tragically, in August 1951, Glen Hudson was killed when his PA 20 crashed at Disappointment Creek. His widow sold the air service to Cliff.

It was a difficult time. The loss of his brother had left him despondent. He flew some freight and took non-flying jobs to make ends meet. He drove a truck, and trapped. Some days, without a job, he would just fly around, scouting the territory, landing on glaciers, or marking future landing sites. Finally, he got his commercial flying license and got down to the business of flying freight and people.

It wasn't easy. In a small community like Talkeetna, many people survived by taking on small jobs as they came along. Hudson was no exception. He was determined to make Hudson Air Service a thriving business, but still jumped at income opportunities of every kind.

Now, as he refueled his small aircraft, fine-grained snow was bouncing off the wings. The wind was definitely picking up. He had needed to apply lots of rudder on landing. His weather eye was keen, honed by flying experience. One more run today would have been profitable, but he decided to stay on the ground. A front seemed to be moving in from the southwest. Hudson was a careful man in all areas of his life, but especially as a pilot. It would be an afternoon to catch up on some hangar work.[34]

Lt. Betscher, the pilot, had invited Col. West-Watson to sit forward in the radio operator's seat. West-Watson had to keep adjusting the radio dials to keep the music clear of static. It had been fine when they were closer to Anchorage, but now, as they entered the mountain ranges farther north, the signal kept breaking up. Airman Ed Olson, a couple of seats away, had kindly tuned in the station for him not long after taking off.

I was drowsy and having trouble concentrating on my book. Looking around at the other men, I could see several with closed eyes. One man stood and loosened the chute straps around his legs. Good idea, I thought. My straps were so tight they were beginning to cut off circulation. I immediately felt better after letting them out a few inches. As I was sitting down again, we hit a downdraft and the airplane dropped a hundred feet or more, but then popped right back up, causing a peculiar sensation in my stomach. I thought about putting on my seat belt but saw no one else doing so. I decided I couldn't read any longer and put my book and glasses in my bag. An Air Force man up front had moved over to sit on a duffel bag.

Then things got rough. It felt like riding in a truck, on a rutted road at excessive speed. It was normal, I assured myself. It would stop in a little while. However, I reached for my seat belt.

I never got it fastened. I gasped as the bottom seemed to drop out of the sky. All I could do was grip my seat straps and hold on. We plummeted hundreds of feet, still in a horizontal position. Just as quickly, I was pressed back into my seat with great force as we were tossed skyward again. We seemed to be under full power, but even so, the airplane began to shudder and shake as if it were going to fall apart. The engines changed pitch, first shrill, then normal. Then, just as quickly as it had started, we leveled off.

That was temporary, for suddenly we went into a steep dive. It seemed to me that we were in a nearly vertical position. Objects in the cabin were flying around. The man who had been sitting on the duffel bags was now up on the ceiling. I tried to hold on. The engines were screaming. I could feel, more than see, the men on either side of me grasping at their seat webbing. *We're going down*, I thought. I felt completely helpless.

The engine noise was deafening. Then there was a loud "bang" and a bright flash from the left side of the airplane. I held on with all my strength.

In a surreal, slow-motion moment, I saw the top of the cabin coming apart. There was a screeching noise as a large section of roof disappeared. The air rushed onto my face and body with a force that threatened to crush me; I could no longer see or breathe. The combination of sounds became one continuous roar. Then I felt myself being pulled from my seat. Something struck my face, and I lost consciousness.

Chapter Seven

Other men in the C-47 had their own terrifying experiences:[35] Airman First Class Edward Fox had decided to vacate his seat near the door. He'd been nauseous since leaving Anchorage. His parachute pack "seemed to weigh fifty pounds." He moved forward to a seat-shaped depression in the pile of baggage close to another man sitting on the floor. In the new position, he was facing the men sitting in the seats along the left side.

The sudden downdraft surprised him, since most of the trip had been smooth. The airplane seemed to bank to the right. Then it pulled up and he felt the G-force on his body. He held onto the baggage and closed his eyes. The engines were racing; he could tell they were diving.

He opened his eyes when the explosion occurred. A "fireball" appeared, and he closed his eyes again. Then it was quiet. He opened his eyes and could see blue sky. *We've hit the side of a mountain*, he thought. He seemed to be lying in a snow bank—and somehow he had survived.

Then, he was jerked back to reality by the scene below him. There was an open parachute; a body tumbled past it. In the midst of falling debris, the C-47 in which he had just been sitting was spiraling downward with the right wing bent back at a grotesque angle. The tail was still intact.

Fox got his hand on his D-ring and pulled it. As the chute opened, he could see that the shroud lines were twisted. He was spun around twice, enough to cause disorientation. He lost sight of the airplane and the other chute.

The wind carried him into a snow squall. He could barely see the top of a windblown ridge below him. He felt himself being pulled left of the ridge top and down the slope. Then, thirty yards directly below him, he saw an animal leaping uphill through the snow, struggling mightily to escape whatever had encroached on its territory.

"Damn," he said, as the white he was falling through merged with the white below, making it impossible to see. "Damn!"

He had been in rough air before, but Airman Second Class Eli LaDuke knew something was different. There had been little warning before the sudden horrific drop in altitude and the bounce back up. As the aircraft began to shimmy and shake at the top of its recovery, he felt as if something had to give. Then, as they nosed down with engines roaring, he realized they might not be able to pull out.

LaDuke was in the fourth seat from the front, next to Ed Olson. The luggage pile in front of him was suddenly illuminated with bright light as the whole right side of the airplane just seemed to disappear—torn out, or blown out, his dazed mind couldn't grasp which. He had the sensation of "somersaulting" forward and landing on the edge of the hole. He lost consciousness for a moment; then he became aware of being outside and lying on his back on a large piece of metal. The metal was attached to the airplane, he realized, because he could see the darker interior of the cabin. He twisted his body sideways and pushed against the flat surface under him. Moments later, he saw the airplane spinning before him, whether above or below, he couldn't tell.

There were parachutes—probably above him—maybe two or three. He realized he was falling at great speed. He gave the D-ring on his chest a yank and waited for the chute to open, but nothing happened. He tried again, and soon felt the jolt of the opening. At the same time, he saw the outline of a snow-covered peak. Three seconds later, he slammed into a snowdrift, buried to his chest. The jarring pain was the most intense he'd ever experienced.

Huey Montgomery, Airman Second Class, had moved from his fourth seat position to the baggage pile. He purposely chose a spot where he could look out a right-side window. The window was partially fogged up. They were flying through thickening clouds, but Montgomery was able, every so often, to see snow-covered peaks. They were high and rugged looking, nothing like the Alabama hills where he'd grown up.

Sitting on the floor, he could feel the movement of the airplane better than he had in his seat. The ride had been smooth; now he could feel every little air pocket through his rear end. It got bouncy, but he supposed that was normal in that kind of airplane. His job as a cook didn't normally take him into close proximity with airplanes. That was good, since he wasn't crazy about flying. He was, however, in the U.S. Air Force and knew he had to put up with it occasionally.

He was taken by surprise when the plane suddenly lost a lot of altitude. It felt like "riding a roller coaster down a big drop and hitting the bottom—only stronger." He was lifted off the floor and then suddenly pushed back down for several long seconds. Then the airplane started rocking from side to side with violent vibrations. He was relieved when it was over. The engines were still sounding funny, though, like when you hit "a slick place in the road with the motor racing."

The engines seemed to rev up to full power and then the nose dropped. It seemed to Montgomery that they were spinning. He looked at faces of other passengers who were hanging on to their seats and he could tell they were worried. He was worried, too.

There was an explosion from somewhere in back and things started to come apart. His thought was, "How are we going to get out? How will I ever get to the door?" Then he realized he couldn't move at all. All he could do was hang on to the ropes holding the baggage—and pray.

Then, when a large hole suddenly appeared over his head, he launched himself toward it. He managed to clear all the jagged metal, and then was miraculously outside. He saw another man falling near him, but then he entered a cloud and couldn't see the man or the airplane. He got his hands on the D-ring and pulled it. As the orange and white chute filled out above him, he said a prayer of thanks.

It seemed less than half a minute later that he hit the top of a mountain ridge. Jagged rocks bruised his body as he was dragged across them. He passed out.

The little bit of bumpiness was insignificant, he concluded. He had been in plenty of rough air and what they were experiencing was nothing to worry about. Airman First Class Bobby Sallis had settled in for the last leg of a long trip. He'd be stationed for two years at Ladd Air Force Base at Fairbanks. He wondered if Alaska's winter fury was as bad as he'd heard. It would certainly be different from his native Arkansas.

He shifted his six-foot frame sideways to get more comfortable. His seat belt was constricting, so he took it off. From his position in the next-to-last seat from the door, he could see most of the cabin ahead of him. A couple of men had moved over to sit on the baggage. The blond-haired crew chief had been moving around, but was now standing at the cockpit door, which was open. Knickerbocker was his name, Sallis remembered. Before they took off, Knickerbocker had shown him survival kits near the door, and had told him that if he had to bail out, to grab one and hook it onto his chute.

Sallis started a conversation with the Army tech sergeant seated to his right. Siplivy was his name. Sergeant Siplivy was on his second hitch.

Their conversation was interrupted when the airplane dropped several hundred feet, as if it had been sucked into a void. The drop came as a surprise, and Sallis reached up and grabbed the metal bar to which the seats were attached. Siplivy reached up, too, but missed the bar and grabbed Sallis' arm. For a moment, their eyes met. They held on like that as the aircraft pulled back up and started to shimmy and shake. Then it went into a dive.

A loud noise, sounding like an explosion, rocked the cabin. Sallis was horrified to feel the side of the airplane fold out, and to feel himself being pulled out with it. He braced his body to prevent that from happening, but the force was greater than he could resist. The sound of metal tearing apart was predominant in his ears. Then he was outside, lying on a table-sized piece of metal that seemed to be still attached to the fuselage. He pushed away as hard as he could and found himself in a free fall. He quickly pulled his D-ring.

Just as his chute opened, he saw a large object go by. It looked like an engine. He saw a man falling. The man's chute hadn't opened. Seconds later, he braced himself as he saw the snow-covered terrain coming rapidly up to meet him.

Airman Second Class Edward Olson, a member of the Security Service, was headed out to St. Lawrence Island as a radio operator with the 3rd Radio Squadron Mobile. A year in that part of Alaska's frozen wilderness! He'd be surprised if it turned out to be the best year of his life, but looking at it philosophically, the sooner started, the sooner finished. It was beautiful country, he conceded, but a long way from his native Iowa.

The Air Force takes good care of the troops, he thought, as he stretched his legs out into the aisle. The thoroughness with which they'd been briefed on using parachutes was a good example. One pilot had personally checked Olson's chute and made minor adjustments. The passengers had then been given further instructions after getting on board.

They were more than half an hour into the flight and the crew chief had just passed along a message from the cockpit that seat belts could be unfastened and passengers could smoke if they wanted to. Olson took the opportunity to loosen the uncomfortably tight leg straps of his parachute harness.

The cabin was warm and the drone of engines made him drowsy. The two men in seats toward the forward bulkhead were also nodding. Eli LaDuke, sitting on his right, had been rather quiet. They were headed to the same place, so maybe LaDuke was doing some contemplation about that. Huey Montgomery, the other member of their St.

Lawrence Island-bound trio, had abandoned his seat and had gone to sit on the floor.

It became a little rough, but nothing he wasn't used to in flight. He started to doze. Then, suddenly, the plane dropped like a rock. It took him by surprise and he could see shock on the faces of the others. He had to hold on to keep from being torn from his seat. To his relief, the airplane lifted up again. These air pockets are common, he reasoned as he felt himself being pushed back down into his seat. It felt as if they were climbing at a high angle. The engines were wide open, but Olson sensed their air speed had dropped. Then came vibration and shaking, followed by a dive. The first drop had been flat, but now the nose was down and they were at full throttle.

Olson was horrified to hear an explosion and see things coming apart. The right side of the aircraft opened up and he lost orientation. It seemed as if he were flying sideways and upside down. He was aware of his body striking the cockpit door very hard. Then he was outside.

It took him a few moments to comprehend the situation. Two or three parachutes below him made him realize he had to open his, too. He easily found the D-ring and yanked it.

It was a rough opening. Just as the chute deployed, he caught sight of baggage falling around him. There were also pieces of flat metal. Then, the risers pulled his parka hood over his head and twisted the fabric halfway around, knocking his glasses from his face. Olson had few debilitating deficiencies, but severe nearsightedness happened to be one of them. In his present situation, sight was something he had great need of.

He descended that way, with his parka hood partially covering his face, and with only blurry glimpses of what lay below. He tried not to panic, and concentrated on how he was going to land without being able to see.

I was slowly regaining consciousness after being struck in the face. At first, I thought I was in a storm. Bright light flashed before my eyes and wind whistled in my ears, but not loud enough to drown out a strange flapping noise. I was cold. *Pull your hood up tighter and lean into the wind*, I told myself. The flashing light soon revealed itself as alternate sunlight and shadow, changing as I fell through the clouds. The flapping sound, I came to realize, was my parka bottom, caught in the rush of air.

Understanding came slowly. *The airplane had broken apart. I was outside—falling.* As incomprehensible as it might be, I was calm, as if suspended between two worlds, and not feeling any particular urgency for taking action.

Then I became aware of things falling with me. There were duffel bags, handbags, and small and large pieces of metal. What appeared to be a wing was below me, oscillating like a flat rock descending through water. I saw another man directly opposite, falling at the same speed. Then his orange and white parachute opened, and I lost sight of him. I saw another open chute.

The second parachute brought me to full awareness just as I entered a heavy layer of clouds. A sense of urgency came then. I needed to open my parachute—*right then*! How do I do that?

The voice of Capt. Hill came quickly to mind, "Just grab the D-ring and throw it away."

I looked down at my chest and tried to focus my eyes. I got my right hand on the metal. *Throw it away—quick*! I saw the small drogue chute coming out above my head just before I lost consciousness again.[36]

I regained my senses quickly, immediately becoming aware of my situation. The comfort of feeling taut risers and seeing orange and white above me was short-lived. I could tell I was in the middle of a snowstorm and less than fifty yards above the ground. There appeared to be a cliff below me—and I was being blown straight into it. The wind was fierce, a momentary advantage, for it carried me to higher ground instead of against the cliff.

I seemed to be going sideways. I had missed the cliff, but directly ahead were two large boulders, one about twice as high as the other. I quickly maneuvered my risers to see if I could control the direction of my flight. I had enough response to avoid the higher rock and just managed to clear the top of the other. I was coming down fast on a steep hillside that sloped to my left.

My friend Jerry Adkins, a paratrooper, had told me that it was best to bend your legs just as you hit, otherwise you could break them. With twenty feet to go, I tried to get ready. At that moment, in my peripheral vision, I caught a movement uphill to my right. An animal about fifty feet away was leaping through deep snow as if trying to escape with its life. *A wolf!* I knew it without a doubt!

I hit, and my momentum drove me to my waist in the snow. Immediately, I was yanked up again. I found myself flat on my face as the wind dragged me across the snow.

Hill had demonstrated the quick release on the front of the harness. I tried to find it, but it was impossible to see or feel anything. I twisted and turned as I skidded across the surface. Snow entered the top of my parka and packed down inside my clothing. I was being dragged around, and down, the slope of the hill at a high rate of speed. I bounced over large and small rocks.

I knew I must spill the wind from my parachute. I managed to get my arms up to grasp one of the risers. I yanked until one side of the chute seemed to be collapsing, but it only slowed me slightly. I had to get my feet up in front of me to use as brakes. I knew it was only a matter of time until my head found one of the rocks that seemed to be everywhere.

Somehow I managed to pull my legs up and twist, so that my feet got ahead of my upper body. They dug in, and I was pulled deeper into the snow. For a moment, I slowed and thought I was going to be able to stop. Then I popped up again and was once more in a head-first position, moving faster than ever.

I was near the end of my strength.

"Help me God," I prayed. "Jesus—help me!"

I summoned the energy to jerk my body around and fling my feet out in front. At the same time, I used all the strength in my arms to pull on the right riser. At that moment, I passed over a windblown portion of the slope, allowing my feet to be free of the snow. I bounced several times but kept my feet aimed to the front. I dug them into the rocks, and in one last effort, jerked one side of the chute down, and came to a stop. I quickly pulled the canopy in and stood on it.

For perhaps a minute, I stood motionless, catching my breath. It was snowing heavily. I heard no sounds except the wind—and my pounding heart.

Chapter Eight

The breakup of our two-engine transport over the Susitna Valley didn't go unnoticed. At 1:18 PM, William Thompson, a member of an Alaska Railroad maintenance crew, was at milepost 269.7, shoveling snow from the tracks. He heard "an airplane with motors apparently at full throttle." The sound lasted approximately twenty seconds, followed by an explosion sounding "just about like a dynamite report." Shortly afterward, he was able to make out an orange-colored parachute. That was immediately followed by what he believed to be a falling airplane wing.[37]

Nearly five miles south, Nick Botner was part of another four-man railroad crew that had recently left the warmth of the Gold Creek section house. They rode their motorcar south one-quarter mile to the south switch, where they were to remove snow from the tracks. The northbound passenger train was due at 1:19 PM. When the crew arrived at their destination, Botner hopped off the car and began to shovel. It was a constant struggle to keep the tracks cleared and inspected. New snow and wind could erase hours of work in just a few minutes. Frost heaves often misaligned the rails, necessitating installation of shims. The winter had been worse than most.

As Botner shoveled, the hood of his parka fell down and he caught the drone of distant engines. His ear was attuned to aircraft flying over the valley. He was a pilot himself, living on a homestead not far away. It had become a game to identify aircraft types. He looked south in the direction of the sound. The peaks to the west were covered with clouds, but a few patches of blue showed over the valley. A minute later, he saw the airplane directly overhead. He recognized it as a C-47, the military equivalent of a civilian DC-3. The sound receded gradually as the aircraft traveled north.

Then the distant engine noise altered, sounding like propellers changing pitch. That wasn't unusual for large airplanes, but something didn't sound quite right to Botner.

"Listen!" he said to another man working next to him.

The labored engine sound continued for several seconds. Botner focused his attention on the portion of sky from which the noise came. Then it sounded normal again.

Botner went back to his shoveling until the same labored engine sound came again. It continued for several seconds. Then Botner's sharp eyes caught a flash of light in a blue patch of sky, followed a few seconds later by the sound of a distant explosion.

"Did you hear that?" he asked.

"I heard it," the other man said.

The engine sound had stopped. Botner frantically searched the blue patch, but could see nothing. Several seconds passed before he spotted two small dots moving like ants down toward cloud layers that covered the ridge of mountains.

"I think I see parachutes," he said.

"I see something too, but I can't make out what it is."

Botner went to Joe Burshiem, his foreman.

"That plane either exploded or crashed," he said. "I saw it and heard it!"

Burshiem was skeptical.

The fourth man on the railroad crew said, "What you heard was probably blasting ice down at Sherman. They're still at it. Listen!"

"Be quiet," Burshiem said to the men around him. After a few moments he asked, "Is that what you heard?"

"No," Botner said. "I know that sound. This was something different. We have to report it!"

Burshiem looked at his watch.

"Well—I don't know."

"We *have* to!"

Burshiem studied his feet for only a moment.

"Nick, if you're sure about this, we'll call ACS."[38]

"I'm sure!"

"All right! In four minutes, number six will be by here. When she clears, we'll move the motor car from the siding to the main line and go into Gold Creek and make the call."

As Fox landed roughly on the slope, he saw another chute about two hundred feet below him. It was open and moving swiftly away. Fox never had the chance to dig in. His chute, filled with wind, took him skimming over the snow, bouncing over frozen rockfalls and windblown ice flows. Try as he might, he was unable to spill air from the chute. Eventually, he was carried over the crest of a ridge and far down another slope. Then, just when he had lost hope of ever stopping, the wind lessened and the chute caught on a small exposed rock formation. The canopy quickly collapsed.

He lay still for several minutes, getting his breath back. Slowly, he recovered enough to roll to a sitting position and finally was able to stand. He checked his body carefully for injuries. His elbows, legs, back, and jaw were all painful, but nothing seemed broken. He eased himself out of his harness. By that time, he was able to breathe without gasping, but his teeth were chattering and he was shaking uncontrollably. The feeling of being alone all but overpowered his senses. He could hardly believe what had just happened. However, the bitter wind stung his face and quickly brought him to a state of reality.

It seemed as if he'd been dragged a mile after landing. He stood still and listened to see if he could hear anyone. There was no sound except the howling wind. Trying hard to look objectively at the situation, he could see that he'd been carried down the hillside and concluded he was out of sight and hearing of anyone else who might have survived. He needed to get back within earshot, and to do that, he'd have to climb back up to the top. Below him was a wide river valley, white with ice and snow, and only partially visible through low-lying clouds.

He forced himself to concentrate. There might be others alive. He'd seen at least one chute in the air and another on the ground. He made up his mind to walk into the wind. That would take him either to the man or to the crash site. The C-47 had been going straight down when he saw it, so it couldn't be far away. He scooped up his parachute harness and canopy, clutching the weighty pile in front of him with both arms.

Fox labored up the slope. At the crest of the ridge, he stopped to listen again. The wind was blowing without letup, and blocked out all other sounds. Walking was torturous. Deep snow made it impossible to make headway. He needed both arms to pull himself forward. Trying to carry the chute and move through the snow brought him near exhaustion. He thought of his friends and family back in Utica, New York, and of his wife, Flo. That helped him keep going. He soon realized that he'd have to abandon the chute. He'd come back to it if he didn't find anyone. Fox had no illusions about the seriousness of his situation. He pressed on, hoping frantically that he'd find another human being. Two men together would have a better chance.

LaDuke hit facing upwind and was quickly yanked out of a snow-drift by his full parachute and bounced over several bare rocks before abruptly stopping twenty feet away. The jolt of hitting the ground had jammed his body, and the pain had not subsided before he realized the sky was giving up objects all around him. Separate pieces of airplane, mostly fragments, were still falling. A few pieces of paper flew by. Snow was falling and blowing, so his view was distorted.

He heard a loud grunt back near where he had landed and became aware that the oval shape of a parachute was traveling at considerable speed toward him. It passed him a few feet up the slope, but close enough for him to see the shape of the man being dragged behind. He couldn't move fast enough to cut it off and watched helplessly as man and chute sped by and disappeared into the snowy mist. Several minutes passed as he stood listening. His pain slowly subsided, and as his head cleared, he decided to try to get over to the man if he could manage it.

Then he heard a distant call. At first, he thought it was from the man he'd just seen, but soon realized that, although the cry came from the same general direction, it was actually from somewhere farther down the slope.

"Hello!" LaDuke called back.

"I'm here!" came the answer.

"I'll try to get down there. Hold on!"

LaDuke shucked his parachute with rapidly numbing hands. He still had his mittens. They hadn't been on during the descent, but luckily, the strap holding them together had remained around his neck. He was chilled throughout his body. His right leg and backside felt especially cold. Feeling back there, he was horrified to discover that his pants had been torn and a large flap of material hung down his leg. Since his undamaged parka covered most of his hip, he speculated that something, probably jagged metal, had grabbed the cloth and ripped its way up toward his pocket. Even in his present plight, he couldn't help being amazed that his skin had no apparent cuts. However, his early-morning decision not to wear long johns loomed large. His body still ached from hitting the ground, but he knew he had to muster the energy to assist the two men around the slope.

Looking back in the other direction, he saw, for the first time, part of the wreckage. It appeared to be a large section of the fuselage. The silver skin had freakishly reflected an errant ray of light that caught LaDuke's attention. A section of cabin had apparently slammed into the little valley two hundred yards away. His dazed mind tried to take in the enormity of all that had happened as the wind whipped his face without mercy.

Chapter Nine

Olson came in hard. He was nearly blind without his glasses and barely caught sight of the ground before he made contact. Fortunately, he was facing the direction of drift, but even so, he was dragged at great speed over snow-covered rocks for a considerable distance. Through sheer determination, he managed to pull the canopy down enough to collapse it.

He stood, stunned at his surroundings. Snow on the steep slope was waist-deep and the wind was blowing so hard that he had to lean back into it.

Olson remembered the instructions for getting out of a chute harness, but his hands had little feeling and his fingers refused to work. He still had his mittens, held together by a strap around his neck, but they hadn't been on his hands. He blew on his fingers and rubbed them. It was a long time before he was able to manipulate the metal catches and step free.

Now what do I do, he thought. Earlier that day, Iowa had seemed far away. Now, it was on another planet.

Cliff Hudson had just finished refueling when his phone rang. Having already grounded himself for the afternoon because of worsening weather, he was set to turn down any job offers. However, it was a sergeant from ACS that Hudson knew.

"Cliff, there's a military aircraft down in the Gold Creek area," the man said. "Nick Botner just called. His railroad crew heard it go down and saw chutes!"

Hudson glanced at his watch. It was one-thirty, still time to fly the thirty miles up there in daylight.

"How's the weather in Curry?" Hudson asked.

"Wind is up, and it's starting to snow. Elmendorf's confirmed losing contact with a C-47 heading north to Fairbanks. It'll take a little while for them to get search planes up here. Could you check it out?" Then he added, "There are sixteen on board!"

"Which way were they going?"

"North. Be careful, Cliff. It's not good weather to be out."

"I'm on the way," Hudson said, slipping into his parka.

Within minutes, he was speeding up the Susitna Valley, eyeballing the forested slopes and mountain peaks through low-lying clouds.

When Montgomery regained his senses, he realized he was lying in deep snow. His parachute canopy was stretched out beside him. He had no way of knowing how long he'd been unconscious or how far the wind had dragged him. There was intense pain in his right shoulder. He thought it might be broken. His mittens were missing and his hands were bleeding and numb from the cold. The howling of the wind was the only sound. Fear was beginning to knot his stomach when, down the slope a hundred yards, he spotted another man shedding his chute harness. He called out as loudly as he could.

For almost a minute Montgomery tried to get the man's attention, but he seemed not to hear. To Montgomery, it seemed as if the wind was just throwing his voice back at him. Sometimes he could see the man's shape clearly, but then he would be gone, hidden in the swirling snow. Maybe it was an illusion—like seeing an oasis in the desert where there really was nothing but sand.

He fumbled with the quick-release mechanism on his harness, but without success. His fingers could feel nothing. He felt extreme frustration and tried to make himself concentrate.

"Hello!"

The voice came from the direction where he'd last seen the man.

"I'm up here!" Montgomery called as loudly as he could.

Then again he heard, "Hello," but it came that time from another direction, from a small valley, or meadow, lying below him.

Montgomery was quick to realize there were two men, and they were calling to each other. They appeared to be closer together than he was from either of them.

"Are you okay?" he heard the first man say.

"I think so, but I need some help with this harness," came the answer.

Montgomery watched as a figure emerged from the mist and took lunging steps down the slope, perpendicular to him. Actually, he was doing more rolling than stepping. Several minutes passed before he reached the second man. Montgomery watched them stand close together for a few minutes, and then the first man seemed to be helping the other get out of his parachute harness. A long period of time, seeming like hours, elapsed before they started moving—away from him.

Montgomery had scooped up his parachute canopy in his arms and was trying to walk toward them, but the snow was so deep that he was making little headway.

"Hey! Hey!" he called. "I'm up here!"

Finally, the two men turned and looked in his direction. Montgomery waved frantically with his good arm. One man started toward him. Montgomery kept walking as fast as he could to meet him. The snow gradually became shallower and he was able to cover a greater distance. It took several minutes, but the two weary men finally stood face to face.

Montgomery recognized Eli LaDuke at once. He had been going to St. Lawrence Island, along with Ed Olson. LaDuke recognized Montgomery and greeted him by name. LaDuke was breathing hard.

After a while, when his panting had subsided, he asked, "Can't you get out of your harness?"

"No. My shoulder aches and I can't feel my hands at all. I lost my mittens. I can't stop myself from shaking."

LaDuke struggled to free the release on the chute harness.

"Snow's packed in and it's frozen solid," he said. "It's the same problem Bob Sallis had with his. He's the other fellow back down there waiting for us."

"He hurt?"

"His knee's banged up. Nothing else I know about, except he's bruised and has scrapes and cuts."

Finally, after an agonizingly long time, LaDuke freed the frozen mechanism and the straps dropped off Montgomery's shoulders.

"We've got to get down this slope," LaDuke said, motioning in the direction from which he had come. "We need to get down to the wreck. There might be others alive."

"Did you see it? The airplane?"

"Some of it. It's in pieces. We need to get down there before it gets dark."

As if to emphasize the importance of haste, LaDuke started back along the trail he had made. Montgomery followed, hugging himself to keep his arms and shoulders as immobile as possible. Walking was arduous. It was necessary to lift a leg high to clear the snow, and then to lunge forward and down to get ready for the next step, an unnatural action that jarred his upper body and sent pain to his injured shoulder. He could see LaDuke was having problems also, although he had no apparent injury to contend with. Montgomery tried to keep up, but soon fell behind. LaDuke waited for him. It was slow going.

"I think my shoulder might be broken," Montgomery said.

After that, they rested often until the three of them were together. Sallis was hunched over, apparently trying to make himself as small a target for the wind as possible.

The three men continued on, breaking a new trail and having to go even slower. LaDuke led, followed by Sallis, and then Montgomery. Sallis was limping, but kept up. They'd go a few feet, then stop to rest. They went on like that for several minutes. The wind was blowing right into Montgomery's face, numbing his exposed skin. The terrain gradually leveled out, making walking easier.

It snowed hard most of the time. Occasionally, it let up at the same time as the wind died down and Montgomery would catch a glimpse of a far-off valley, a land that looked frozen as hard as iron.

Then he started seeing parts of the airplane. It didn't look like an airplane at all. There were pieces scattered all around him—and baggage, too.

"This is a terrible thing!" he said aloud as the impact of what had happened fully hit him.

I'd been alone in woods before. I had hiked and camped solo in southwestern West Virginia while growing up. Realistically, though, it had been impossible to get more than a mile from civilization, and I'd always known exactly where I was. I had never before experienced the loneliness I now felt. Minutes before, I'd been sitting in the warm cabin of a C-47. Now I was alone on the side of a snow-covered mountain *somewhere* in interior Alaska.

Questions came to my mind in rapid succession. What had happened to the others? Was I the only one alive? What about Knapp and McDonough? I'd seen other parachutes. Maybe my friends had survived.

I was trembling excessively. There seemed to be little feeling in my body. I touched my face to see if I had injuries there, but my hands were like chunks of wood. I alternated between putting them in my armpits and rubbing them together until circulation started to return. When I could feel my fingers again, I started rubbing numb areas of my face until it began to feel normal. After several minutes, it dawned on me that I had to get rid of the parachute harness. Somehow, in spite of its frozen condition, I managed to free myself.

Snow was packed into my clothing. I shook it out of my hood and pulled as much as I could out of the top of my uniform. I unzipped my parka to remove what had packed in there. If my body heat melted it, I'd be wet, which wasn't good. Fortunately, my bunny boots were tight enough that no snow had gotten into them.

The snow let up a little and I could see the terrain better. I started calling. My voice seemed lost against the wail of the wind. I tightened my parka hood with the neck strap. Not only had I lost my mittens, but my pile hat, as well. The hat would have covered my ears, but the parka hood would partially serve that purpose. The mittens, though, were a serious loss. The wind chill must be minus thirty or lower, I guessed. Hands uncovered for long would be in danger of frostbite. I kept them in my armpits except when I absolutely had to use them.

My right leg hurt. I must have twisted it or maybe banged it on a rock in my long glide across the slope. I tried to examine my leg, but my hands fumbled as I felt around. I rubbed them some more to improve circulation. Then I noticed a few spots of red in the snow around my feet. Blood! Immediately I thought of the wolf I had seen just before I landed.

I reexamined my legs, but found nothing. I had two layers of clothing, which consisted of my long johns and my dress blue trousers. The latter were quite thick. I couldn't see any rips in the cloth. I felt around my face. My hand came away red. I felt my lips and found them thick and swollen. That was probably where the blood in the snow had come from.

I fought my panic. My situation was clearly desperate, but reason told me to think things through. I didn't know where the airplane had come down. There was maybe another hour of daylight left. What could I do? To head upwind seemed the most logical thing. The wreckage would most likely be in that direction. *All right, but try to find someone first.*

I called again, "Hello! Anybody there? Hello!"

I called out the same words repeatedly for several minutes. I hadn't moved more than a few feet from where I had stopped. I considered going farther up the slope before heading into the wind. I might be able to see a greater distance when the snow let up. I didn't want to stay where I was without shelter. The larger boulders I had nearly hit when coming in might provide some protection—if I could make it there.

It was then I heard a faint call from above me. It sounded like a "Hello!" Then again, more distinctly, "Hello-o-o! Hello-o-o!"

"Down here!" I answered, and began moving toward the voice.

It took us several minutes to find each other. The spot where I'd been standing was windblown and snow was sparse, but as I moved away, it became deeper. Then, out of the white swirls appeared a brown parka-clad figure, struggling through drifts with the folds of his parachute clutched to his chest. As he got closer, I could see a round face with blond hair through the front of his hood.

I don't think two strangers were ever happier to see each other. We didn't shake hands, or even speak at first, but just stood close together for a few moments as he got his breath back.

Finally, he said, "You hurt?"

"No, I don't think so—just cold. How about you?"

"I don't think anything serious."

"You see anybody else?"

"No, no one."

"Did you see where it went down?" I asked.

"Not really. I saw parts falling, but I'm not sure which direction that was from here."

We briefly shared our experiences. We'd both been dozing when we hit that first downdraft.

I introduced myself, almost as an afterthought. Names hadn't seemed important.

"Well, Pratt," he said, "I'm Ed Olson, and it looks like we're in a bit of trouble."

"They'll surely have planes out looking for us," I said.

"This weather makes it tough. It does seem to be clearing a little."

Indeed, it was a little lighter and the wind had died somewhat, but visibility could still be measured in yards.

"I heard something!" Olson said, pointing a mitten into the whiteness.

Sure enough, a lone figure, leaning into the wind, soon appeared, fifty yards along the slope at about our altitude. As he got closer, we could see he was having difficulty. He'd struggle along through waist-deep snow for four or five steps, then pause to rest. When he finally reached us, he was near exhaustion. Ice had formed all around the rim of his parka hood. His eyebrows were exaggerated mounds of white fluff. Puffs of condensation came from his mouth and nostrils with such frequency that he seemed to be emitting one single long breath.

"I heard you yelling," he gasped, and then started brushing snow from his pants. His name, he said a little later, was Ed Fox.

We gradually made our way back to where I had left my parachute. It was then that we heard an airplane high overhead.

"A jet," I said. "They're looking for us."

"He can't see through these clouds," Fox said.

The whine of the distant jet fighter eventually disappeared—and with it hopes for an early rescue. It would soon be dark and, ready or not, we were going to be there for the night. We couldn't stay in the open. We needed shelter of some kind. Silently, I said a prayer of thanks that we'd found one another. I hoped that if any others were alive, they had also gotten together.

We had no chance of reaching the crash site before dark. We decided, after a little discussion, that the best action for us was to find a spot right there and try to make a shelter from the two parachutes. There was a rock about four feet high upwind from us. We made our way there. The snow wasn't as deep in the lee of the rock, but we spent several minutes clearing away what there was.

"I think I saw blood back there in the snow," Olson said to me.

"I cut my lip. It bled pretty good for a while." After a moment, I added, "I saw a wolf as I was landing."

"Was he going up the hill?" Fox asked.

"Yeah—like something was chasing him!"

"I saw that, too—but I think it was a fox."

I didn't feel like being assertive, but I knew what I'd seen.

"I'm pretty sure it was a wolf," I said.

We were quiet for a while. I knew their thoughts were similar to mine. Blood! Wolves! A real Jack London kind of thing. But this wasn't a story from the pages of a book. I tried to put wolves out of my mind.

Chapter Ten

The other three men trying to reach the wreckage were finding it tough going. They had stopped to rest and stood close together with their backs to the wind.

LaDuke had an urgent matter to address.

"I need to get this covered up," he said, indicating the rip in his pants. "I'm going to be in trouble soon if I don't."

"There's a duffel bag back there in the snow," Montgomery said. "It's open. We might get something out of it. I need gloves."

"Show me!"

Montgomery led him back a few yards along their trail. The bag was split and the contents were scattered, most of it covered by new and blowing snow. There were still a few articles of clothing in the bag. Montgomery tried to dig something out, but his hands were practically useless.

"Here, Huey, let me," LaDuke said. There were no gloves, but he soon found what he needed for himself, a pair of dress blue trousers. "They look like they might fit," he said.

It was a clumsy exchange, taking several minutes. He had to remove his boots in order to pull the borrowed trousers over his own. It was with relief that he finally got the laces and buckles of his boots refastened. Then they trudged back to Sallis.

"We need to get to the wreckage," Sallis said. "There's survival gear there. Knickerbocker showed it to me when we boarded."

They resumed their trek down the little valley. The snow had let up and they could see more of the scattered airplane parts. One large dark shape, the one LaDuke had seen earlier, was probably the fuselage. Farther away, a flatter shape might be a wing. All around them were baggage items, some intact, some broken open with their contents scattered. Without doubt, there were things they could use, but now wasn't the time.

They moved slowly, helping one another when they could. LaDuke thought he had prepared himself, but he was still stunned when they came upon a body lying in a crater in the snow, partially covered by an open parachute.

"Is he dead?" Montgomery asked.

"Yeah," LaDuke replied after moving close enough to make a judgment. "His chute must have opened too late."

He shuddered as he remembered what a narrow escape he'd had himself. They were all quiet for several moments, and then LaDuke pulled the canopy over the body.

Not far away, they found another body. Again, LaDuke got close enough to determine that the man was dead. A briefcase was close by. LaDuke picked it up and saw it had Capt. Hill's name on the flap. He tucked it under his arm. He'd put it somewhere for safekeeping.

They finally reached the fuselage section. It lay alone, sheared from the cockpit and tail sections, neither of which was in sight. LaDuke figured the fuselage was lying in a northwest position, based on subtle light he could make out in the south. That made sense because of the direction the aircraft had been heading. There was a gaping hole high up on the left side, about midway on the shortened cabin area.

"Hello! Anybody here?"

There was no answer. LaDuke had not really expected one.

"I guess we have to go in there," Sallis said.

LaDuke was even more assertive.

"We *must* get that survival gear—if it wasn't dumped out on the way down."

They crouched on the leeward side to rest. Montgomery was still shaking.

"I'm freezing!" he said.

LaDuke had seen Sallis favoring his left leg and he knew that he was in pain, too, but he wasn't complaining.

"We've got to either get inside—or build a shelter," LaDuke said. "It'll be dark soon. We have to get out of the wind. Either way, we need what's inside."

He looked at the other two and knew neither of them was up to the effort.

After carefully planning his route and letting Montgomery and Sallis initially steady him, he managed to climb through the big hole. The fuselage lay tilted slightly to the right, so he had to climb up and then down. The metal was extremely slippery; there were jagged edges everywhere. The aluminum skin seemed to have been ripped, as if by giant hands.

Once inside, he moved slowly into the rear section. He had dreaded the possibility of finding more victims, but found himself quite alone. Maybe up front. However, he wouldn't be able to get up there, anyway. Snow was packed into a severely compressed space. It looked as if the open front, devoid of the cockpit, had scooped up snow and ice on impact. There was a strong smell of aviation gasoline, but no evidence of fire. Objects were scattered all around and covered with snow. He dug into several masses, shoveling with his hands.

Sallis called from outside, "What are you finding?"

"Sleeping bags!"

"Do you see anybody?"

"No, but I can't get into the front section. Anyway, we can't stay in here. Too many things to snag on in the dark."

LaDuke gathered what useful items he could find and placed them under the hole. From there, he tossed them up and over the top, where the others could retrieve them. Then he retraced the treacherous route he had followed going in. He was more than happy to be outside again. They inventoried the recovered items. There were several sleeping bags, a couple of survival kits, half a dozen parachutes, about a dozen flares, and two tarps. Sallis had also found a piece of plywood outside, probably part of the cargo floor. They stacked everything next to the fuselage, where it could be covered with one of the tarps. They had just finished when they heard an airplane motor.

The little green aircraft was on them almost before they had time to react. It flew out of clouds not far from the higher peak to the north. Luckily, LaDuke was right beside the pile of recovered items. He snatched a flare from under the tarp, and despite trembling hands, managed to light it and fire it toward the small airplane.

Montgomery was waving as best he could with his good arm. Sallis was yelling and trying to jump up and down.

"He had to see that!" Sallis said. "You almost hit him."

LaDuke was also screaming, but he wasn't sure what he was saying or even if it made sense. He watched the airplane disappear into clouds that covered the surrounding hills. The motor sound faded.

"Come back!" pleaded Montgomery, softly.

It wasn't long before they heard it again, and then it appeared once more, coming straight down the narrow valley between the peaks. LaDuke held his breath as it seemed one wing might hit the steep mountainside. The airplane roared barely a hundred feet overhead, swooping up only when it had passed over the wreckage site.

"He sees us!" Sallis said.

They could tell from sound and direction of the engine noise that the pilot was making another approach. That time, there was a wing dip, short and quick, but definite. *They had been seen.* Then the little airplane went to full power and turned south. The sound finally faded.

Their spirits were lifted, despite worsening weather. Someone knew their location. They could wait it out. However, they needed to look to their immediate needs. All three men worked with renewed energy, even with their aches and pains. They found metal pieces large enough to act as windbreakers. With darkness swiftly approaching, they simply chose a spot on the leeward side of the fuselage, one that looked reasonably sheltered. They popped some parachutes and put them on top of the snow. The plywood flooring went on top of that. Their sleeping bags would be on the plywood, which they hoped would block some of the cold. They hung another canopy over jagged edges of metal on the fuselage and back over the makeshift beds. It was dark when they finished. They were exhausted. Montgomery had simply collapsed in a heap next to the fuselage and appeared unable to get up.

"You okay, Huey?" LaDuke asked.

"Tired . . . and cold."

His head was down and he was still shivering.

"We need to get inside, out of the wind," LaDuke said.

Sallis was grim-faced.

"We've got to do something for him. I think he's in shock. He needs to be kept warm."

"All we have is body heat," LaDuke said.

They helped Montgomery into a sleeping bag and threw a tarp over him. Sallis and LaDuke lay on either side, practically on top of the big man. They would survive the long night, LaDuke knew, and they had hope of rescue the following day.

Cliff Hudson's aircraft had no radio, so he headed back toward Curry to report his find. Running low under the overcast, he spotted the Curry airstrip through snow squalls. Visibility was low and the field had no lights. He landed, using the local pilots' accepted method of lining up an approach with nearby railroad signal lights. As he taxied up toward the big Curry Hotel, he was surprised to find that an advance detachment of the 10th Air Rescue had just arrived and was setting up operations. A military helicopter and a Beaver sat ready, not far from the runway.

Hudson went directly to the officer in charge and gave him detailed directions for finding the downed aircraft. The helicopter left at once. Hudson thought it would have been expedient to invite him along, but they didn't, and he watched them fly north and disappear into the squalls. A part of him felt relieved that, having done his duty, he was out of it, but he was also concerned that they might not find the site.

He'd been lucky, he thought, as he made his way back to his airplane. He went over recent events in his mind. As soon as he'd gotten the telephone call, he had flown up the valley, pretty much under the worst of the weather. Visibility to the ground was generally not bad, but the ridge to the west was covered with clouds. There were high winds there, he had concluded.

He hadn't had much information to go on. ACS had reported what Nick Botner had called in. Parachutes had been seen near, or somewhat north of, Gold Creek. Hudson, on reaching Gold Creek, began to section off the valley in his mind. He'd fly a pattern of sorts over the wide flats between river and ridge. He knew military aircraft followed the valley in their flight pattern, so it was unlikely the C-47 would have been over the ridge or over the Talkeetna Mountains to the east.

He was making his first pass west of Gold Creek toward the ridge at about four thousand feet, letting his eyes roam over a broad expanse of forested valley as he went. He pulled up sharply as he approached the dark outline of the ridge to make his turn. He knew the ridge was about four thousand feet high for most of its length, with some higher peaks close to five thousand. He was also well aware of the danger of being low there, especially with the capricious winds lurking around the tops, wanting to suck his little airplane down. Even knowing that, whether by luck or premonition, he had swung wide at the top of his turn and entered thicker clouds surrounding the ridge. Maybe—just maybe—they could be over that far.

Then he saw the flare. It was unexpected, and too close to his wing for comfort. Elated, he completed his turn, went out over the valley, and circled to go over the area again. He held his altitude at about forty-five hundred feet and aimed for the valley he had spotted between the north peak and lower hills to the south. Through his wire-rimmed glasses, he focused on the spot, daring hardly a glance at his instrument panel. It would be tricky going in there, he knew. Nevertheless, he had committed his aircraft and himself without inner debate. The peak on his right seemed close as he throttled back to get a better look. Finally, through a break in the clouds, he had spotted the scattered wreckage. Much of the silver and red surfaces had been covered with snow, but there was enough showing to let him know that he'd found what he was looking for. It was hard to believe he'd found it so quickly.

Three men were jumping up and down near what looked to be a fuselage section. He pulled up and went around again. He had hastily scribbled a note, promising to return with help. Stuffing the note into a weighted message bag, he had again made the tricky maneuver through the narrow valley. Slowing down once more, he dropped the message bag. The wind caught it, and judging by the direction it went, he feared the men would never see it. As he had sped away from the crash site, he saw that the whole valley had become engulfed in a general snowstorm.

Safely on the ground at Curry, Hudson scrapped his decision to go to Talkeetna and decided to stick around awhile and see what happened. His fears were soon realized. The helicopter returned, forced back by high winds and low visibility. Hudson decided to stay overnight with a friend.

Darkness came swiftly, even before we had time to find and uncover stones to hold the chutes in place against the wind. We ended up laying one chute on the ground and putting the other over us as we lay in the lee of the rock.

That provided us some shelter from the wind, but not from the cold that seemed to emanate upward from the earth. We lay parallel to one another, as close together as we could. All three of us shivered excessively, our bodies fighting against the penetrating cold. I tried to think warm thoughts, thoughts of home, family, friends—anything that might take my mind off the situation. The effort was largely wasted.

Maudie Betscher was anxious, but not frantic. Bob's plane was down, but at least he was alive. She had just returned from the Cunninghams' in Anchorage when Lt. Mercer had stopped by their trailer to give her the news.

"The wreckage has been spotted in the mountains," he had said. "Two or three people waved at a bush pilot who flew over the site. That's about all we know, except that rescue operations have been set up close by. They'll start the recovery in the morning."

She put Keith to bed and prepared to retire. She knew she should get some sleep, for tomorrow would be a long day. Bob could be injured, even though he'd managed to wave. Nevertheless, there was the long night ahead. Even with the survival gear she knew was in the Beaver, it wouldn't be a comfortable night. She was thankful that even though it was snowing, it wasn't bitter cold. Then it occurred to her that it would be much colder in the mountains.

At least his position was known. She was sure he'd said he was to have only one or two passengers. If three men had been spotted, then they must all be alive.

As she was about to retire, there was a knock at the door. Three of Bob's squadron members stood there with the overhead light illuminating the snow swirling about their heads. The expression on their faces told her they bore news—and it wasn't good.

"Mrs. Betscher," one of them said, "we don't know if Lt. Betscher is one of the survivors seen at the crash site, but we felt we had to come and tell you something you may not be aware of. He was scheduled to fly a Beaver to Fairbanks—"

"Yes, I know."

"Well—they made a change at the last minute. The aircraft he was taking to Fairbanks was a C-47 with several passengers. Thirteen, I think it was."

The ache in her heart was almost unbearable.

Chapter Eleven

LaDuke was aroused from a fitful sleep.

"What's that?" he said.

"Wolves!" Montgomery replied. "They've been howlin' and snarlin' all night."

LaDuke listened intently, but heard nothing beyond the persistent wind and the hammering effect it had on their flimsy shelter.

"I don't hear them now."

"They come off and on. They'll be back."

"You sure it's wolves? Maybe it's somebody from the airplane."

"No—he's right," Sallis said as his head emerged from his sleeping bag. "It's wolves, all right!"

"What can we do?" Montgomery asked, sounding anxious.

It worried LaDuke, too. Being stranded on a stormy mountaintop was bad enough, but the new fear seemed worse, and immediate. Wolves, from what he knew about them, were unpredictable.

"One of us should stay awake to keep watch," he said.

Sallis and Montgomery grunted their approval.

"I don't mind watching," Montgomery said.

"No—I'll go first," LaDuke answered, making a judgment that, although Montgomery seemed improved, he was probably the most in need of rest. Then he told Sallis, "I'll call you next."

"I don't expect I'll be asleep," Sallis replied.

We passed the greater stretch of the night trying to keep our circulatory systems going. I pounded my feet on the ground and bumped them together repeatedly. I crossed and uncrossed my arms. Keep something moving all the time, was my thinking. My shivering was constant. I'd read somewhere that shivering is nature's way of protecting mammals from the cold.

About every hour, we exchanged places so that each of us could have a turn in the coveted middle position. In the beginning, I tried to hold onto the chute fabric to keep it from blowing. When my hands became numb, I gave up and put them in my armpits.

It seemed as if the night was going to last forever, but eventually I had brief periods of sleep—if it could be called that. Several times I emerged from semi-consciousness with numb feet and joints aching. Once, I heard wolves yelping. I thought I heard sniffing just outside our shelter. The other two men were moving, and I knew they'd heard it also.

I tried to think of other things, of my Salt Rock friends, of Eve, of Rose, and, of course, of Millie. What was she doing tonight? She'd be sleeping, no doubt; it was five hours later in the East. Would she know what had happened? No—how could she? She might never know if I didn't make it. She'd just think I stopped writing because I'd changed my mind about her.

Mother was another matter. She and Dawson would be notified. I hoped we'd be rescued before they heard about it. Despite Mother's strong faith, she became panicky over things like that.

Leaving home for the first time in the spring had been stressful. With packed handbag in the early morning light, I prepared to leave Salt Rock for the induction center at Ashland, Kentucky.

I called to Dawson through his bedroom door, "I've got to go now."

His voice quivered a little as he said, "All right. You be careful."

Saying goodbye to Mother was gut-wrenching.

"Be faithful," she said.

"I will be, Mother."

"Be faithful to everything we've taught you. Be faithful to God."

"I will, Mother!"

"Go to church."

"I will!"

"I'll pray every day that God will watch over you."

I patted Spike's head.

"Stay, boy," I said, as I closed the gate and headed for Atchley's store to catch the early bus. I didn't dare look back.

Was I being watched over? Had my mother's faith saved me? Did *my* faith enter the picture? If so, did I have enough to see me through? Throughout the night such thoughts assailed me, bringing both discomfort and support. Friends and relatives marched before me in seemingly endless numbers.

It came as a surprise when the first evidence of daylight penetrated the chute fabric. It seemed incredible that we had really left the miserable night behind. I dropped the hood from my head, and immediately my face was enveloped in the icy fabric of the parachute. Our combined breathing had created condensation in the enclosed space. I pulled the cloth from my face and struggled to get outside. When my head finally emerged, it was not yet daylight, but it was definitely getting brighter. There were several inches of new snow, but the wind was no longer at blizzard strength. The air was frigid. I could see stars. The storm had lifted, as had my spirits. *Now they would find us!*

I managed to get out from under the snow-covered canopy. Rolling onto my knees, I tried to rise. My entire body was sore. I stood up in stages, taking more than a minute to complete the process. Fox and Olson were also out and appeared to be experiencing similar problems.

My hands were sore and swollen, and a couple of my fingertips had no feeling. I thought I might have some frostbite. We stomped our feet and raised our arms repeatedly in calisthenic-like motions. After several minutes of getting my body working, I walked a few feet away and unzipped my parka. Besides needing to urinate, I wanted to look at my right leg. It had throbbed during the night and was now quite stiff. I eventually got my trousers down.

I was surprised at what I saw. The right upper leg of my long johns was caked with blood. I quickly pulled the long johns down to see what injuries I had. Olson and Fox came over to see why I was undressing.

"I guess this is where the blood came from," I said.

On the inside of my thigh, about seven inches above my knee, was an open hole nearly the diameter of a quarter. I twisted my leg from side to side and blood oozed out and ran down. The wound looked deep.

Fox turned away, but Olson was more analytical. He had some trouble seeing, but moved in close enough to examine my wound.

"I'll bet a piece of pipe did that," he said.

I'd been thinking the same thing. There must have been all kinds of exposed tubing in the airplane as it came apart. The injury, as gruesome as it looked, didn't cause me great concern. I knew I could walk, and somehow the tubing had missed hitting an artery or bone. It had gone through my dress blue trousers and my long johns. There was a rip in the long johns, but I had to feel around to find the hole in my trousers. The tubing had punched through, and the wool fabric had closed up. I got my clothing back on quickly.

In the meantime, dawn was slipping in. The sky was overcast, with patches of light here and there, but the wind stayed moderate. In the distance, from the direction in which we'd been blown in our parachutes, was a valley. The sky showed light above the mountains beyond the valley. That way was east.

We'd known from the beginning that we were on a mountain, but now our location was more clearly defined. It was a high mountain, judging by the apparent distance to the valley. The slope on which we were standing extended upward to an undetermined height, appearing to touch the roiling clouds. Below us, at a distance of a hundred yards, was a gully where our slope met an equally high hill to the south. Looking west, in the direction from which Fox had walked, the two hills met at a higher elevation. We could see no farther. Of course, Olson had trouble seeing anything more than a few feet away.

Then, the barely audible wail of a train whistle drifted up from the valley. It was so unexpected that we looked at one another for confirmation. It was light enough to see now, and we strained our eyes to make out anything looking like railroad tracks or civilization.

The valley was broad and covered with forested areas, but over at the far side was a long streak of white, paralleling the distant range, most likely a frozen river. Beyond the river was a darker streak that could be a railroad.

"How far is it?" I asked.

"Ten miles—maybe more," Fox said.

We didn't hear the whistle again. Our eyes searched a long time, looking for smoke or anything else that might indicate the presence of people. We could see nothing that resembled civilization. Nevertheless, we knew there was a railroad there somewhere and took some comfort in that.

"We need to decide what to do," Olson said.

We discussed options. We could stay where we were, as our basic survival training instructors had taught us, or we could move up to the top of the ridge where we might be able to spot the wreckage. A third choice would be descending what was probably a steep mountain face and heading east toward the railroad.

The subject of rank didn't really occur to us. As it turned out, we were all enlisted men, with Fox having the highest rank of Airman First Class. Olson was Airman Second Class. I was lowest rank at Airman Third Class. Nevertheless, we made our decisions by consensus.

The first point of agreement was that we couldn't stay where we were. We had no shelter but the parachutes and greatly feared the consequences of having to spend another night there. If it got colder, we could freeze to death.

We discussed climbing up on the ridge to look for the wreckage. There would be enough daylight for that. However, if we didn't find it, we would be no better off than we were now. In fact, we'd probably be in worse shape, since the wind could be at gale force up there.

The most logical thing, we decided, was to get off the mountain and into timber, where we could build a fire. Fox had a few matches.

"These will get a fire going," he said, pulling a couple of crumpled envelopes out of his pocket. "I found them yesterday while I was walking. One of the mail bags must have broken open."

We reluctantly decided to leave the parachutes behind. They were just too heavy and cumbersome to carry, even though they would have made handy shelter in the woods. If we had a knife, we could cut the canopies off the heavy harnesses. But we didn't have a knife, and we made the tough choice.

We set our eyes and our hopes on the distant valley. The white expanse stretched out tantalizingly below us. We believed that once we were in the woods we could survive, even in colder weather. We could piece together a shelter of sorts from branches and deadwood and we could have a fire. However, without the parachutes for cover, we had to get into the woods that day—before dark. Another problem was developing even as we talked; the weather seemed to be deteriorating once more. The blue areas of sky had disappeared and the wind had picked up again, although not with the force of the day before. It was hard to determine whether the swirling snow now hitting our faces was falling from above or being kicked up by the wind.

We started diagonally down the slope toward the gully. From there, we'd make our way straight down the mountain, if that was possible. The mountainside would be steep, if the brief glimpse I had the day before was real and not just something from my imagination. We'd proceed with caution until we could get a feel for what we were facing.

Earlier that same morning, my mother, with a nose for trouble, had experienced anxiety when she heard on the radio that there had been an airplane crash in Alaska and that several men were missing.

Dawson was still sleeping. He worked the 4-to-12 shift at the Rail Mill in Huntington and hadn't gotten home until after 1 AM. She went about her morning chores, feeding her chickens and milking the two family cows.

Cline Adkins, her brother, who lived down the lane with my grandparents, had dropped off the morning newspaper. She scanned it quickly. There was a small article about the crash, but it revealed nothing she hadn't heard on the radio. She picked up a letter that had arrived the day before, written on January 31. She looked at it again.

I am still at Ft. Rich. I give up. I don't know when I'm leaving.
I'll let you know when I get there.

The part that bothered her most involved the weather:

We had a cold spell here this week in which the temp. went
down to -28. That's cold for Anchorage. It was -52 at Ladd
at the same time.

She heard Dawson getting up and met him at the foot of the
stairs.

"Dawson—there's been an airplane crash in Alaska!"

"When?"

"Yesterday. I think Rupert's in it."

"Ah, Glenna—that's not likely. They have thousands of airplanes
flying every day up there. Anyway, they would have let us know by
now."

"He's in it—I know it! I want you to go down to the store and
get word to Della McComas and Nona Gill. Tell them to pray for
Rupert. They'll get the word around."

"Aw, Glenna—"

"Do it right now."

Chapter Twelve

The other trio passed much of the night watching for wolves, taking turns in one-hour shifts. While one watched, the other two tried to rest, although numbing cold invaded their sleeping bags and any slumber consisted of brief excursions just below consciousness. Awakening brought immediate and lucid recall of their predicament.

Finally, LaDuke saw the morning light begin to filter through the canopy. The wind had died to an irritating whimper and the snow had stopped, but not before a new foot-deep layer of white had accumulated. The men pushed their way out of their makeshift shelter.

It was an eerie scene in the predawn light. No longer were the small scattered parts of the airplane visible. Instead, there were white mounds all around. The main fuselage, to which their shelter was attached, was covered, except for some windblown surfaces.

All three men had trouble getting around. They were sore from bruises, cuts, and scrapes, and stiff from cold. Sallis' knee seemed to be improved, but apparently still restricted his movement. Montgomery was more active than the day before, but was still favoring his shoulder. LaDuke walked a few yards around the shelter, hoping to find something that might be of use. Finding nothing except some tracks that could have been made by wolves, he rejoined the other two men.

"It's cleared up," Montgomery said. "The search planes will come back."

Sallis was more cautious.

"Look at the clouds," he said, pointing west. "I think we have to prepare to be here awhile."

"You're right," LaDuke said. "It's nasty weather—and unpredictable. We could be here several days. They know where we are. That's the good part. They'll get us out eventually."

"I heard a train whistle this morning," Montgomery said. "Way off."

"I heard it, too. To the east."

No one spoke for a while as all three men strained their eyes to see across the valley toward the distant hills. LaDuke thought he could make out a line above a river that could, just possibly, be a railroad. It was, however, too far to be sure—and who knew what lay between them and it. It might as well have been on the moon. He could see no other signs of civilization—no smoke, no buildings.

"The railroad's there," Montgomery said with new determination. "Maybe we'd be best off to try and get to it."

"Huey, we're up high on a mountain," LaDuke said, trying not to show impatience. "Look how deep the snow is. We'd never make it. We've got to keep in mind that they know we're here."

Montgomery didn't push his point, but LaDuke could see he wasn't convinced.

Sallis had his mind on something else.

"Why don't we get out and see if we can find some things to use?" he said. "We saw duffel bags over there yesterday. Under the circumstances, I think it's all right for us to take what we need."

"Good idea," LaDuke said, then added, "I'm worried about wolves. We need a way to protect ourselves. There might be guns or knives in somebody's luggage."

LaDuke was relieved that the snowy mounds where the two bodies lay were undisturbed. The sounds of wolves during the night had initiated all kinds of gruesome thoughts. Going back to the fuselage again, they searched more thoroughly without the time pressure they'd felt the day before. They found more flares, smoke bombs, and several containers of canned heat. In the back section of the fuselage, they discovered frozen, dehydrated cheese and candy. Hoping to thaw the food, they took turns trying to light the canned heat containers. They did get some to flare, but then they sputtered and went out. Finally, they gave up and nibbled at the candy and cheese in its frozen state and ate snow to quench their thirst.

Sallis had been right about the weather. It was snowing again and visibility had been reduced to a quarter mile. They made their way carefully around the area, digging in the snow, searching for anything they could use. Montgomery found an undamaged handbag. The zipper was frozen, but he managed to force it open.

"Look at this!" he whooped, holding up a large, dark-handled pocketknife.

It was a lucky break. A knife would serve many purposes, LaDuke figured, especially for protection against wolves. They soon found an immediate use for the new tool when they uncovered an intact duffel bag, still locked. The knife easily slit the canvas and someone's wardrobe lay open before them. Necessity overcame guilt about taking what they needed from the bag. Montgomery found a much-needed pair of gloves. They all took items that would help layer out the cold.

"Here's what we need!" LaDuke cried. He held up a forty-five automatic handgun. He removed the clip. "Empty!"

They searched the duffel bag and clothing thoroughly, but found no ammunition. Disappointed, LaDuke put the gun beside Capt. Hill's briefcase under the front of the fuselage.

Through their plundering, they became better acquainted with the crash area. LaDuke could see that they were in a depression or little valley a hundred yards across. To the south were rounded low hills, stepping gradually higher in a southwest direction. It was back there that he and Montgomery had landed. Sallis had been slightly north of them, at a lower altitude, but in a higher part of the depression. To the east, the land sloped down and just seemed to disappear into the backdrop of the faraway valley where they had heard the train. Whether it descended gradually or dropped off suddenly, he couldn't tell. Not far to the north were steeper and higher peaks.

There were high mounds of snow everywhere, indicating the locations of several large pieces of the C-47. They seemed to form a straight line. A hundred feet behind the broken fuselage and their shelter lay the tail section, or what was left of it. Behind that, about the same distance, was a shape resembling the middle wing section. In the other direction, up ahead of the fuselage about a hundred feet, was a mound LaDuke thought might be the cockpit. It was another hundred feet beyond that to the base of a high, steep hill. Other smaller pieces were under the snow all around them. They had seen them the previous evening. Apparently, the wreckage was widely scattered.

They tried to uncover some of the larger pieces so they might be seen from the air, a task soon discovered to be impossible. The wind picked up again and new snow squalls seemed to materialize within seconds. Falling and blowing snow quickly covered everything again. LaDuke was silently thankful for the flyer who had spotted them before the new snowfall.

They dragged some manageable pieces of wreckage to their shelter to strengthen it against the wind. The snow was so deep that they had to "roll" through it to get from place to place. The weather continued to be unpredictable. The sun would come back for a time and then disappear behind moisture-laden clouds. The wind was consistently difficult.

U.S. Air Force messengers were visiting several homes across the country. The telegram delivered to my mother read:

MRS. GLENNA A. MORRISON
SALT ROCK, WVIR

IT IS WITH DEEP REGRET THAT I OFFICIALLY INFORM YOU THAT YOUR SON, A/3C RUPERT C. PRATT, HAS BEEN MISSING IN FLIGHT SINCE 5 FEBRUARY 1954 BETWEEN ELMENDORF AFB AND LADD AFB ALASKA. EXTENSIVE SEARCH NOW BEING CONDUCTED. WHEN FURTHER INFORMATION IS RECEIVED YOU WILL BE NOTIFIED IMMEDIATELY. A LETTER CONTAINING FURTHER DETAILS WILL BE FORWARDED TO YOU AT THE EARLIEST POSSIBLE DATE. PLEASE ACCEPT MY SINCERE SYMPATHY IN THIS TIME OF ANXIETY.

MAJOR GENERAL JOHN H. MCCORMICK
DIRECTOR OF MILITARY PERSONNEL
HEADQUARTERS UNITED STATES AIR FORCE

Olson led the way and I brought up the rear. We hadn't gone more than a few yards before I realized the snow depth was going to be an even bigger problem than we had anticipated. It was up to Olson's waist, and he had to lunge forward with each step in an effort to penetrate the wall of white. After five or six steps, he'd stop and rest. He struggled for thirty minutes before finally looking back at us with a face revealing desperation. We hadn't gone more than a hundred yards.

"We can't get down to the timberline at this pace," Fox said.

"Pratt, you're taller," Olson said. "Maybe you'd better break trail."

I went up front. After a few yards, I saw what Olson had been up against. Normal steps were impossible. I used my body weight to fall forward, making a trough ahead of me, then I'd get up and take a high step into the trough. I repeated the difficult maneuver until I was sweating, despite the cold.

I had another problem. Keeping my bare hands in my pockets or in my armpits was difficult while breaking trail. I had to stop every few yards to warm them.

The slope became steeper, making it easier to move forward. The weather seemed to change every few minutes. It was snowing harder now, and we could no longer see across the valley. At times, visibility was reduced to a few yards. I kept looking behind us at our trail. I thought that if we could keep the line straight we could stay on course. We had been walking nearly two hours, traveling maybe a quarter mile. My leg hurt, and my spirits began to sag.

"Pratt, you're bleeding again," Fox, right behind me, said.

I looked at my leg, but I didn't see anything.

"You've been leaving a trail in the snow," Olson said from the rear, "for a while now."

Fox went up front. We didn't discuss the difficulties we were encountering. We just kept going. We knew we had to. There could be no stopping, except for short periods to catch our breath. I wished they hadn't told me about the blood. It made me conscious of my leg and reminded me again of the wolf I'd seen.

Without warning, we broke out of deep snow onto a windblown ledge where walking was easier. We had been traveling downhill, but now we seemed to have reached a point where the eastern slope made a big drop. We proceeded with greater caution.

Sometimes, when the snow let up, we caught sight of the valley below us. For a few minutes we paralleled the mountain face, moving in a southerly direction. The slope below was dangerously steep. We were looking for the best way down. Our progress brought us into deep snow again, and I went back up front to give Fox a break.

We found a place that looked less perilous than others we had passed.

"I think we should go down here," I said. "Not as many boulders—and it seems smoother."

The others agreed, and I started down. The slope was rounded ahead of us, and deep gullies lay on either side. We could see only a few yards. I worried about what lay below us. For the first time, I was glad for the deep snow. It kept us from sliding into unknown trouble.

We took turns in front as we painstakingly made our descent. There was little talking. Even going downhill was tiring work.

As the morning passed, the forested area gradually came closer. I was up front when we broke out of the snow onto a windblown ice field. The footing was treacherous. We all skidded around and fell down several times. I couldn't see over the crest, but hoped there'd be some snow there to stop us if we lost our footing. I kept moving.

We were close together when I started sliding. I went down on my rear and picked up speed as I went over the edge. I heard yells and knew Fox and Olson were sliding right behind me. Fear gripped me as we slid down what appeared to be a steep field of ice. Visibility extended only a few feet ahead.

I picked up speed and became airborne several times. There was no point in trying to stop or even attempting to slow down. Gravity had taken over; we were as helpless as when we'd been falling through the sky. Now, however, we had no parachutes. I heard Fox and Olson yelling and grunting behind me.

Then, miraculously, the slope leveled off and I slid into deep snow. I cartwheeled several feet and landed face down. I quickly dug myself out to find Olson and Fox right next to me, doing the same.

As soon as we realized we were unhurt, except for a few new bruises, we began to shake snow out of our clothing. My hands were completely numb. As I'd done so often in the past hours, I held them in my armpits until they regained feeling.

We had lost altitude fast, although not the way we would have chosen. The slope behind us looked formidable, far steeper than we had imagined. The glacier-like sheet of ice extended upward for hundreds of feet. How we had escaped serious injury from such a slide was beyond my comprehension.

"The snow's deeper here," Fox said.

There were high mounds all around us. The land rolled eastward, at first fairly steep, but becoming less so in the valley. I could see trees several hundred yards below us. That was where we needed to be.

Higher up, we'd often been able to pick our way through areas of less snow. In our new location, the snow was not only deeper, but consistently so. I tried walking a few feet. It required real effort. The mounds around us revealed themselves as bushes covered by several feet of snow.

It had stopped snowing again. We rested several minutes. Then we took stock of our situation. Olson was worried about dehydration.

"We need liquid," he said. "Try eating snow."

I'd been sweating and knew he was right. I scooped up a handful of snow and shoved it into my mouth. The cold hurt, but I left it there to melt, letting the water trickle down my throat. It was difficult to swallow. Strangely, I hadn't thought about water until Olson mentioned it.

I repeated the process several times until the dryness decreased. My lower lip was swollen and my lower front teeth ached. I gingerly wiggled them and could feel that some were loose.

"Let's get moving," Fox said, taking the lead position. "We've got to get into the timber before dark."

I had lost my wristwatch in the accident, but I judged it to be nearly noon. Our progress was extremely slow. We had to rest after only a few steps. We exchanged places often, but it was discouraging. One thing helped, though. The sky cleared again and the sun lifted our spirits.

"They'll be out to look for us," Olson said.

Fox quickly brought us back to reality.

"We can't wait here for that. We still have to get down into the timber. There's only a few hours of daylight left—and the weather could get worse."

Olson and I knew he was right. We had to push on.

I'd been thinking about snowshoes. Snowshoes would put us up on top of the snow, where we could walk and not have to struggle so hard. I'd never worn snowshoes. No one growing up in southwestern West Virginia needs them. Curiously, my mind became fixed on the subject.

"I could take off my shirt and get some branches to twist around through the sleeves." I said hopefully. "Then I could use my shoelaces to tie the snowshoe to my foot."

Fox and Olson didn't laugh, but Fox said with the beginning of a smile, "Yeah, Pratt—that's only one foot. What're you going to do, hop to the railroad?"

I was too tired to be embarrassed. Perhaps they thought I was delusional, and there might have been some truth in that, but I was desperate to do something to help us move faster. It seemed warmer at the lower altitude, but I wondered if we could stand another night in the open. Just a few days earlier, temperatures had been down around minus 30 degrees in Anchorage and minus 50 in Fairbanks. At our location, it had probably been somewhere in between. It could plunge again in a few hours.

Maybe it would be best to keep going in the dark, not stopping at all. Just keep going! All these thoughts percolated in my brain, keeping the seriousness of the situation before me. We continued on, lunging and high-stepping, until we finally reached an area of small scrub pine. It was getting late; I didn't want to contemplate the consequences of not making it into the woods before dark.

Chapter Thirteen

The morning wore away as Cliff Hudson waited in the Curry Hotel restaurant. He had decided to get back into the action. It was nearly noon before there was a break in the storm. He was out ahead of the Air Force men, clearing the snow from his airplane when another Talkeetna pilot, Don Sheldon, arrived.

"I think I know about where it is," Sheldon said.

"Well," Hudson countered, "I was up there yesterday and I know *exactly* where it is."

"Ride with me," Sheldon said. "I have a radio."

The two men were uncompromising rivals in the air service business, but Hudson recognized the logic in the suggestion. He transferred two pairs of snowshoes from his Aeronica Chief into Sheldon's Super Cub and then climbed into the backseat.

As soon as they were off the ground Hudson said, "Fly over to the hills and turn up toward the highest peaks."

The ceiling was still low and Sheldon flew under it all the way to the base of the ridge.

The small single-engine airplane was on us almost before we heard it. It was traveling north, close to the mountain, only five hundred feet above our level.

Fox shouted, "Jump up and down!"

We jumped as best as we could and waved our arms wildly. We yelled until our voices broke. Finally, we stopped when we realized the airplane was out of our sight.

We looked at one another in wordless desperation. Obviously, the pilot hadn't seen us. Uppermost in my mind was the thought that he would search other areas before coming back. It was a civilian aircraft. As if to accentuate our mood, a fast-moving cloud obscured the sun, putting us in shadows again.

I tried to be positive, to stay upbeat. Keep the faith, my mother would likely say. It is amazing how one event can alter one's outlook. Nothing in our predicament had really changed from five minutes before. We were no more or less stranded in the wilderness. However, with the unexpected appearance of the airplane, and then its departure, my mindset changed. I accepted the reality that we'd never have the stamina for the days of difficult travel it would require to cross the valley, even if reaching the railroad on foot was possible. I was beginning to feel the limiting effects of my leg injury, something I had largely ignored up to that point. Then there was the weather issue. What we were experiencing was mild by Alaska standards and subject to rapid change. A plunge in temperature equated to a plunge in our chances of survival.

As if to accent that thought, Olson said, "It's going to snow again."

On the mountain ridge, sometime after midmorning, the other three men heard an airplane engine.

"Flares!" LaDuke shouted.

Sallis tossed him one. LaDuke got it lit, but because of his haste, he received a burn. The engine sound disappeared. Apparently, the flare hadn't been seen.

Angrily, LaDuke nursed his hand. It had started snowing heavily again. The wind blasted fine icy grains into their faces.

Something had caught Cliff Hudson's attention. He leaned forward and shouted over the engine noise, "Down there behind us! I saw something!"

He pointed to a line in the snow extending from near the top of the ridge, down the steep face, and almost into the timberline.

"Could be moose tracks," Sheldon said.

"Check it out anyway," Hudson insisted. "That's too high up for moose!"

We heard the engine again, farther away, and soon saw the airplane moving east across the valley. It's going away, I thought. Then we saw it bank south. We watched its progress in a daze. Seconds seemed to plod with infinite slowness. Then, miraculously, it turned west toward us.

"They're coming back," Fox said. *"They saw us!"*

Sheldon banked the Super Cub to the right and flew around again over the lower end of the trail.

"There—in the short spruces!" Hudson said.

"I count three men," Sheldon said, "up to their waists in snow!"

He wagged the wings and then made an exploratory pass over a clearing about a mile away. Going around again, he expertly put the skis on the snow. For several seconds he skimmed the surface, skillfully adjusting the throttle to balance the airplane between commitment to landing and abortion. When no branches, boulders, or tree trunks materialized, he cut the throttle and came to a stop.

Hudson exited, donned one of his two pairs of snowshoes, and carrying the other pair, set off through the woods at a lively pace.

"I'm Cliff Hudson."

"We sure are glad to see you, Mr. Hudson," Olson said.

Hudson was medium height and thin; his wire-rimmed glasses gave him an owl-like look. His appearance, however, was the least of our concerns. His presence was enough.

"By golly," he said, "It looks like you could use some help! Anybody hurt?"

"Pratt has a hole in his leg," Fox said, his voice still high with excitement.

All three of us were elated by the turn of events. Even now, it's hard for me to find words to describe my feelings at that meeting just above the woods.

Hudson looked me up and down.

"Can you walk?" he asked.

"Came down from up there," I said, jerking my thumb toward the ridge.

Then I realized his question centered on the snowshoes he was carrying. He grinned, apparently satisfied that I wasn't going to collapse right away.

"I'll help get these snowshoes on you first, then you can get back to the clearing for pickup."

I found it impossible to get my fingers to perform the motions necessary to fasten the straps. He knelt and started to cinch them for me.

"Have you found anybody else?" I asked.

"I dropped a note to three men up on the hill yesterday by the wreck. Was that you?"

"No—it wasn't!"

For the first time I felt real hope for the others. Three more, at least, were alive. Maybe McDonough and Knapp had made it after all.

"Did you see them again today?"

"We were just now on the way back up there when we spotted you. Dagnabbed weather kept us from getting out earlier."

When Hudson had my snowshoes securely attached to my feet, he said, "Just follow my trail. I packed it pretty hard so you won't have much trouble." Then he added, "Sheldon went back to Curry to get one of the Air Force doctors. They'll be back before you make it to the clearing."

I started walking. My first thought was that it was wonderful to be up on top of the snow and not down in it. My confidence was short-lived. I caught one snowshoe under the other and tumbled face first. Hudson helped me up and I tried again.

"Just kind of shuffle along, and keep your feet farther apart," he said.

I soon got the hang of it, at least enough to stay upright and make progress. The new range of motions put a strain on my leg. Despite that, my spirit was soaring. We were safe—and there were other survivors.

I entered taller timber, the elusive area we'd been trying all day to reach. The drone of an engine came from the south. I heard the airplane land somewhere below me.

Several minutes passed as I kept walking, following Hudson's tracks. Then, ahead on the trail, I saw a form moving toward me. As the distance between us closed, I saw an officer insignia on his pile hat.

"Major Carl Russell," he said when he reached me.

I gave him my name and rank in as military a style as I could muster.

"How many more behind you?"

"Two more."

"Are they injured?"

"Mostly cuts and bruises. We're all pretty tired out."

Then I mentioned my leg.

"Let's take a look," he said, opening the bag he'd been carrying under his arm.

I complied as best I could, balancing on my snowshoes and trying not to fall on my face. Finally, I got my trousers and long johns down around my knees.

"Oh, yeah! Nice, clean puncture wound," he announced. "Seems to have stopped bleeding. You're extremely lucky. Whatever went in there could have cut an artery."

He wrapped gauze around my leg and secured that with tape.

"I think it'll be okay for now," he said. "They'll fix you up when you get to the hospital."

Major Russell went on up the trail toward the other men and I continued toward the landing site. Taller trees surrounded me now and it seemed warmer. The wind wasn't blowing nearly as hard.

When I reached the airplane, the pilot was outside, dragging items from behind the backseat.

"Don Sheldon," he said, extending a free hand to me.

No sooner had I given him my name than he started peppering me with questions. I told him briefly about the accident and of our problems on the ground. He listened, seemingly absorbed by every detail.

It wasn't long before Fox, on Hudson's snowshoes, and Major Russell reached the clearing. The doctor immediately left again, carrying the snowshoes back to Olson and Hudson. It took over an hour to get everyone to the airplane.

Sheldon went on the radio to give Air Force Rescue our names. Although no one was to blame, what transpired in that conversation caused my family an extra twenty-four hours of anguish. Sheldon was sitting in the cockpit and Ed Fox was standing right outside. I was a few feet behind Fox. I couldn't hear the conversation very well.

"Your name is?" Sheldon asked Fox.

"Fox—Ed Fox."

At that point, Fox stepped aside and Sheldon looked toward me. "I didn't hear that," he said.

I thought he hadn't heard Fox, so wanting to help, I repeated Fox's name. Sheldon said something into the mike. I understood later that he'd called in Fox's name and then had turned to me to get my name. When I repeated Fox's name, Sheldon had misunderstood me, hearing it as "Block." Since I'd already introduced myself to Sheldon, I mistakenly assumed he had included my name in his call to Curry. In fact, he reported there were three survivors, Olson, Fox, and *Block*. The misunderstanding caused the military some confusion as there was, of course, no "Block" on the manifest.

The new snow had a hard, fine-grained consistency. As it pelted the three men at the crash site, they decided to get inside their shelter. They spent most of the day there, coming out only when they heard an airplane. That a search was in progress was obvious. Sometimes they'd have time to light a flare, but most often it wasn't before the sound had died away. From time to time, they'd nibble on the cheese and candy.

Conversation was subdued, and centered mostly on the situation. LaDuke kept worrying about wolves. What if they were attacked? He devised a plan—of sorts. He'd keep the knife, and in case they were attacked, he'd be the aggressor to draw the wolf's attention, then fall backward as it attacked. The other two would jump on the wolf from behind. While they held the animal, he'd stab it. It was a plan that didn't have much chance of success, he knew, and it wasn't met with a lot of enthusiasm, but just having a plan somehow made him feel better.

They talked and worried about the fact that the Air Force hadn't been able to get close enough to rescue them. There wasn't even a clear indication that their location was known. True, they'd heard airplanes all day, but the weather had never cleared at the right time. Squalls seemed to come in, one right after the other.

As the snow continued to pile up and as dusk began to swallow the landscape again, Sallis said, sadly, "They're not going to get here today!"

"Another night on this mountain," Montgomery said with a moan. Then, abruptly he laughed, and his voice took on a musical tone, light and lifting, "But we'll get off of here! We'll get off of here! You can be sure we'll get off of here!"

Montgomery had a way with words, charming his listeners with uninhibited chatter, although it was often chatter oozing with meaning. He hadn't been himself since the accident, and LaDuke was glad that he seemed to be pulling out of his lethargy. That he'd suffered severe trauma had been evident.

The comic relief was welcome, but the seriousness of the situation weighed on LaDuke's mind, as seemed to be the case with Sallis.

"How long can we hold out here?" Sallis asked.

"We've been lucky," LaDuke said. "As cold as it's been, it could be a lot worse. This is Alaska. It can drop to fifty below in just a few hours. With the wind blowing the way it has, that would be really serious for us"

"Maybe it would be better to get off this mountain where the wind's always blowing and walk over to that railroad," Montgomery said.

LaDuke, in his calculated manner, rattled off his reasons for staying where they were.

"There's a drop-off in that direction. We don't know how steep it is. It's miles over to the railroad. Even if we got down into the valley, how much headway would we make? Look how much trouble we have moving around here—and the snow's probably deeper down there in the woods."

Sallis and Montgomery listened, but were silent. LaDuke couldn't tell whether they agreed with him or not.

The wind was whipping the nylon canopy covering their shelter. It was getting colder.

"I'll take the first watch," LaDuke said.

It had grown late, and snow was falling heavily again. Hudson thought there was time to ferry us to Curry, but Sheldon disagreed.

"I can only carry one passenger," he said. "That means five trips. It's better if we stay together."

As the pilot-in-command, the decision was his to make.

Major Russell had a parachute, and he soon had it open and draped over saplings Hudson had bent and tied together. A large campfire was roaring. Russell had also brought a gallon jug of coffee, prepared by his wife, Virginia, he said. It was laced with about a pound of sugar. Sheldon had a jar of orange marmalade and some crackers among his survival gear.

Sheldon cut pine boughs and the rest of us rocked the Super Cub while he placed them underneath the skis to keep them from freezing to the snow. He radioed Curry again. We'd heard a helicopter and other aircraft, and were anxious to hear how the rescue was going. They informed us that the Air Force had been unsuccessful in finding the crash site. Even during the times the weather had cleared, the ridge had remained socked in. Land parties with dog teams had left Curry and Gold Creek, but were having major problems in the deep snow.

We sat around the fire far into the night. Hudson kept cutting deadwood and dragging it into camp.

"This'll get you all warmed up, just like home," he said.

He was right. We let our heat-starved bodies soak up the radiating heat until the surfaces of our parkas were too hot to touch. I felt somewhat at peace during that interlude. These three men were strangers, yet their presence gave me great comfort. They represented safety and normalcy.

Major Russell, although professional, was affable in manner. In addition, his persona projected something of the adventurer. He told us about some of the other rescues in which he'd been involved and about the problems he'd encountered in getting to Curry that day.

"Had to land at one of the outposts. I'm not even sure exactly where we were. When we tried to leave, the snow was heavy, so it took us several tries to take off. We'd barrel down the runway and then abort, because we couldn't get up enough speed to take off. I had to climb out, swing the tail of the Beaver around, climb back in while we taxied back, then get out again and swing her around again. Well—we did finally get off, as my presence here suggests."

Don Sheldon was the most talkative and seemed to have a storyteller's flair for the dramatic.

"Alaska's a big country, and being lost in it is a lonely deal," he said after having listened again to our individual stories.

Then he launched into a story of his own.

"Fellow I knew flew back into the boondocks. Hadn't told anybody where he was going—and as it happened, he had to make an emergency landing on a lake. They later found his tracks where he had left his airplane, walked across to one shore, then back to the other shore, then back to the airplane, where he put a bullet into his own head." He paused as if to let the tragic events of the story sink in.

Fox asked, "Why'd he do *that?*"

"Don't know," Sheldon said. "He had the things he needed to survive. Had heavy clothing. Had matches—and a gun. And, as it turned out, they reached him within a week."

"A little hasty," Hudson said.

"Only thing I can figure is a lack of will to survive," Sheldon said. "He just gave up—long before he should have."

I believed that Sheldon was giving us a compliment—maybe his roundabout way of telling us that we had good survival instincts.

Cliff Hudson, although quietest of our rescuers, was more direct.

"I don't see how any of you got out of there. That goldurned wreckage is scattered all over the hill. You're lucky to be here!"

I had begun to understand the truth of that, now that I'd had time to think of something besides survival. Our escaping from a disintegrating transport plane in the manner we had seemed to be a miracle.

Hudson told us about sighting the wreckage the day before, but included only the barest of details. He seemed almost reluctant to talk about himself. I concluded that he was a humble man, although, obviously, an able one.

I couldn't help noticing that Hudson and Sheldon said little to each other. In fact, they seemed to avoid any contact unless necessary. I put it out of my mind, for on that night all three—Hudson, Sheldon, and Russell—were my heroes.

Fox started shivering and couldn't stop. Major Russell ordered him to bed. Olson and I soon followed. The huge fire had started to dig its own hole into the snow. Ed Knapp and Don McDonough were much on my mind. I prayed for them. Even though the night was spent in relative comfort, I slept fitfully.

Don Sheldon
Photo supplied by
Roberta Sheldon

Cliff Hudson
Photo supplied by Ollie Hudson

Dr. Carl Russell
Photo supplied by
Dr. Carl Russell

Chapter Fourteen

Bobby Sallis forced himself to roll out of his sleeping bag into the subzero air. It was Sunday morning, he realized. Thoughts of home and his folks were strong. Did they know yet? Surely, by now.

Moisture had collected and then frozen on everything inside the shelter. He touched the canopy and crystals sprayed the air. On sticking his head outside, his spirits immediately lifted. It was bitter cold, but clear, and the wind had died. If they were going to be rescued, it would be today. He called to the others. They soon emerged, still nursing aches and pains, but looking more alert than they had a few hours before.

Crawling outside, Sallis stood gingerly. There were several inches of new snow, but it didn't keep him from walking around the area on one of the several trails they had established. Sallis' knee was improved. They had each taken their watch during the night, and thankfully, there'd been no wolves.

LaDuke and Montgomery were now outside and moving around. LaDuke appeared to be pleased at what he saw, but he spoke cautiously.

"Remember how quickly it can change," he said, and then added, "but it does look good."

"Y'all can come and get us anytime now!" Montgomery shouted into the clear dawn.

A few miles away, six of us greeted the same clear cold morning. I had slept fully clothed, minus my boots and parka. Although sleep had been intermittent, I felt rested. I had difficulty getting my right boot on because my injured leg had stiffened. I kept at it, though, until I had the boot on and laced.

Olson and Fox were already up. Olson looked to be in good spirits. Fox was more subdued, looking gaunt and pale. I took in the details of the scene around us, knowing it was something I'd want to remember. The lean-to, whose construction consisted of the white parachute draped over the saplings Hudson had pulled together, was set in among medium growth pine and cottonwood. The campfire was no longer burning, but was still emitting smoke from the bottom of a wide deep hole.

Fifty feet away, Hudson, Sheldon, and Russell were vigorously rocking the Super Cub to free the skis of accumulated ice. Their breathing created translucent white vapor clouds around their heads. After a few minutes, Sheldon, apparently satisfied, approached us.

"We're getting out of here," he announced.

Major Russell arranged the order of departure.

"Fox will go first," he said, "followed by Pratt, and then Olson."

Sheldon started the engine, let it run a couple of minutes, and then moved out into the open. I soon realized he was marking off a runway. The new snow had obliterated the ski marks from the previous day. There were small trees all over the clearing and the route he marked was anything but straight. The takeoff path didn't look long enough to me, but, of course, I couldn't second-guess the expert. After all, he'd already landed and taken off from there the day before. In a few minutes, the little airplane came back and got into position for the takeoff run. The wind was practically nonexistent.

Hudson and Russell helped Fox into the seat behind Sheldon. There was an anxious look on Fox's face. Then they were moving. I held my breath as the Super Cub bounced and swerved along, slowly gaining speed until finally it lifted into the air, seeming to barely clear the taller trees at the end of the makeshift runway. I listened to the receding sound as the airplane flew south.

Sheldon didn't waste any time. Hardly half an hour had passed before we heard him coming back. In a short time, he'd landed, pulled up to us, turned around, and was ready to take off again.

It was my turn. Major Russell and Cliff Hudson assisted me as I climbed into the back. Hudson shook my hand after I was strapped in.

"They'll fix that leg up just fine," Major Russell assured me.

Then Sheldon pushed the throttle all the way in and we surged forward over the frozen surface. Pine branches slapped the undercarriage with loud whacks as the pilot maneuvered back and forth. Several times I thought we were lifting off, then we'd be skimming the surface again. All the time, I was looking over Sheldon's shoulder at the rapidly approaching tree line.

I'd made up my mind up not to be nervous.

Hudson had repeated the old adage to us the night before, "It's like falling off a horse. The best thing you can do is to get right back on."

It made sense when he'd said it, but right now, such wisdom was easy to ignore. I was heavier than Fox. Maybe my added weight would put us at a disadvantage.

We did finally lift off and cleared the trees, although not by much, it seemed to me. As we gained altitude, I began to feel better. The mountains we'd left the day before lay to the right. I could see now that they formed a ridge, with most of the higher peaks to the north. Most of the linear crests were now in sunlight, but the highest elevations still had some clouds around the tops. I thought of the three men still up there. Surely, they'd get out today. Again, I wondered if McDonough and Knapp were among them.

Sheldon shouted back at me, "That's the Susitna River to our left. We'll follow it down here a few miles to Curry. Curry's only about fifteen miles from where we were, so it'll only take a few minutes to get there."

Like a travel guide, he instructed me to observe this or that point of interest. We were over a railroad and following it south. That would be the railroad that had seemed unreachable the day before.

"That's Curry right up there. You can see the hotel. That's where we're going. The airstrip is right in front of it."

Sheldon eased the throttle back and set his landing speed while we swung around over some low hills southeast of a cluster of buildings. He became a study of concentration as we approached the landing strip. We quickly lost altitude, crossed the railroad and telephone wires, and settled onto the hard snow surface.

We were able to pull up fairly close to the hotel. Two corpsmen helped me out. As soon as I had exited, Sheldon gave me a thumbs up and started moving back toward the airstrip. The corpsmen led me to a waiting jeep.

Don Sheldon extracted us from the wilderness that day, one at a time, all except Cliff Hudson. I learned later that Hudson had stayed at the campsite until, by arrangement with the Air Force, a helicopter had picked him up. He was still the only one who knew where the wreckage was located.

An airplane flew up the valley about midmorning. LaDuke shot off one of the few remaining flares. Although the single engine aircraft made some turns in their direction, he was unsure if the flare had been seen. He felt frustrated.

The morning wore on and LaDuke worried. There were clouds coming in closer now, and more formidable ones forming around the distant hills to the east. They couldn't see much to the west because of the elevation rise in that direction. He'd noticed that the wind currents were strange. Generally, fronts came from the west, but there the wind blew mostly from the east. There seemed to be a chimney effect of some kind, making weather prediction difficult.

"I heard that train again last night," Montgomery said.

"Yeah," LaDuke replied, "I heard it too."

"I'd be better at walking than I am at waiting."

"I still think we should stay here."

"Maybe they've given up on us."

LaDuke had begun to have his own doubts about staying at the crash site. Montgomery wanted to try for the railroad. What if he was right? What if the Air Force was giving up the search? What if the airplane that had spotted them had crashed and they didn't really know their position? What if their only chance lay in setting off for the railroad? It had gotten colder, and could get colder still. They might be better off in the woods below. No—he couldn't change his mind. At least, not yet.

"Huey," he said. "I'll tell you what! If they don't get to us in a couple of days, you can lead the way over there."

Whether to leave or stay became a moot question shortly before noon, when the clatter of an Air Force helicopter brought the three men hurriedly out of their shelter. The craft hovered overhead and LaDuke could see the pilot and another man gesturing to them. The wash from the rotors was kicking up snow all around the fuselage and shelter. Then the chopper quickly pulled up and moved westward. LaDuke panicked for a moment, since he thought they were leaving. Then, to his relief, they settled on a rise about a hundred feet from the shelter. The rotors stopped turning and three men exited and came toward them on one of the trails they had packed down during their stay. One of the men was a corpsman.

The young Air Force lieutenant reached them first. LaDuke mustered his best military protocol as he saluted sharply.

"Airmen LaDuke, Montgomery, and Sallis, *sir*."

The lieutenant grinned and snapped back a salute.

"Sorry it took so long," he said. "Are there just the three of you?"

"I guess we're the only ones who survived," Sallis said.

The third man was quick to speak up. "No—there are six of you. We got the other three over to Curry this morning."

"This is Mr. Hudson," the pilot said. "He spotted you right after you went down. He and Mr. Sheldon picked up the other men. We've been trying to get in here for two days. Every time we thought we had you located, the weather closed in again. I just picked up Mr. Hudson a few minutes ago because he had pinpointed the location. He led us right up here. Good thing, too. The snow's coming in again."

Hudson kept fidgeting with his steamed-over glasses, ignoring the chatter of the young officer.

"The other men you rescued?" LaDuke inquired. "I have a friend named Olson."

"Olson was one of the three we rescued," Hudson said. Then, almost hesitantly, he asked, "Are there bodies here?"

"We saw two," Montgomery answered.

"Show me!"

Hudson picked up two of the parachute packs stacked next to the fuselage and followed LaDuke as he led him to the two white mounds. At each site, Hudson popped a chute and reverently covered the mound with the orange and white canopy.

They were soon ready to go. LaDuke had one more heart-pounding moment as the helicopter rose from the crash site and fought the wind to get over the eastern edge of the ridge. The drop-off about which they had speculated was indeed steep, and he gasped as it seemed they were about to be sucked down the side of the mountain. Then—they were clear, and quickly sped off toward the southeast and safety.

The helicopter took Montgomery, Sallis, and LaDuke to Talkeetna, and from there they were flown to Elmendorf in an SA-16 Albatross. Fox, Olson, and I spent most of that day in the big Alaska Railroad hotel at Curry.[39]

As I was entering the hotel, I hobbled past the bar and dining area where breakfast was being served. The aroma of bacon filled my nostrils and I realized how hungry I was. I hadn't had any nourishment since breakfast on Friday morning, except for some of Virginia Russell's hot coffee and a few of Sheldon's crackers with orange marmalade. A middle-aged woman quickly slipped from behind the bar and put an arm around my shoulder.

She said, "Come back here as soon as you can and there'll be breakfast for you—anything you want."

I thanked her and assured her I'd be back. An Air Force corporal led me upstairs, showed me to a room, and told me I could rest before a doctor would come to examine me. It felt good to remove my outer garments. My dress blue uniform jacket had large sweat rings under the arms. Out of habit, I checked to see that my reading glasses were in the inside pocket, only to remember they'd been in my handbag and lost in the accident.

I tried to rest, but couldn't. After a few minutes, I slipped out to the bathroom down the hall. The face in the mirror was unfamiliar. It was red and swollen, and my cut lip protruded grotesquely. One eye was black and the other red and puffy. I could wiggle several of my lower front teeth. I used a washcloth to remove some of the grime from my face and then went back to the room.

The floor was quiet. Nobody seemed to be around. I wondered where Fox was. Olson should get there soon. The doctor didn't appear, and after a few minutes I went downstairs.

The woman behind the bar said, "I prayed for all of you while you were out there."

I sat at the long wooden bar. A couple of men came over and offered to buy me a drink. I declined, with the excuse that I'd be seeing the doctor in a few minutes. The kind woman asked me what I'd like to eat. I ordered steak and eggs and a big glass of orange juice. I managed the eggs all right, but the steak was difficult to chew with loose teeth. I had to cut the meat into small pieces and shove the pieces into the back of my mouth with my finger. I had an audience watching me with interest, but people were respectful enough to keep their distance.

I made it back up to my room just before an Air Force doctor arrived.

I don't remember his name, but he examined me and then said, "They'll want to do X-rays when you get to the hospital. You can drink liquids, but don't have any solid food."

I thought it best to keep quiet about my recent feast. I asked him about Fox and Olson.

"They're both resting in the rooms right next to you," he said. "We're going to get you to Elmendorf as soon as we can."

About mid-afternoon, they put the three of us in the caboose of an Anchorage-bound freight train. An officer rode with us. It was from him that I learned the names of the other three survivors. Tears flowed as I realized McDonough and Knapp weren't among them. We arrived in Anchorage in the early evening and were taken by ambulance to the 5005th Base Hospital.

Eli LaDuke, February 7, 1954
Photo supplied by Ginger LaDuke

Bobby Sallis,
February 7, 1954
*Photo supplied
by Bobby Sallis*

We were all X-rayed soon after our arrival. After that, I had a two-hour operation on my leg. My puncture wound was explored and cleaned. The injury was unusual and attracted a crowd of observers. I counted twelve doctors and nurses around the table. They pried my pants off, then cut off my long johns and left me naked from the waist down. I swallowed my modesty and endured it. They gave me a local anesthetic. I was awake throughout the procedure. It was late at night when it was over and I was allowed to eat. A nurse brought me a hamburger and a glass of milk.

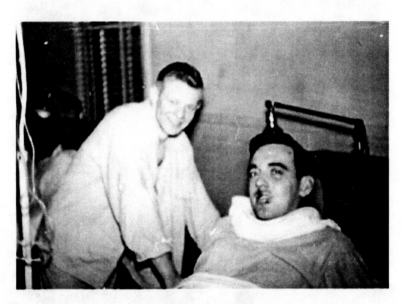

Ed Olson and Rupert Pratt, February 8, 1954
Photo supplied by Ed Olson

Chapter Fifteen

About noon Monday, the same Air Force NCO who had delivered the Saturday telegram stood again at my mother's door. She had watched the government car come up the lane, turn around just before the bridge leading to the barn, and stop in front of the house. Ann Harbour, a neighbor and friend, stood close beside her.

"It's good news this time, Mrs. Morrison!" the sergeant said.

She tore open the envelope to read:

I AM PLEASED TO INFORM YOU THAT A REPORT JUST RECEIVED STATES THAT YOUR SON, A/3C RUPERT C. PRATT, HAS BEEN RETURNED TO MILITARY CONTROL. HE IS PRESENTLY HOSPITALIZED AT THE USAF HOSPITAL, 5005TH HOSPITAL GROUP, APO 942, C/O POSTMASTER, SEATTLE, WASHINGTON. HIS PHYSICAL CONDITION IS UNKNOWN AT THIS TIME. HOWEVER, IT IS NOT BELIEVED THAT HE IS SERIOUSLY ILL. WHEN ADDITIONAL INFORMATION IS RECEIVED, YOU WILL BE NOTIFIED. I HOPE THAT YOU WILL SOON HAVE THE COMFORT OF HEARING DIRECTLY FROM HIM.

MAJOR GENERAL JOHN H. MCCORMICK

The following day she received the third and final telegram:

REFERENCE MY TELEGRAM OF 8 FEBRUARY 1954 REGARDING YOUR SON, AIRMAN THIRD CLASS RUPERT C. PRATT. REPORT JUST RECEIVED FROM THE 5005TH HOSPITAL GROUP, APO 942, C/O POSTMASTER, SEATTLE, WASHINGTON, STATES THAT HIS CONDITION IS GOOD. HIS INJURIES

HAVE BEEN DIAGNOSED AS MULTIPLE CONTUSIONS AND
LACERATIONS OF THE FACE, BODY AND EXTREMITIES;
PUNCTURE WOUND RIGHT THIGH. HE IS NOT CONSID-
ERED SERIOUSLY ILL. I HOPE THE NEWS OF HIS RECOVERY
WILL SOON BE FORTHCOMING.

MAJOR GENERAL JOHN H. MCCORMICK

The six of us were together for a week in a ward at the 5005th
Hospital on Elmendorf Air Force Base. "Together" had special
meaning for us. There was much to say to one another because of our
shared experience. Eli LaDuke, Bobby Sallis, and Huey Montgomery,
having been at the crash site, had stories different from Olson, Fox,
and me, and in many ways, more traumatic.

Lt. Col. John McAfee, Alaskan Air Command Public Information
Officer, held a formal interview with us the day after our arrival.
Anchorage television, newspapers, and radio stations had representa-
tives present. Our group picture appeared in the *Anchorage News* and
was carried by national news services, as was the story.

The rest of that week was filled with paperwork and recuperation,
in that order, it seemed. I had limited pain and was allowed to walk
short distances. Mostly, though, I was ordered to use a wheelchair.
None of the others had serious injuries. Montgomery's shoulder had
been severely wrenched, but nothing was broken. Our scrapes and
bruises healed quickly. We were all in our early twenties and found it
hard to stay inactive.

One of the nurses, an attractive redhead, told me a few days after
our arrival, "You know, you looked terrible when you came in here,
and now you don't look half bad."

I told her she didn't look half bad either, and received a cold stare
and silence for my imprudence.

Paperwork became time-consuming, but of course we had no
shortage of time. The Air Force needed statements for its accident
report. It was important to discover the cause of the crash. All Alaska

Command C-47s had been grounded. An extensive chain of interviewers paraded through our ward each day, having us fill out lengthy questionnaires and answer a myriad of questions. The same questions seemed to appear repeatedly. Where were you sitting? Who was next to you? Are you sure it was really an explosion you heard and not the sound of the plane breaking up? Did you lose consciousness? Did you smell fuel? They were thorough.

We filled out forms itemizing every piece of clothing and personal belongings we had lost. We would be reimbursed. An officer appeared one day and informed us that we were eligible to join the exclusive Caterpillar Club because parachutes had saved our lives. That sounded like a good idea, but required more paperwork.

We were well-informed about recovery efforts. They seemed to be particularly careful to bring me the latest information; they knew I had two friends still missing. It was Monday or Tuesday before the ground party from Curry made it to the crash site, and Wednesday, February 10, before the Air Force got its experts to the scene. They found wreckage scattered over a square mile area. Winds had been at moderate levels, but came back furiously at midweek. As a result, the scene changed as some wreckage was covered up again and some previously undiscovered parts were revealed. Overall, they were having a hard time.

Because there were six of us, many visitors came into our ward. Visitors, regardless of who they came to see, seemed to want to talk with each of us. The lab men came to see me nearly every day the first week, bringing books and sweets. Altogether, there were about twenty patients in the ward, and I shared the food with them.

A strange incident occurred. Some visitors came in to see one of the other men, Olson, I think, but I can't be sure. One of them kept glancing at me. Finally, he came over and stuck out his hand.

"I'm Sonny Carter, and I can't help noticing that you look like someone I know."

I was stumped.

"From the service, or before?" I asked.

"From before. Way before! I think we went to elementary school together."

Then it came to me. I had known the Carters all my life. They had been friends of my family at Salt Rock long before I was born.

"Sonny Carter! I remember! At the old school across from the church. Velma Matthews was our teacher. That had to be first grade, because we moved into the new school across the river at midyear."

"That's it! That was the only year I went to Salt Rock School."

I don't think I had seen him since then.

"And you remembered." I was flabbergasted. Although I was recovering, I didn't even look like myself. "Maybe you saw my name in the newspaper," I suggested.

He assured me he hadn't. I still suspect he had notice that I was there. In either case, we had a long visit. We remembered sitting on the grassy bank below the road and eating our lunch together. We also remembered a dog show we had seen on the baseball field by DeJarrnet's store. The troop had stopped at the store and T. E. Walker, our principal, went down and asked them to put on a show for the school. It was an unscheduled stop, but they agreed, and it was an exciting time for the students to see the tricks and antics of about a dozen dogs. I was to see Sonny only once or twice after our meeting in the hospital—and that was after we had both left the service.

Another unlikely visitor came calling. Capt. Reardon, the Fort Richardson company commander, apologized for ordering me to get us aboard the doomed airplane. He tried to maintain a military demeanor, but his emotion was evident. I was embarrassed and shrugged it off.

"Not your fault, sir. No one can know things like that."

When he left, he told me the company would still like to have me back in the petroleum lab.

"I can't think about that yet," I said.

Over the course of the week, bodies had been discovered and brought to Elmendorf. One day, a hospital staff officer came in and sat beside my bed. He was straightforward, though kind.

"There's no chance your friends are alive."

It wasn't what I wanted to hear, of course, but it confirmed what I already knew and brought some closure.

George Hyek was broken up about Knapp and McDonough. The four of us had grown close.

"I'll never forget that trip up the mountain on Christmas Eve or the party in the lab. I just can't believe they're gone," he kept saying.

New alliances help in such matters. I had shared an ordeal with the five other men with me now and it bound us together in a special way. I got to know them quite well in the few days we were together.

Ed Fox, the oldest of the group by a couple of years, was in some ways the youngest. Lighthearted and carefree, he kept us smiling with his jokes and stories. He had telephoned his wife, Flo, in Utica and was excited about prospects of her joining him in Fairbanks. That is, if he ever got to Fairbanks, he quipped. He didn't think he'd ever set foot on an airplane again. He was going to request a train ticket to Fairbanks this time.

Eli LaDuke, also a New Yorker from Au Sable Forks in the northern part of the state, was youngest of the six, and in many ways the oldest. A "take charge" person, he was deliberate in speech and manner, serious in conversation, and a paragon of logic and good sense.

Bobby Sallis, from Arkansas, was quiet, almost shy, appearing to be, in some ways, the "southern gentleman" stereotype. Nevertheless, in a week, we dug out the real Sallis, who was wise and thoughtful, unobtrusive in his ways and highly interested in people.

Large framed, with huge hands dwarfing ours, Huey Montgomery, an Alabama native, had the epithet "character" written all over him. He made us laugh with his chatter and homey expressions, delivered in a squeaky little voice. It took a few days for me to see that it really was Huey, and not some part he was playing. He was generally uninhibited. I was intrigued by his expressive metaphorical speech, used in an easy, natural way.

Ed Olson had a ready smile and helpful ways. From Elkader, Iowa, he still possessed small town manners. Underneath lay deep intelligence and an expressive nature. That expression soon surfaced. He hadn't been long in the hospital before securing paints and paper. His resulting creation showed himself underneath an open parachute,

white bunny boots pointing resolutely toward a snow-covered landscape. Ed seemed to me as solid as an Iowa silo.

I'm not sure what I contributed to the group or what they thought
of me, but I guess they accepted me for what I was, a slow-talking
hillbilly from the nurturing, but sometimes smothering protection of
an Appalachian culture. I suppose that underneath, we weren't much
different from one another. We shared the same time in history, and
that seems, with hindsight, more relevant than geographical roots.

We were all quick to get letters off to our families. I started mine
at 8:30 Monday evening.

Dear Mother,

I guess I've got a lot to be thankful for now. As you
probably already know, I was aboard a C-47 plane that crashed
about 100 miles from Anchorage. It happened Friday 5th and
as yet only six of us were rescued out of 16 aboard. There are
a lot of things I could tell you about it, but right now I'll only
tell you the most important things. First of all I'm not hurt
in any way except my face looks as if I had been in a fight
and I have a puncture wound in my leg that will keep me in
the hospital for about a week. It will be fine. In fact, I walk
around on it now.

There is not much hope that my buddies Donald
McDonough and Ed Knapp are alive.

We were all on one side and the baggage was on the other
side. We went into a power dive and when we tried to pull out
the engine right where I was sitting exploded and the whole
plane came apart. I remember seeing everything falling and I
could hardly realize that I was out in the air and falling too. We
had on parachutes but I couldn't find the rip cord for awhile,
but at last I did and got the chute open. It seemed like only a
couple of seconds until I was in the snow. I couldn't spill the
wind out of the chute and it dragged me down the mountain
for about 200 yards. That was the first opportunity that I
had to pray but I really did and finally I got it stopped. It was
snowing and I couldn't see anyone or hear anything except

the wind. In about three hours I found two other guys. We had to spend that night on the mountain. The next morning we couldn't find anyone else or the wreck so we started off the mountain and toward a railroad we could see about 22 miles [the actual distance was more like five miles] away. I believe the most shallow snow we encountered was 3 ft. deep. We got about 10 miles when two bush pilots, Don Sheldon and Cliff Hudson, spotted our trail and found us. They had skis on their plane so they managed to land in a clear space about 3 miles from us. One of them brought snowshoes to us while the other flew back to the nearest settlement of Curry for a doctor. When he got back the weather was so bad that he couldn't take off again, so we had to spend another night out there. They flew us out the next morning. From Curry, they put us in the caboose of a train and brought us back to Anchorage. They had already [gotten] out three other guys that [were] close to the wreck. I've been in the newspaper, radio, and television up here. They are taking good care of me. Don't worry. Use my Ft. Rich address.

Love, Rupert

Chapter Sixteen

With hardly any notice, the other survivors were discharged from the hospital. That came as a shock to me. I had expected to be discharged about the same time, but it didn't happen.

I was required to sit in a bathtub filled with a medicated liquid for an hour, three times a day. One day, early in my second week, the red-haired nurse came into the room to check on me. She was pretty, and I couldn't help but be interested. Previously, in a moment of weakness, she had told me her name was "Jane." After that, she threw up a wall between us. I suppose she was unwilling to break the military protocol between officers and enlisted men—or more likely, just had no interest.

"How long will I have to do these soaks?" I asked.

"Three weeks—maybe a month."

"A *month*?"

She patiently explained it to me.

"Your injury is deep. We have to keep it packed so that it doesn't heal from the top and then get infected underneath. That takes a lot of time. In the meantime, we have to give you penicillin and do these baths to keep out infection. You'll be here awhile."

I was disappointed, but determined to make the most of the situation. It wasn't easy. I developed a problem the doctors called "delayed shock." I called it "walking nightmares" when I reported it. It had started about the time the other men left. Just as I was drifting off to sleep, I'd feel as if I was falling over backward and would try to grab onto something. Sometimes I'd involuntarily scream as it happened. I wasn't getting much sleep. Then, in a few days, it progressed to the point where I was having the same attacks during my waking hours. It would happen when I least expected it, while eating, while in my wheelchair, or while reading a book. Sometimes it would hit me four or five times a day.

The hospital had a psychologist who talked to me for an hour. As I recall, he thought the problem was because of the way I had left the airplane, or that maybe I was feeling guilt about being alive while my friends were dead. He prescribed a sedative and said the anxiety would subside with time. It did, slightly, while I was in the hospital, but remained a real problem for me for several months, and to a lesser extent for years.

I had told Hyek I wasn't sleeping well. One evening, he appeared with a paper bag in his hand.

"This will help," he said.

I opened the bag to see a laboratory flask inside, filled with a clear liquid.

"What is it?" I inquired.

"Alcohol. From the lab."

"To drink?"

"Sure. Just mix it with a little water before you get ready to sleep. Works like a charm."

It did seem to help. I used it for several nights until a nurse discovered the flask in the bottom of my nightstand where I had concealed it.

"What's this?" she asked, pulling the cork and sniffing what was left of the contents.

I played dumb.

"Probably something left there before I came," I said.

She took the flask and I didn't hear any more about it for a couple of days. Then Jane confronted me. She was angry.

"Are you an alcoholic?" she demanded.

"No, of course not!"

"Then why did you have ethyl alcohol in your nightstand? The lab tested it. Were you drinking it?"

"Well, I—"

"Of course you were. Airman, don't you know you could be court-martialed for this? Who gave it to you?"

There was no way I was going to betray Hyek.

"A friend brought it to me—a civilian."

I was glad she didn't persist with the questioning.

"Well, I want you to know I went to bat for you," she said, her voice becoming less cutting. "They're not going to pursue the issue."

"Thanks, Jane."

"Don't think you're out of the woods yet. I've been ordered to watch you carefully to see that there's no reoccurrence of this kind of thing."

"There won't be!"

I meant it.

"And you're to address me as 'Nurse' or 'Lieutenant,'" she said, glancing at the men in beds on either side who had been listening with interest.

I was sufficiently humbled after that. I warned Hyek not to bring any more "sedatives."

Another developing problem was my isolation from almost everyone I knew. The other survivors were gone. Our time together had been all too short. Although I had listened to their stories as they told them to others, there were things I would have liked to talk to them privately about. Visitors no longer came, except for George Hyek, and he came less often. I longed for familiar faces. I did enjoy talking to Jane, but there was always that barrier between us.

There were good times, too. I'd been feeling sorry for myself because I had received no letters from home. It normally took a week for mail to get there. One day about the time the other men left, a nurse walked up to me with a fat paper bag containing thirty-five letters. For days afterward, I continued to receive large bundles of mail.

The same nurse jokingly said, "If this continues, they'll have to put an extra person in the mail room."

Letters came from relatives, old friends, and members of the Salt Rock Church. Eve, my dancing partner, wrote. I got mail from Schenectady, too. One a day, if not more, started arriving from Millie Mereness. Thankfully, she hadn't known about the crash until after our rescue. Tom DeVito, Sr. wrote too, telling me all about Tom's activities in England.

A series of letters, sometimes accompanied by cookies, served to confuse my emotions. Rose, riding the gentle breeze of familiarity, had slipped back into my life. I was not unaware of my fickleness, but not particularly bothered by it either. *Was it possible to be in love with two girls at once?* I wallowed in that fantasy for some time before I realized I couldn't have them both. I'd declared my love to Millie, and I wouldn't abandon the idea that we had a future together. Nevertheless, I answered Rose's letters and said little about my feelings, perhaps an indication of a growing fear. Millie, despite my love for her, was certainly not a sure thing. Letting go of Rose was like burning a bridge. That was hard for me.

Mother's letters were full of wonder and worry. I had to keep reassuring her that I was all right. In a letter on February 16, I responded to what must have been an inquiry about my feelings before our rescue:

> I knew I was going to get out no matter how long it took. We knew where the railroad was and eventually in three or four days we could have reached it and found civilization by following it.[40]

My mind dwelled on "home" much of the time. Upon entering the service, I had experienced moderate homesickness. Now, my thoughts seemed to constantly linger on Salt Rock, family, and friends. My family was close-knit, as were most families of that time and location. I was especially close to my mother's family because of proximity. My father, Rupert Pratt,[41] had died three months before my birth, forcing Mother to go back to live with my grandparents, Lucian and Jenny Adkins.[42] She soon, however, built her own house—but on the family farm. When Mother married Dawson Morrison a few years later, she traded houses with my grandparents and we took up residence at the old homestead, only a short distance away.

Community ties in Salt Rock were sometimes nearly as strong as family ones. In an era before television, at a time when few people even had telephones, where our links were through church, store, post office, community events, and what we could see from our front porches, we knew one another quite well, often down to intimate details. It was a time, in our agrarian culture, when a person's integrity was likely to be measured by the state of his or her vegetable garden. It seemed to me that Salt Rock people supported each other in good times and bad. I was sure that my friends there were concerned for my welfare.

The twenty beds in my ward were occupied most of the time. Men would come and go frequently. During my second week, we had an influx of soldiers. A large Army maneuver was being held in southern Alaska at the time and the weather had turned bitter cold. Frostbite cases rose significantly, filling the hospital.

I wasn't entirely without visitors during the remainder of my hospital stay. Don Sheldon spent an hour regaling me with stories about the Alaska frontier. His knowledge of flying and his self-assurance were impressive. I figured if he didn't kill himself making rescues like ours, he'd make a name for himself. On the other hand, maybe he'd do both.

Cliff Hudson came, too.

"Thought you might need some company," he said, handing me a few Milky Way bars. With mischievous twinkles in his eyes he added, "Had a six pack, but they confiscated it at the door."

He too had stories, told in his usual low-keyed fashion.

"Come to Talkeetna," he said before leaving. "I'll show you around."

I resolved to take him up on the offer.

Capt. Wilson, commander of the 5001st Supply Squadron at Ladd, appeared one day. I was napping and he kidded me about sleeping on duty. I wanted to think he had made a special trip to see me, but he was probably at headquarters on business.

"Is there anything I can do for you?" he asked before leaving.

I wasn't really prepared to discuss it, but the opportunity was so good that I quickly said, "I think I'd like to apply for a transfer here so I can work in my field."

He was cautious.

"Well—I'll try, but understand that it's not wholly my decision to make."

They weren't words that gave me confidence.

The man who led the search team from Curry to the ridge came to see me on February 16, still smelling of campfire smoke and sweat. He told me many details of the crash site area, some elements of which I shared with my mother:

> He said the parts were scattered over a square mile area. I guess that the plane just came apart and the pieces fell straight down. Their theory is that the engine didn't explode but in the force of trying to pull out of the dive the engine was literally torn loose and knocked the side right out of the plane.

Sometime during the period of my hospital stay, Maudie Betscher left Alaska. She had mixed emotions. She would later put it in her own words.

". . . in the dark of evening and flying over the craggy, towering, snow-covered slopes bathed in moonlight. I marveled at their beauty and yet was aware how violent they could be."[43]

Another grieving wife left the continent. Jill West-Watson, with her two young children, Liz and David, and accompanied by friends, left her Virginia home and set sail on the Queen Mary toward the British Isles. The body of her husband hadn't been recovered, and she hoped she might bear the pain better in the presence of family.

I was finally released on March 9. My twenty-first birthday had passed almost unnoticed. I could have been released a day earlier, but discovered most of my clothing had been discarded. They quickly outfitted me with a new dress blue uniform, which had to be fitted. Actually, I did recover my old trousers and later wore them, since the hole in the fabric was practically unnoticeable. That same day, I was given a long-promised eye examination to replace my missing glasses. They'd be shipped to Ladd, I was told.

My new orders were to report to the Casual Squadron on Elmendorf and wait for railroad tickets to Fairbanks. I had followed Fox's lead and decided that for now I'd be more comfortable on rails than in the air.

Nurse Jane was on duty when I took my departure. She was busy, so I waved to her and mouthed a goodbye. I imagined that her smile was a little broader and her countenance a little less stern as she waved back. Then she turned back to her duties and I made my way out to the bus stop.

Chapter Seventeen

I took up residence in one of the Elmendorf Casual Squadron barracks near the Alaska Command headquarters cluster. I was to wait for orders and a voucher for the train ticket to Fairbanks. I soon settled into a routine. Each morning and each afternoon, I reported to the squadron headquarters to see if my orders and voucher had arrived. That was my only duty, taking no more than five minutes. After breakfast, I'd walk to the base library, where I stayed all morning, except for a coffee break at the Airman's Club. I had always read extensively, and my time in the Casual Squadron was no exception, even though I was without reading glasses. After lunch, I'd go back to the Airman's Club and spend the afternoon exploring the world of hard liquor.

I'd never been a drinker—if you don't count our party at the lab or an occasional beer. We had never had liquor at home. I knew about Dawson's bottle in the barn and the one in the hen house, but I hadn't been tempted. I really gave no thought to what I was doing. I just drifted into it because I discovered that time passed quickly when I was drinking. That's the quick explanation. Closer to the truth might be that I was seeking a pain-deadener—an anesthesia for something that had nothing to do with physical pain.

Money soon became a problem. I hadn't been paid since the end of January. At that time, as I recall, an airman third class received between eighty and ninety dollars a month. I had recently told my mother that I was going to save my money so I could go home the following Christmas. I'd forgotten that, and my wallet was conspicuously flat. Lodging and meals were free; it was the booze that was taking my money. Since I hadn't been paid at the end of February, I went to the Alaska Command headquarters and explained the situation. After filling out a few forms, I got the money and, embracing the short view, continued to spend.

The days passed, far more of them than there should have been, in my opinion. "Military time" had a meaning beyond the method of keeping track of hours in the day. It could also be defined as the speed at which something got accomplished. Sometimes the military wasn't good at that. After all, it took only a few minutes to draft orders, and less than a day to deliver them anywhere in Alaska.

I drank alone, mostly in the afternoons. In my defense, I did spread my drinks out so that I didn't get beyond "high." Evenings were less of a problem, since there were things going on to occupy my time. I went to movies, attended some of the many entertainment events on base, and occasionally stayed in the barracks and read.

There was little mail. I had informed everyone to send mail ahead to Ladd, since I expected to be there shortly. I did receive a letter from Capt. Wilson that said, in effect, that I couldn't transfer to Elmendorf or to Fort Richardson. They were still shorthanded at Ladd. It was what I had expected, and such were my feelings at the time that I was neither sorry nor glad—just resigned. What I wanted now was to get the two years done.

The same brush that applied shades of gray to my military expectations began to color another area of my life, as well. I was thankful for Millie's letters and her concern for me, but her casual mention of dating caused me concern. Of course, we had never agreed not to date others, and although I applauded her candor, I felt helpless to protect the romantic bond that I had allowed myself to think might last forever. I suppose it was my overall frame of mind that put me into such a state of uncertainty.

My "delayed shock" was still a problem. The frequency of "attacks" had lessened and I was no longer having them in my waking hours. They came at night, sometimes occurring several times. I would arise tired and irritable each morning. I'd promised Mother that I would attend church, and made one effort to keep my word. I attended an Episcopal Church service the first Sunday after I left the hospital. My experience with other denominations was obviously limited. It's amusing now to see what I wrote home about it:

I went to church Sunday to an Episcopalian service. They are something like Catholics, but they put on beautiful services. They have an image of Christ in the front and everyone bows to it as they go in and come out. They all kneel when they pray or the priest prays. Instead of a sermon they read a long list of responsive readings and after a little bit, everyone sings "Glory to God in the highest," or "Glory to his name."

I didn't realize it at the time, but I had entered something of a spiritual wasteland. To apply my mountain metaphor to the situation, I had encountered a brier thicket along the trail. Many people in the hospital had told me how lucky I was to be alive, and some even said God had spared me "for a reason." I knew the former was true, but I had major trouble with the latter. What about McDonough and Knapp? Why had they been "taken" and I hadn't? And the others? Weren't their futures as important as mine? "God is a just God," I'd been taught. It was easier for me to accept luck. Luck meant that God didn't have a hand in it—I could let Him off the hook.

The hospital Protestant chaplain had visited often during my month there. I liked him and enjoyed his visits, but he seemed to be more interested in being my friend than in providing spiritual guidance. Over chess games, we talked of such things, but not in the depth I was in need of. God—or perhaps more accurately, God's actions and motives—had become quite a mystery for me. I wanted answers.

My mother, had she known about my condition, would probably have said, as she often had, "We can think too much about things. It's better to be simple. Just accept things on faith."

That wasn't easy for me. Certainly, I had cried out to God for help on the mountain—and accepted it without trying to understand it, but now, in the aftermath of the tragedy, I was floundering in uncertainty. Despite the many questions emerging from the hinterland of my mind, I believe that the foundation of my faith, though shaken, remained intact. It would be some time, however, before I'd know that.

I was in the Causal Squadron for three weeks, and when I finally shipped out on March 31, I had no money left. I was going to get hungry on the trip to Fairbanks. Meals weren't supplied.

Nevertheless, I enjoyed the ride. The last time I'd been on a railroad had been in a caboose with other things on my mind, and the time before that was during the night, on the troop train. I hadn't experienced the splendor of the countryside then. Now, there was still snow, but bare ground was beginning to appear.

We stopped briefly at Talkeetna, which was even smaller than I'd imagined. I thought of Hudson and Sheldon and wondered what their lives must be like living there.

As the train moved up the Susitna Valley, I studied my map. On our approach to Curry, I couldn't help feeling some fascination. As we pulled up in front of the big hotel where Sheldon had dropped me, the conductor announced a ten-minute stop. I got off, along with several other passengers. To my great surprise, I spotted Cliff Hudson standing near the main doorway. I rushed up and shook his hand.

"Thought you'd be back up north by now," he said.

"I got sidetracked."

"They're still taking things out up there. Trying to get one of the engines here to the rails. Hard job. Still haven't found that British officer. Plenty of snow left up there. How you doing?"

"I'm good. I'd like to thank you again for—"

He wanted no part of that.

"You going to come here and visit sometime?"

"Sure."

"Come in summer. We'll fly out to some fishing holes I know."

The train whistle sounded—the signal that it would leave soon.

"I've got to get back on," I said.

I shook his hand again.

"Come and see me," he repeated.

"I will. *I promise!*"

A few miles up the tracks, the mountain ridge was easy to spot, looking only a little less foreboding than I remembered. Although it was a clear day and the snowy peaks merged softly into a cerulean sky, the ridge was almost black in its exposed parts. I couldn't help contrasting it with hills of home, for which I often longed. My hills, full of light and life, were a comfort for my soul. These were dark and solemn—deathlike. Nevertheless, I was drawn to the ridge and gazed at it with morbid fascination. I knew the sight would always be vivid in my memory. Someday, I thought, I might want to go back there—but not for a while.

I was famished, but the chow hall was closed by the time I got to the 5001st Supply Squadron. I'd have to wait for breakfast. No one was at headquarters except the CQ.[44] He managed to find the corporal from supply so I could draw linens, blankets, and my stored footlocker. The corporal didn't look especially pleased to be called back to duty.

"Name, please?" he said, without looking up.

"Pratt."

His head jerked up, and there was recognition.

"Oh, yeah—Pratt!" For a moment, he looked as if he didn't know what to say. Then he added, "We've been expecting you. Sorry about Knapp and McDonough. That must have been rough."

He brought out my footlocker, record player, and linens.

"What else do you need?" he asked.

"Mittens and pile hat. Well, really, I need more than that, I guess. I lost all the winter gear I wasn't wearing. My parka's still good, except for a little rip."

He disappeared for several minutes. I could hear him shuffling things around on shelves in back. When he reappeared, he had an armload that he deposited with a thud on the counter. He went back for another load, which he placed beside the first.

"That should do you awhile," he said, a smile on his face.

I couldn't believe what lay in front of me. There were duplicates of all the things I had lost: sweaters, heavy socks, pile hat, a brown light jacket, and some things I'd never seen before. They were all new, still in boxes. What left me speechless was a new pair of bunny boots, a slightly used, but clean, brown parka, and incredibly, lying atop the pile, a new *blue* parka.

When I got my voice back, I managed a humble, "Thank you."

I started to remove my old parka, with the thought of relinquishing it, along with my now-battered bunny boots. He waved me off.

"Keep them for spares," he said. "Least we can do."

I soon learned that the whole squadron, and even many in other squadrons, knew of the accident. There had been a memorial service for Knapp and McDonough in February. The story of the crash had already been elevated to folklore level. I had to tell "repair" versions numerous times.

Returning to Ladd was bittersweet. Finally arriving afforded a degree of comfort, but I missed Knapp and McDonough. I was back in the same barracks, and back at the refueling shack doing the same work, but it felt different. It *was* different.

Sergeant Crawford was a kind man.

"Take it easy on that leg now. One of the other men can climb up on that tank."

That theme continued for several days, until I couldn't stand it anymore.

"Look, Sarge," I said as I slammed my right foot down hard on the ground several times. "I'm in good shape!"

I didn't want pampering or sympathy. I wanted to get on with everything, so I worked hard. The carpentry job we had started before going to Anchorage was complete, which had tripled the size of the building. Two new men, Airman First Class Leo Shamka and Corporal Lyndle Main, had been added to the crew.

Main and I quickly became friends. He'd been assigned to the military police for a few months, but hadn't been well-suited for it and transferred to POL. He was mild-mannered, always telling funny stories about growing up in Griggsville, Illinois. He became an excellent friend. He was also quite familiar with the bars of Fairbanks and vicinity and introduced me to them soon after my arrival.

Shamka, a college graduate, was from Minnesota, I believe. It took me longer to get to know him, but I found it a rewarding friendship when I did. His hobby was photography. He was friend to another POL airman named Kenneth Haab, who also dabbled in photography. Through Shamka, I came to know Haab quite well.

The four of us became friends, but for months it was Main to whom I was closest.

POL really was short of personnel, even though the ranks had swelled to forty-four men.[45] The shortage was mainly in flightline refueling. We were servicing transport aircraft as well as three fighter squadrons. The 18th, 433rd, and 449th fighter interceptor squadrons of F-89 Scorpions were flying several missions a day. That took a lot of jet fuel. Crawford worried that they'd pull people from fuel storage to drive refueling rigs.

Spring came and went. Summer, surprisingly warm, arrived. Winter darkness had fled, and sunny days prevailed. Sunshine soothed my spirit for a time. I went out and explored the countryside on my days off and even went swimming in a rock quarry on the other side of Fairbanks. A shadow, however, lurked over me. I was drinking heavily.

I hadn't been back long when I found Ed Fox. He was in an interim job as cook in the Maintenance Squadron right next to us, a fact I discovered when I ate in their mess hall one day instead of my own. He still hadn't been able to get Flo up from the states.

"Sallis is here, too," he said. "I'll get us together."

The three of us saw one another as often as we could, but our schedules were different and we couldn't get together as much as we would have liked. One Sunday, we went to town together, and on impulse attended service at a little Methodist church. We didn't talk much about the accident. Sallis eventually left for the outside and a discharge.

My life at Ladd wasn't a bad one. I had friends. I didn't dislike my job or the base environment. I managed to juggle work and private activities with some skill. Nevertheless, darkness continued to dominate my spirit and color my perception, even though I was essentially ignorant of its presence.

Chapter Eighteen

Fall came. The 5001st Supply moved from the ancient Quonset huts into wooden barracks, greatly improving our living conditions. About that time, I was promoted to Airman Second Class. I was again invited to join our squadron basketball team. My leg was healed and I committed to playing, although Main and I were still visiting the many barrooms of Fairbanks. It was hard to get to practice and do that too. Too often, the barrooms won. I wasn't a bad basketball player. My dependable layups and soft fall-away jump shots, combined with a passable defense, gave me a strong position on the team. However, Sergeant Dale Watson, the coach, let me know that he was aware of a problem.

"Pratt, you drink too much!"

I was defensive, saying, "I do the job, don't I?"

"There's more to it than that. I don't care how good an athlete you are, if you don't keep in shape and you don't measure up to certain other standards, I won't keep you on the team."

I was taken aback. It seemed to be an attack on my integrity—and my integrity was something in which I took great pride.

"Sergeant," I said, "if ever I'm not doing my best, you won't have to kick me off the team—I'll quit!"

Watson had the last word.

"Just so you understand me."

Crawford's fears were realized when Sergeant Hoover called me to his office one day in October to inform me I was to attend a winter driving school in preparation for operating a refueling rig. The order came soon after my decision to switch my MOS from Petroleum Analysis to POL. I was abandoning any effort to get into a lab.

The school lasted two weeks and I was then apprenticed to a rig with Derril Pilkington. Two more weeks of that and I was considered safe to refuel all types of aircraft on the base. I liked driving the big five thousand gallon tankers. It also got me close to aircraft. I still loved them and still had the desire to learn to fly. However, the first time I refueled a C-47 alone was rather traumatic. After finishing, I retracted and stored the hose while the crew chief went inside and up into the cockpit. He asked me if I'd bring the paperwork inside. I stood in the doorway, hesitating to go farther.

"Up here," he called.

"I'll just leave it here and I'll wait outside," I said.

I could feel my heart pounding. It was unexpected.

"I can't leave this. Come on up."

I forced myself to step inside and up toward the front. The interior was a duplicate of the one that had crashed. I looked at the location where I had been sitting, at seats to either side, remembering the faces of the men there. The hardest part was seeing the seats McDonough and Knapp had occupied. I would have been up there, too, if I hadn't been so slow getting my parachute on.

The flight chief was staring at me.

"You all right?" he asked.

I didn't feel like telling him the story.

"Yeah—just a little claustrophobic."

That winter, Main and I continued to frequent the bars. We weren't out every night during the week, but enough, and on weekends we did our best to make up for lost time. Main seemed to thrive on that routine, but it was dragging me down. Looking at the letters I wrote home, there was little evidence of what was really going on. Evidently, I was telling Mother only the things I thought she wanted to hear.

Millie's letters continued to come, three or four a week. I enjoyed hearing all about school and other details of her life. In one respect, however, the letters continued to disturb me. Despite words of love and expression of hope that we might one day be married, she spoke often about dating. Over the past year and a half, several names had surfaced, then disappeared. I hadn't forgotten our "deal" about dating, but I couldn't refrain from asking her if I should be concerned. No, she told me; she'd be there when I returned. I continued to drink.

My salary couldn't support my lifestyle. Whiskey was expensive, especially off base. Then, a moneymaking opportunity came my way. About once every three weeks, we'd have to do KP.[46] It was a hellish job required of most airmen up through the rank of Airman Second Class. We had to get up at 4 AM and were on our feet in the mess hall for most of the day until about 8 PM. It came to my attention that POL noncommissioned officers and cooks would look the other way if one airman pulled KP for another. It would be just one absence from the

Millie Mereness, 1954

section, in any event. One day I was offered twenty dollars to pull someone's KP. That was a lot of money, and I took the job. Word got around and I was swamped with extra work. Once, I pulled KP three times in one week. I now had excess funds. How long that way of life could have continued is anyone's guess, had not three things happened to change my wayward direction.

The first revolved around a purchase I had made late in the summer of 1954. I bought a car. I got it cheap, and there was a reason: the black 1948 Pontiac wouldn't start half the time, and it sounded like the engine was filled with gravel instead of oil. Anyway, there weren't many places to go. I did go blueberrying with "Charlie," a civilian base employee I had befriended. Charlie, his wife, and several children were from an Eskimo village somewhere farther north. They all piled into the Pontiac and we labored up a big hill north of town. Another time, I took the same family farther along the same road and dropped them off for a caribou hunt, then went back three days later to pick them up, along with their game.

Not much later, the car stopped running, and Main talked me into having the two of us overhaul the "straight eight" engine. We were able to leave it outside the POL maintenance shop during the day, then push it into the garage to work on at night. To say that I had expertise in mechanics would be a gross overstatement. Main had some rudimentary skills, but was handicapped by overestimating what they were. The job turned out to be a major endeavor, taking most of the winter. The upside was that it cut into our barhopping.

The second event affecting my life was the arrival of Ed Fox's wife, Flo. They lived briefly in a trailer on the base before moving into a cabin in Fairbanks. They'd invite me to dinner about once a week, and those home-cooked meals helped me remember what home life was all about.

But the thing most responsible for putting me on a different path is painful to remember, and even more so to write about: I was dropped from the basketball team. "Kicked off" would be more accurate. It was early March, as I recall, and I'd been struggling. I was used to scoring eight to ten points a game, but that average had dropped a few points. I was tired. We played two games a week against other squadrons at Ladd and Eielson, with occasional games against other organizations around the area. In addition, we practiced once or twice a week. That schedule alone wasn't difficult for a twenty-two-year-old, but combined with the late night work on the car and trips to town on other nights, it was taking a toll. I made it to the games, but sometimes not to the practices.[47]

I showed up for a game one night after having a few drinks in the Airman's Club. We didn't have an official code against drinking, but players knew how Coach Watson felt about it. I had disregarded that. He stopped me as I was beginning to dress.

"I'm not starting you tonight," he said. "In fact, don't even dress. It would be embarrassing for us to have you falling down on the court."

I stormed out of the locker room, angry with the coach and vowing I wouldn't go back. After a while, though, I saw Watson in the chow hall and apologized. He accepted my apology with some coolness.

The next game was in two days, with no practice in between. I joined the pre-game strategy session, not knowing what to expect. I was rather surprised and elated when Watson put me in the lineup. I went into the game determined to show him that he'd made a wise choice.

It was my best game. My defense was nearly perfect and I scored fourteen points in our victory. After the game, Watson came and sat beside me on the locker room bench as I was lacing my boots.

"You played a good game, Pratt," he said, "and I'm glad, because it's a good way to finish up. I'm dropping you from the team."

I was too dumbfounded to do anything except nod. I left that night, shamefaced. I never learned why he chose that particular time to drop me, but it turned out to be the best time for me, and I'd like to think that was why he did it. Whether through his wisdom or not, I fully realized that I was being removed from the team not because of the way I played basketball, but because my values had declined to the point where it affected not only me, but others as well. It was an invaluable lesson that has stayed with me for a lifetime.

During my remaining months in Alaska, I slowly climbed back to a state of rational living. I didn't stop drinking, but I curtailed it greatly. There was one setback to my resolve. Rose and I had continued to exchange letters for many months, but the frequency had declined. After a long period devoid of communication, she wrote to say she was getting married, a blow that took several days to absorb. She had been my first love. I realized then that I had put her on a shelf, with the idea that I could take her down if I wanted to. It hurt to know that she had removed herself from my life, and I grieved for a couple of weeks before coming to grips with the truth; *whatever we had before, it was over now.* I accepted it and sent her a note wishing her well.

Main and I got the car finished that spring and I sold it to Staff Sergeant Eugene Posey at a profit. I think he later sold it to Adam

Gathers. Main rotated back to the States, and I began to spend a lot of time with Leo Shamka. We'd go to town occasionally, but any drinking consisted of nursing one or two for the evening and carrying on good conversation.

My dream of going home for Christmas of 1954 hadn't been realized; I didn't have the funds. Now, with a new focus, I continued to pull KP in an effort to recover some of the money I had been wasting for a year. Then, the POL workload got so heavy that our men were excused from KP, and that put an end to the extra money. I couldn't really be sorry, because I hated pulling KP.

My promotion to Airman Second Class had given me a few more dollars each month. I had already opened a bank account with the windfall I had received from the sale of my car and was encouraged by how it had started to grow. I was starting to think ahead. Millie was much on my mind. I had managed to become philosophic about the situation. I prepared myself, as best I could, for the eventuality that things might not be the same when I saw her again.

However, in the event that she really did love me enough to marry me, I needed to save money. She'd be graduating from high school in a little over a year. My imagination saw us getting married even before I finished my time in the service, then me completing my senior year in college and finding a teaching job. The cloud shadowing my dream was that she might not love me enough to marry me or that she might fall in love with someone else. I bolstered myself to wait a few more months for the answer. I knew I'd stay sober now.

Chapter Nineteen

Nearly a year and a half had elapsed since my return to Fairbanks. I had passed through some uncertain times, and had a few scars to show for it. Now, I was getting on with my life and feeling good about it. True, I was still experiencing "panic attacks," as they are now likely to be called, but they were less frequent, about one a week. They always occurred as I was about to fall asleep.

It was a warm June and a hot July, a welcome change after a bitter cold winter. Most of the long days of summer were spent on the flightline. All three fighter squadrons were scrambling several times a week, which kept us hopping. My time off was spent exploring the area, often on photographic jaunts with Shamka and Haab. They gave me many duplicates of their slides and photographs, which I mailed home.

One day, Haab and I drove an oil truck to Birch Lake, about sixty miles south on the Richardson Highway. The Air Force had a rest and relaxation camp there. The facility needed heating oil about every two weeks and Sergeant Hoover spread the detail around so that most of us were able to make the run at least once during our tour of duty. The truck had a top speed of thirty-five miles per hour. Even on the concrete road it was a jolting two-hour trip. We were expected to take the whole day, so we had a few hours to enjoy ourselves on the lake. We checked out a rowboat and went exploring. Haab and I became better friends that day. Not long after that, the short-timers[48] moved into barracks with rooms. Haab became my roommate. From a Montana ranching family, he had retained the values of that environment. His friendship was a good influence on me.

I was more relaxed now, part of it having to do with my "short-time" status. Mid-October wasn't far away. Any time now, I'd be getting the opportunity to choose three stateside bases. I could order my three choices, but there was no guarantee that I'd get my first choice, or any of the three, for that matter. Wherever I went would be where I'd finish my enlistment.

Even as my excitement about going home mounted, a nagging element gave me cause to reflect. I'd come to love Alaska, even though it wasn't quite the "Jack London" setting I had envisioned. Nevertheless, it hadn't lost capacity to intrigue me. I knew others who felt the same way. Another POL airman, Bob Metcalf from Massachusetts, had acquired land in the Fairbanks area. He explained the system to me. You could apply for a forty-acre homestead from the United States government for a dollar an acre, make minor improvements, live on the land for thirty days a year, and in five years it became yours to keep or sell. That appealed to me. I put homestead acquirement high on my list of possibilities for after military service.

I continued to see a lot of Ed and Flo Fox. They had a car, ancient as it was, and would often pick me up at my barracks. At their cabin one evening in early summer, I shared an idea that had been incubating for several weeks.

"Ed, I've only got three months left and you're not far behind me. I'd like to go to the crash site. If we don't do it now, we might never get the chance."

"I can go next month," he said quickly.

I had to smile. I was prepared for discussion, maybe for having to convince him. However, in Fox's mind, the idea had immediately become a plan, and the next step was to do it.

When Ken Haab heard about the intended trip, he said, "I'd like to go along."

We prepared over the next few weeks, applying for five-day leaves, buying train tickets, and filling out forms to obtain camping gear and weapons. On Fox's kitchen table, we scrutinized topographical maps to find the best access to the mountain. While in the hospital, Sallis and LaDuke had pointed out where they thought the crash site was located. We found where we thought we had been also, but there was no way to know for sure except to go there and find out.

We never discussed why we wanted to go, and I'm not sure it even occurred to us, except maybe subconsciously. I realize now, in my case, it was because of Knapp and McDonough. They had been removed from my life in an abrupt way. Although I was still in awe of the "mountain," something in me knew the site of the crash would be the best place to say goodbye.

On July 30, I wrote to my mother:

> I have my leave orders and everything set to take off Monday morning. Three of us are going. My roommate Ken Haab is going along too. We got our provisions and everything set up yesterday. All we have to do is catch the train at 8:30 Monday morning.
>
> We expect to get back Friday, so we are taking five days rations. We got mostly C-rations from the supply room, but we got a few extras at the commissary. We are taking sleeping bags, a pup tent and arms. We are taking a 30–30 cal. rifle, a 12 ga. shotgun, and a 38 cal. automatic revolver. We are also taking a couple of cameras.

Before leaving, we gave our respective squadron headquarters a detailed schedule of our intended itinerary, with maps. We wanted people to know where we were—just in case.

On the morning of August 1, Flo drove us to the train station. We checked our firearms into the baggage car. With our fully loaded knapsacks, we boarded one of the gold-and-blue coaches. We had divided heavy things, tent parts and supplies, among us. Wearing our fatigue uniforms and exuberant countenances, we would, no doubt, have attracted attention anywhere else, but to passengers on the Alaska Railroad, the sight we presented was probably commonplace.

Soon after getting underway, Fox struck up a conversation with the conductor, who was highly interested in our plans and kept coming back to ask more questions. He knew Sheldon and Hudson and was himself a pilot.

"If you could bring something back, I could always use instruments," he said. "My old Piper is pretty bare."

"We'll look around," Fox said, and then added cautiously, "They told us to leave things alone. They covered up a lot of the wreckage so it wouldn't be spotted from the air."

"If you can find anything without disturbing the landscape, I'd appreciate it."

The summer scenery was different from the snowy landscape I'd seen on the last two trips. We moved along the slopes of the hills between Fairbanks and Nenana. Game was abundant among the clusters of trees and shrubbery. Haab took numerous photographs, some through the windows and some from the outside steps with his long thin frame hanging out over the ties to get advantageous shots.

After a brief stop at Nenana, we moved across low flat country before beginning a gradual climb up into the Alaska Range. It was sunny, but hazy. We had hoped to see Mt. McKinley, but the clouds around it were thick. Higher up, at Healy, it was foggy. Even so, the mountains within our sight filled me with awe. From Healy, a gradual descent took us down through Cantwell and Summit, to Hurricane Gulch. I had crossed that expanse on my return to Fairbanks in the spring of 1954, and now, as then, I gasped in wonder, not only at the natural splendor but also at the engineering marvel of building a bridge hundreds of feet over the chasm.

The train slowed to a crawl before moving out onto the wooden structure. Were it not for being able to look down at the narrow platforms on either side of the tracks, I would have readily accepted the illusion that we were suspended in midair. Fox and I sat nervously. Haab, however, was up and moving from side to side, snapping pictures.

From Hurricane Gulch, we proceeded through Chulitna Pass and into the Indian River Valley. I had a feeling we were getting close to our point of disembarkation.

We soon crossed a steel-framed structure and our conductor friend said, "Indian River Bridge."

We had told him we wanted to get off at or near Gold Creek. On the map, that seemed like a good place, and Fox and I remembered that one of the rescue teams had started from there. Now, however, we were ready to exit at any likely spot. The conductor was standing by to signal the engineer for a stop. We had taken three seats along the right side of our car and were straining our eyes to get a good look at the ridge of mountains to the west.

"That's it!" Fox said, jabbing a finger against a window pane.

"We'll get off here," I told the conductor.

We started removing our gear from the overhead racks. Some of the passengers who had been following our conversation wished us luck.

"The next place is Canyon," the conductor said. "It's not far, but it's three or four miles short of Gold Creek."

"We'll get off at Canyon then," I said.

We had everything piled by the door as the train slowed, and finally screeched to a stop. The conductor jumped out and put down the stepstool.

"Pound on the baggage car door," he said, "unless you want us to take your guns to Anchorage."

We complied and soon had everything at our feet beside the tracks.

"Good luck, fellows," the conductor said. "When will you be back?"

"Thursday or Friday," I replied.

"We'll look for you. Just flag us down. He waved toward the engine, pulled up the stool, and jumped on board as the train began moving.

"Don't forget to look for instruments," he called back to us.

The train receded in the distance. Canyon turned out to be a two-story brown building beside the tracks. It had a bare, almost military look. No one seemed to be around. A sign on the door declared it to be the property of the Alaska Railroad. We were not to enter.

One lone set of rails, with its accompanying telephone wires, stretched a mile or more in either direction. To the west, partially enshrouded in clouds, was the mountain ridge that was our destination. It was difficult to judge the distance. We looked at our map. It appeared to be three or four miles to the base, a shorter distance than the five or six we had figured from Gold Creek. Below us, and in our way, was the Indian River. Thirty to forty yards wide, it was swift and noisy, a barrier we'd given little thought to, but which now loomed enormous before us.

"We should have gotten off at the bridge," Haab said.

"That's almost a mile back," I replied. "We can walk it, but it'll take a while."

"Too long," Fox said. "It's already three o'clock. I'd like to get across and maybe a couple of miles in before we camp. We should try to ford here."

I was cautious, saying, "It looks deep."

Fox was persistent. He walked up and down the bank for several minutes, throwing in stones and staring at the water.

Finally, he called to us, "Here's the best place to cross."

He pointed out the route we should follow. Several large rocks were protruding from the water and if we navigated carefully from one to another, we could make it, he assured.

"It's not as deep as it looks. Mostly up to the knees. It's swift, though."

We tied all our gear to our knapsacks and tied ourselves together with the twenty-five-foot rope Fox had insisted we bring. With my first step into the frigid water, I knew it was going to be difficult. It was up midway on my thighs, and the force nearly swept my legs out from under me. I learned to compensate by leaning upstream and gauging each step carefully. The rocky bottom was slippery, and each step had to be carefully calculated. It took several minutes to cross, but at last we climbed out onto the opposite bank, none the worse, except for being soaked from the waist down. My boots sloshed as I went up the willow-covered bank into the woods.

The land was mostly swampy; we had to zigzag back and forth between little streams to keep to higher ground. We actually came within sight of the bridge we had chosen to avoid. The distance was hard won. Moreover, we had another problem. Mosquitoes attacked us in swarms. As soon as our pants legs hit bushes in our path, clouds of hungry insects would fly up and attach themselves to our exposed skin.

"I can't stand this!" Fox finally said, throwing down his pack. "Get out the nets!"

We had used an oily repellent my supply corporal had given us, which was now revealed to be useless. The mosquito nets had been thrown in almost as an afterthought. They were large and fitted over our heads like hats, cutting down visibility considerably. Nevertheless, the situation was immediately improved, and we proceeded through the brush in better spirits.

We soon found that we couldn't go straight west. A steep hollow, or canyon, stretched in a southwest direction before us, making it necessary to veer southward for nearly a mile before coming to its head.

Progress was tortuously slow. We traveled until it was nearly eight o'clock. Mosquitoes had penetrated our nets and were eating at our still exposed hands as we stopped for the night. Our tent was up in record time. We climbed in and never came out until the following morning.

There was a chilly mist in the morning, with mosquitoes only slightly less ferocious than the day before. We ate cold C-rations in the tent, as we had the evening before, and then hurried to pack up and get going.

Elevation was gradually gained and the walking surface improved. The ground wasn't as spongy and the mosquito population diminished. The forest was a mix of spruce and birch, with cottonwood and white cedar in abundance. There were lots of birds and small game. We'd seen no large animals except a moose close to the river.

I was wearing the thirty-eight in a holster on my belt and Fox was carrying the 30-30. Haab had the shotgun, but it was broken down and tied to the top of his knapsack. Around noon, a covey of ptarmigan flew up to the right of us. In a lightning fast move, Fox brought the rifle up to his shoulder, swung it around in line with the

A section of the mountain ridge from the east side, August 1955

flight of the birds, and knocked one to the ground. Haab and I stood openmouthed. I'd been a hunter since the age of twelve, and I'm sure Montana-born-and-bred Haab knew a thing or two about guns, but I'd never seen anyone shoot down a flying bird with a rifle. Fox scooped the bird up as though nothing unusual had occurred. It had been hit in the head. He stuffed it into his knapsack.

"It'll liven up our C-rations," he said.

It was 1:30 PM when we reached the base of the ridge. We'd been slowly gaining altitude. The east side was far from vertical, but ascent looked to be much harder from that point on, and challenging in places. "Fingers," covered with tundra and interspersed with outcroppings of stone, extended from the top down. I had noticed on our topographical map that the ridge looked Sphinx-like, with fat paws extended out into the forest. We had earlier determined that we were a little north of the area where we had skidded down the mountain face on the sheet of ice and where the pilots had picked us up.

We left the timber behind. It wasn't easy going. Our packs were heavy, and recent rains had softened the soil, making it difficult to maintain traction. We did switchbacks in some steeper parts. Wide stretches of the surface were solid rock, sometimes too steep to walk over in an upright position. We'd seen little sun all day and were getting into clouds, which seemed to always surround the landscape. Whether from the weather or from fatigue, I was beginning to feel dispirited.

We struggled on until six o'clock.

"We're about three quarters of the way up, maybe more," Fox said.

We had stopped to rest on a narrow ledge, barely wide enough for a tent.

"Let's camp right here," Haab said.

Fox and I didn't protest. We'd had enough for the day.

Our campsite provided an interesting view of the valley. The forested plain we had walked over that day, with its gradual elevation increase, looked deceptively simple. I could make out where I thought the Indian River Bridge was located, but the railroad was indistinct at the foot of the Talkeetna Mountains. We looked at our map and compared it to what lay before us. To the southeast was the notch in the mountains where the Susitna River flowed in from the east and where the Indian River joined it. We strained our eyes to pick out elusive indentations where Gold Creek, Sherman, and Curry had to be.

The tent was pitched on the forward sloping ledge. Behind it rose a steep hillside covered with low, creeping vegetation. A rocky cliff was just a few feet in front of the tent. A few scraggly bushes surrounded the ledge. We had to be watchful not to step over the side. Our portable camp stove was too close to the tent, but on the most level place we could find. We tried to get a wood fire going, but were only marginally successful. Fox roasted the ptarmigan, which provided a few not-too-well-done bites for each of us. Hot C-rations and coffee were as appreciated as a meal from the finest restaurant.

It rained all night and the tent leaked. We had tried to dig a trench around it, but the soil over the rocks was so shallow that our efforts had little effect. Water ran down the hillside behind us and came right through the tent, soaking our sleeping bags and clothing.

Rupert Pratt and Ed Fox, August 2, 1955
Photo by Kenneth Haab

In the morning, we emerged, wet, cold, and still tired from the day before. We were, however, energized by the fact that we were not far from the top, and encouraged by a letup in the rain. There were many clouds, but they were mostly above us, obscuring the top of the ridge.

"What's the plan?" Haab asked.

"We're close enough that we can make this our base camp," I said. "We'll travel light, spend the day at the crash site, and then come back here tonight."

We spread out our wet sleeping bags on bushes and, after a breakfast of scrambled powdered eggs, continued our climb toward the top of the ridge. We soon ran out of vegetation, except for the short scrubby groundcover that seemed to overlay all but the rockiest terrain. Gullies on each side were filled with ice floes. The wind picked up and clouds engulfed us every few minutes. Visibility was poor above us. I felt as if we were near the top.

Suddenly, Fox shouted, "Look!"

He was pointing into the gully on our right. There lay one of the tires from the C-47. I was startled to see such physical evidence of the crash right before my eyes. What had happened there again became real for me. I wondered if it might not be more real than I was ready for.

Chapter Twenty

We went into the gully to examine the tire. It seemed unaffected by whatever stresses it had encountered or for having laid a year and a half on the mountainside. We speculated about how it could have been so cleanly separated from the wheel without damage. We weren't able to locate the wheel in the vicinity. I have since wondered if it might have been a spare, stored somewhere in the airplane. Haab took pictures of Fox and me with the tire.

Fox and Pratt with the C-47 tire
Photo by Kenneth Haab

As we were about to continue up the slope, Fox said, "Let's roll it!"

Some boyish madness seized us, and in seconds we had it moving. It skidded over an ice flow, bounced high into the air, and disappeared from sight. I thought at first it must have lodged in the rocks, but then I heard it tearing through the vegetation below. I'd hear it, then there would be silence for several seconds, and then I'd hear it again. That pattern continued for what seemed like a full minute, and then I didn't hear it again.

"Must have gone all the way to the bottom," I said. "I hope it didn't take out our camp."

Haab was standing above us, a disapproving look on his face.

"You could have killed somebody," he said.

I had to smile at the improbability of that occurrence, considering the number of people per square mile.

We finally reached the top. Stones littered the landscape. There was little vegetation. It had stopped raining. Nevertheless, the air was filled with a mist that prevailed, even during the brief periods when the clouds cleared out. Parts of the aircraft were scattered all around, many only inches in diameter. We found a wing section covered with small stones. We left it undisturbed.

It wasn't a nice day, which seemed to increase the aura of gloom I could feel hanging over the mountaintop. I avoided talking. Fox appeared to sense the melancholy too, although he dealt with it the Fox way—with verbal assault.

"Damned mountain sits out here in the sun all summer just waiting to rain on us."

I was surprised at the amount of personal gear still on the landscape. The Air Force had been there in June 1954, after the bulk of snow had melted. That was when they discovered the last body—that of Lt. Col. West-Watson. Why hadn't they removed these things? Articles of clothing were everywhere, spilled from broken duffel bags and handbags. I eventually found my bag, ripped open, with its ruined contents scattered. I came across a pair of blue jeans with Knapp's name on a pocket. Fighting down my feelings, I cut out the part with his name. Nearby, I found a uniform and a shoe, both his. For a long time I sat alone at the spot, remembering my friends. Now, with hindsight, I probably should have continued looking. I could have saved something for the families of the other men. It was, however, an emotional time.

We found nothing of monetary value. We had discussed that possibility before we left Fairbanks and had agreed that should we find something of value, we would turn it over to the Air Force to determine what to do with it. It's likely that the scattered contents had, in fact, been searched during the recovery phase over a year before.

Fox appeared with a hat in his hand. He pointed to his name in the liner. I showed him what I had found.

"Let's go look for the parachutes," he said.

Haab accompanied us as we walked south, down and around the hill. After a while, the terrain began to look familiar. We could see down into a large gully and I realized that we were on the slope where my parachute had dragged me. Fox recognized it, too, and we walked faster, knowing we had to be close to the spot where we'd spent the cold night.

There was a brief interruption. Haab pointed excitedly over to the other side of the gully, a distance of about a hundred yards. A brown bear was ambling down the hillside coming in our direction.

"That's a grizzly!" Fox announced.

He swung the 30-30 up to his shoulder.

"Wait!" I said. "You'll just—"

"Pow!" went the rifle and a second later rock dust kicked up at the bear's feet.

"Just to scare him," Fox said with satisfaction in his voice.

The bear had been startled and reared up, front legs outstretched. I loosened the strap of my holster, ready to grab the .38. The animal stood for ten seconds, during which time none of us said a word, and then, to my relief, he turned and lumbered back up the other side and was soon out of sight.

We continued on, glancing nervously across the gully from time to time. It wasn't long before we found the rock where we had taken shelter. There, right where we'd left them, lay the two parachutes. The site was less than half a mile from the crash site. It would have been difficult walking into the high winds that day, but if we had known, we could likely have made it there to be with Montgomery, Sallis, and LaDuke.

My parachute had been the covering one at our shelter, so I took the top one from the ground and cut out a section of it with my hunting knife. I sliced it so that I could get part of the harness along with the canopy. The orange section of silk had faded somewhat from exposure. I also took the D-ring with cable and pins.

We returned to the crash site and took some more pictures.

"I'm surprised there are no large pieces around here," I said. "Do you suppose they blasted it all up?"

"Maybe—or maybe there's more down the other side of that rise that we haven't seen," Fox said, indicating a higher area to the west.

We had planned to go up there, but it had been constantly covered with clouds since our arrival.

"It's getting late," I said.

Indeed, it was mid-afternoon, the "start down" time on which we'd agreed. We decided to descend to our camp. Just before we left, Fox found the airplane's turn-bank indicator, which appeared to be in working order.

"For the conductor," he said with satisfaction.

Downhill was much faster, and we were soon back at our camp. To our dismay, the sleeping bags were still soaked. Fox had a gleam in his eye.

"Tell you what," he said. "I think we can make it back to the railroad today. I don't want to sleep in that wet bag."

Haab and I were doubtful. I voiced my opinion.

"It took us nearly fifteen hours to get up here. It'd take us until sometime tomorrow morning to get back."

"Well, I'd rather be walking than laying in that thing. It's only dark a couple of hours. We could rest during that time."

Haab conceded, "Sounds good to me!"

I picked up my bag and felt the wet fabric.

"Let's get going, then."

We wanted to travel as light as we could, so we took several cans of C-rations from our knapsacks and buried them in the shallow soil on the ledge.

"Just in case we ever want to come back," Fox said.

We left the ridge, making good time. Well into the woods, Fox, our idea man, had another one.

"That canyon we skirted going up," he said. "If we don't do that this time, but cross it instead, we could save a lot of time."

"It looked pretty deep," Haab said.

"Sure—but we can pick our spot."

His leadership had gotten us over the river and served us well in other respects, so we agreed. That time, though, the idea almost got us into trouble.

Our new route was in a more northerly direction. We kept up the pace, stopping only once to eat cold C-rations. Fox paused occasionally to study his compass. Instead of stopping to rest, we pushed on through the semidarkness of the arctic summer night. Sometime around midnight, we stood looking down into the dark hollow. It wasn't as deep as I'd remembered, not more than a hundred feet, but it was steep. Trees lined the sides, and many stood out at odd angles because their roots weren't deep enough to hold their weight.

We were all running pretty much on reserve energy and probably not thinking straight. We chose the most likely looking spot and launched ourselves over the side. I felt as if I was in a free fall. I tried grabbing at small trees and brush but invariably they would uproot and I'd accelerate on the way down. There was crashing and cursing on either side of me. I saw the 30-30 skidding down ahead of us. I landed hard at the bottom. None of us had serious injuries, but my hands were bleeding from grabbing trees, and I had more than a few bruises.

Once across the small stream, we looked up the other side with some anxiety. If anything, it was higher and steeper than the incline we had just descended. Knapsacks, sleeping bags, and tent parts were still burdens to deal with, even though we had unloaded some weight at the campsite.

I climbed carefully, inspecting each foothold before committing to it. There was no talking. I could hear Haab and Fox matching my labored breathing. It was a steep climb and there was real danger of falling if a handhold broke loose. It was with relief, then, that I pulled myself up the last few feet and fell exhausted onto the tundra. The other two men were in no better shape.

The payoff for our efforts came when we picked up our original trail and found we were near the river. A mile or two had been saved. It was getting dark by that time, but we forded without incident. Soon we were standing before the railroad building.

"I'll go jimmy a window," Fox said.

A few minutes later, he opened the front door and we dragged our gear inside. After spreading tent parts and wet sleeping bags over tables in the big kitchen, we collapsed on the upstairs cots.

I awoke about eight o'clock to the smell of coffee. Fox was up and fixing our breakfast. Haab was sitting on the edge of his bunk, putting his boots on.

We had just finished eating when a four-man railroad crew went past on a handcart. The kitchen lights were on and I saw their heads turn in our direction. They soon halted and backed up to the front of the building. We explained our situation, Fox doing most of the talking and making it seem the most natural thing imaginable that we, "being military personnel," should take refuge in a government building. It turned out that they remembered the accident quite well. A couple of them had even been present when one of the engines had been loaded onto a car near there after being sledded across the "flatlands." They finally left, seemingly satisfied we'd leave things as we found them.

The train wasn't due until early afternoon. After we had thoroughly cleaned up after ourselves, we killed time and mosquitoes outside along the tracks. The train arrived on schedule. We were back in Fairbanks at 8:30 that evening.

In September, the POL men who were to rotate the following month received a hard blow. We were told that we were being extended—indefinitely. The Air Force didn't have enough men to replace us. I moped around for several days, feeling sorry for myself. During that time, I reread Millie's letters, the ones since the crash. She had continued to write several times a week, always assuring me of her love. In my mind, though, there was a question about the condition of our relationship. I needed to see her, to talk to her, to get things straight.

Then, in late October, we received news that we'd be returning to the States after all. The new rotation date was in mid-November. I'd be stationed at Stewart Air Force Base at Newburgh, New York, a mere one hundred miles south of Schenectady. It had been my first choice of the three bases I had requested, and I was greatly pleased.

The days fairly dragged now, but rotation day finally came. I was flying commercial to Seattle, from where I intended to take a bus across the country. With six weeks' leave, I was headed home to West Virginia. But first, I'd make a stop in upstate New York. If things worked out favorably there, I could go home feeling good.

I had thought I wouldn't be nervous about flying, but as the time approached, I found myself dreading it. An airman named Bill Lathrem was traveling with me, so it helped to have someone with whom to discuss the trip. He'd take the bus with me as far as Chicago, where he'd then head south to his home in Kentucky, and I'd continue alone toward Albany. Our plane was scheduled to leave at 11 PM. It snowed all day and the temperature dropped to -30. Ed and Flo Fox took us to the airport near Fairbanks. Flo handed me a bag of homemade chocolate chip cookies and Fox gave me an envelope.

I looked inside and saw two pills.

"What is it?" I asked.

"They'll let you sleep on the plane. Take one now and another in a few hours."

I stuck the envelope in my pocket. I wouldn't take the pills, but I didn't want to refuse a thoughtful gift. I knew Fox had been having some real problems with flying. His job had taken him on a turbulent flight to an outpost the year before and he had returned to Fairbanks several shades paler.

"We'll keep in touch," Fox said, as Lathrem and I were about to exit the terminal.

I hugged Flo and shook Fox's hand, saying, "We sure will."

The four-engine airliner kicked up mountains of snow taking off, and it seemed like forever before we finally lifted off the runway. Thirty minutes later, after reaching cruising speed, we ran into some moderate turbulence. I asked the flight attendant for a glass of water, and took both pills.

Chapter Twenty-one

The cross-country trip on a Greyhound Scenicruiser was long, but uneventful. I sat with a young German woman who'd just seen her soldier husband off to Alaska. She was headed for Maine, so we were together for four days, all the way to Albany. Lathrem left us at Chicago; I wasn't to see him again. "Ester" told me numerous tales about Germany and of the hardships she'd experienced as a young girl during the war. We became good friends and regretted parting.

I had accepted an offer from the DeVitos to stay with them, and Tom, Sr. picked me up at the Albany bus station early in the morning. We had a good chat on the half-hour ride to Schenectady. He was excited about "Tommy" coming home for Christmas.

I called Millie from the DeVitos' before she left for school. She said her mother wouldn't let her skip school, but she would come straight to see me after her last class. I had slept little since leaving Alaska and was exhausted. I was afraid that if I went to sleep now I'd be unwakeable. I showered, dressed, and watched TV, fighting to keep my eyes open. I remember sitting on the couch in the living room about 1 PM. Then, my next conscious sensation was the soft touch of Millie's lips on my mouth. I held her close for a long time, finding it hard to believe that we were finally together.

The Merenesses invited me to stay with them. I accepted, after making sure Tom and Natalie wouldn't take offense. I wanted to be able to spend more time with Millie. I stayed several days and became better acquainted with her mother during that time. I recall a conversation I had with Marguerite one day while Millie was in school.

"You've been writing to each other for a long time," she said.

"Yes—over two years."

"She'll be eighteen in March."

"I know."

"She's a senior. She won't graduate until June."

"I know. You don't have to worry."

Through that brief but candid exchange, I got the message that Marguerite accepted me, but wanted me to understand her concerns for her daughter's welfare. From her father, Floyd, I felt neither acceptance nor hostility. Basically, he ignored me.

I met her brother, Floyd, for the first time. He'd been in the Army and in Korea the summer I met Millie. He was now attending photography school in New York City and came home on weekends. Marion, Millie's sister, was in nurses' training at Ellis Hospital in Schenectady.

Millie had her driver's license, which enabled us to take the family car and get away occasionally. She introduced me to many of her friends. It was our private times, however, that I craved and needed. One day, not long before my departure, we sat in her driveway in the car.

"You know that I love you," I said.

"I love you, too. I've been telling you that."

"You've been dating?"

"You're back now. That's all over!"

"For sure?"

"For sure!"

We had exchanged words of love many times before, declarations that I think we believed would somehow give us a future together, but it was a future that, as yet, had little shape. Now I needed us to plant our intentions firmly in the present.

I got right to the point.

"Can we talk of something more serious in our relationship—like marriage?"

She didn't seem surprised.

After a few moments of apparent reflection, she said, "We will—and soon. But not now—not yet. I still have to finish school."

To me, her words had none of the feelings of rejection, but only of promise. Finally, I had to set my face toward home. Seeing Millie was the balm I had needed. We were okay, she told me again before I boarded the train for West Virginia.

For a time, it was wonderful to be home. Family and friends trooped in to see me. A Huntington newspaper did a front-page article about my crash survival. We had an old-fashioned Thanksgiving, but afterward I began to feel restless. My heart was in upstate New York. I wanted to be near Millie. Tom, who was going to be home before Christmas, invited me to stay with his family. I was scheduled to report to Stewart AFB January 2, but decided to leave home a few days before Christmas. My mother wasn't pleased, but accepted my decision.

There was, however, one last issue I had to face before leaving. I'd only been home a few days when a mutual friend told me that Rose wanted to see me. Her marriage was troubled, the friend confided.

I put it off. It wasn't that I didn't want to see her—but why open old wounds? Finally, I stopped one afternoon at her place of employment. She was as beautiful as ever, but she looked tired. We talked on mundane topics for several minutes, then I told her about the time I had spent with Millie.

"Are you going to marry her?" she asked.

"If she'll have me."

She looked me in the eye as if she had something momentous to say—but then she sighed, "Good luck, then."

"Rose, things never seemed to work out between us. I'm sorry for that."

"Yes," she said, with a wry smile. "Me too."

My love for Rose was an ember that had refused to die. But now, finally, I felt the relief of knowing that I was going to get on with my life.

I bought a car, a 1953 Ford and, feeling liberated, headed out through Ohio and western Pennsylvania toward Buffalo. There, I got on the newly constructed New York State Thruway, and followed it all the way to Schenectady.

Tom was home by the time I arrived; we had a joyous reunion. He had continued to write to Nancy Ross while he was in England, and later in Africa. They were dating, and as before, we became a foursome. Then, too soon, it was time for Tom to head out to Wright Patterson AFB at Dayton, Ohio, and for me to travel south to Stewart.

Stewart was much smaller than Ladd. The vine-covered brick buildings made it feel like a college campus. I was assigned to fuel storage to work with a civilian and two other men. One of them, Sergeant Kellar, was a West Virginian.

Millie Mereness and Rupert Pratt, summer 1956

On September 16, after nearly a year of intense courtship, Millie and I were married. For the next four months, we lived in a little apartment in Rock Tavern, near the base. In January 1957, I was discharged from the U.S. Air Force. We moved to Huntington, where after one semester and one summer term at Marshall, I completed my BA degree. I was hired to teach in the Cabell County School District, where I worked for two years while earning my MA. We decided to move back to New York, where Millie would attend the State University of New York at Albany. I became a teacher in the Schenectady City School District, as Millie eventually would. In August 1959, after a turbulent courtship, Tom DeVito and Nancy Ross made it to the altar.

I held Alaska in my heart for a long time. The homesteading idea I had embraced while there still held me in its grip. I brought the subject up with Millie several times. There was interest, but not at the level I hoped for. I loved her too much to make it an issue. Gradually, careers took over and my Alaska dream diminished in importance.

My bedtime panic attacks slowed, and then all but disappeared. Pushed to some back shelf of my mind was the crash, the pain of loss, and the bad year in Fairbanks. It wasn't that I didn't wonder about Ed Fox and the other survivors. I remembered that we'd promised to stay in touch. Little did I dream it would be near the end of the century before I'd see any of them again.

Part Two

1996–2005

Foreword to Part Two

I received a phone call in April 1996 from Rupert Pratt. He was looking for information about Capt. Earl (Bob) Betscher, the pilot of a C-47 that crashed in Alaska on February 5, 1954.

I remember answering, "That was my dad's airplane!"

So began a journey that continues to this day.

Later that year, I met the six men who had survived and learned their stories of that tragic day. There had been some reservation on my part. I remember driving to Dayton, Ohio, with my wife, Jan, for the first reunion and thinking, *my father died—these guys lived . . . this is going to be a party?* Three days later, we were all one big family, joined by a tragic plane crash—and friends for life.

I grew up knowing my father had been killed in a military airplane crash. My mother remarried back into the Air Force, and my stepfather adopted my sister and me. I'm very close to my adoptive father. He raised me as his son, but I often wondered about Bob, what he was like, how I'm like him, and how different my life would have been if he had lived.

When I went off to college near my mother's hometown, Mom told me there was a special box waiting for me in the attic of my grandmother's house. I opened that box one summer day in 1970. I found Bob's personal effects—letters, C-47 training manuals, newspaper clippings, and copies of the memorial service for my father. I remember promising myself that someday I'd go to Alaska and find the crash site. I didn't know where it was or how I'd get there, but I needed to go and touch the C-47 with my own hands and stand where my father had died. Twenty-eight years after that youthful promise and two years after the first reunion, my wish came true. Not only did I touch the instrument panel of my father's airplane, but I took an oil pressure gage home.

Over the years, we, as a group, mounted plaques honoring the ten men who died on Kesugi Ridge, arranged a medal for a hero who found some of the survivors that day, and set the record straight for the history books. Rupert's story is our story, and it's a good story to tell.

Keith Humphries Betscher
West Chester, Ohio
September 20, 2005

Chapter Twenty-two

On February 5, 1996, the forty-second anniversary of the airplane crash in Alaska, I initiated a search for the other five survivors. I had contemplated such a project for years. My primary excuse for not starting was lack of time. Since I'd retired from teaching in June 1995, that excuse was no longer valid.

Our son, Greg, supplied the means. For Christmas, he had given me a computer CD[49] containing all the listed residential telephone numbers in the United States. I had barely used it, except to look up the names of a few friends. Nevertheless, I recognized its potential as a people-finder.

What about those men to whom I was bound by virtue of having shared one traumatic event? Were they still living? What had they done with *their* lives? Had we been different because of what had happened to us? I had often asked that question about myself, but had found no definitive answer. Maybe knowing about their lives could provide one. Such speculation strengthened my desire to find them. I'd start that very day, I resolved.

Later that morning, I dug out my old newspaper clippings. Long ago, I had given them to my mother and she had pasted them into a big red scrapbook. After her death in 1978, I had placed the scrapbook in my own family archives. As I opened it, bits of paper rained down onto the carpet. The scrapbook pages were in an advanced stage of deterioration. The newsprint, though yellowed, was in good shape.

I carefully removed the pages and laid them out on the floor of my study. I had a picture album I'd purchased in Fairbanks in 1955. It, too, contained old clippings and Alaska photographs. Many of the clippings were the same as those in my mother's scrapbook. They were from the time of the crash, from the Huntington and Anchorage papers. There was also an article from the Huntington paper printed after I returned home in 1955. I soon found what I was looking for: the 1954 home addresses of the other survivors.

Besides the phone CD, I owned a map CD[50]. It was extremely detailed, right down to street level. First, I'd simply try calling names. If that didn't work, I'd zero in on the area, using a map. I'd call people there with the same surname. Surely I'd find a relative who would know the whereabouts of my friends.

My list of names consisted of Edward J. Fox of Utica, New York; Eli LaDuke of Au Sable Forks, New York; Edward W. Olson of Elkader, Iowa; Bobby G. Sallis of West Helena, Arkansas; and Huey T. Montgomery of Eldridge, Alabama. I wondered what the chances were that any of them would still be living in the same area. On the other hand, what were the odds that we'd all still be alive?

I had been closest to Fox after the crash, so it seemed natural to try him first. I fired up my Macintosh and popped in the phone disk containing New York numbers. I typed in "Fox Edward J." and pushed the return key. Eight names came up, but none in the Utica area. I thought maybe his name might appear in a different form in the phone book. I typed in "Fox." Hundreds of names flashed on the screen. Scrolling down, I counted the possibilities. There were four "Edw. J. Fox," and thirty-two "E. Fox," with one from Utica. There were four "E. J. Fox," and seventeen "Edward Fox."

Picking up the phone, I dialed the lone Utica number. The woman who answered the phone listened courteously.

"My name is Rupert Pratt. I'm from Scotia, New York, and I'm trying to locate the Edward J. Fox who was in an airplane crash in Alaska in 1954."

"Sorry," she said. "I don't know of anyone in my family who was in Alaska back then."

I tried a few more numbers with similar results. It began to dawn on me that it might not be so easy. Clearly, I needed to take a different approach.

I pulled out the disk holding the southeastern states. Since "Bobby G. Sallis" wasn't a common name, I'd try it next. Only one name appeared on the screen. The Huntsville, Alabama, address and phone number had to be his.

I dialed the number. A woman answered.

Almost as if she'd been expecting my call, she said, "I think my husband will be very interested in talking to you."

In seconds, Sallis was on the line.

"Pratt—it's good to hear from you," he said in the same smooth southern accent I remembered. "How in the world are you?"

We talked for nearly an hour and covered a lifetime of experiences. Sallis had had an interesting career. After leaving the Air Force in October 1954, he'd worked for Greyhound Bus Lines, but soon left to attend Memphis State College. In 1955, he entered government service as a contracts administrator and negotiator for agencies such as the Army Missile Command and the National Aeronautics and Space Administration. During his time with NASA, he was actively involved in the Space Program.

When I inquired about his responsibilities with NASA, he told me that he'd negotiated and administrated complex government contracts for the acquisition of hardware, software, and other sophisticated space-related products. He later entered the private sector and worked in the same profession. I was impressed. His first wife had died, and he and Ramona had been married for many years. Sallis had four children and several grandchildren, he proudly told me.

I filled him in on my history.

Then I said, "Let's have a reunion."

"An excellent idea."

The reunion bit had just popped out. I guess the idea had occurred to me before, but I hadn't given it much thought. Now it seemed the most logical thing in the world.

I was exhilarated when I went to bed that night and determined to find someone else the next day. Sallis had had no contact with any of the others, but voiced optimism that I'd find them.

The next day, I continued the search. Eli LaDuke had grown up in Au Sable Forks, New York. A computer check brought up only John E. LaDuke from there. A woman told me her husband was a relative of Eli's. Eli was living in Ellenton, Florida.

"I won't give you his number," she said, "but I'll call him and have him call you back."

"Don't tell him who it is," I said. "I want to surprise him."

Five minutes later the phone rang. "I was given your number and told I should call you," Eli said.

As had been the case with Sallis, LaDuke's voice also seemed unchanged from the time of our stay in the hospital at Elmendorf. He seemed to measure each word carefully before releasing it, and then reluctantly.

"Eli, do you remember where you were forty-two years ago yesterday?" I asked.

"Sure do—on a mountain in Alaska! *Who is this?*"

"It's Rupert Pratt, Eli! That mountain is part of my memory, too."

It was a poignant moment, and I think we both felt it.

"Well, it sure is good to hear from you, Rupert," he said.

He filled me in on the intervening years. I already knew some early details from having read letters to my mother from Roger and Rita LaDuke, his parents. After leaving the Air Force, he had worked as a bank teller at Keensville National Bank for two years, during which time he bought a motel with his parents at Au Sable Forks. After two years in northern New York, he went to Indiana to attend Tri-State College. He married a hometown girl, Ginger Sheffield, soon after graduation. Their first child, Alan, was born in September 1962, followed by Lisa in December 1965. They moved to Cincinnati, where LaDuke worked in the electronics field.

LaDuke had a varied and interesting career. From 1962 to 1978, he was with Cincinnati Milacron, where he worked as an engineer, personnel director, assistant marketing director, field engineer manager, and manufacturing manager. In 1978, he cofounded Sentinel Computer Corporation, which specialized in small business systems, personal computers, hardware, and software. In 1986, Eli went with Hunkar Labs, Inc., where he was operations manager. He finished his career with Applied Data Management, as a manufacturing representative. In 1994, he entered semi-retirement, and soon after that, he and Ginger moved to Central Florida. He told me he was loving it.

At the end of our conversation, I asked, "Would you like to have a reunion somewhere?"

"Absolutely! Let's do that."

Two of the men found. Great! Over the next few days, I made some computer passes with "Huey Montgomery" on the southeast disk and "Ed 'Olsen'" on a Midwest disk. I got no results for the first and far too many for the second.

I decided to concentrate on finding Ed Fox. Over a period of several days, I called many of the twenty-nine Ed Foxes around the state. Some were interested in my story and tried to be helpful. For most, I got answering machines or no answer at all. Two-thirds of the way through the list, I became discouraged. I seemed to be no closer to finding Ed Fox than when I'd started. If he wasn't in the Utica area, he could be anywhere.

I still thought Utica might be the most productive place to look. There were eight names on the list, including the one I'd already tried. For some reason, the name "Jane Fox" caught my interest.

A woman with a pleasant voice answered.

"Why, yes, he's my cousin," she said quickly. "He lives in Palm Bay, Florida. Hold on—I'll give you his number."

So easy! One minute I hadn't had a clue, and in the next, I had Fox's number. We had a lot to say to each other. He and I, along with Sallis, had been stationed at Ladd after the crash. Sallis had soon been discharged, but Fox, his wife Flo, and I were there for more than a year and a half. I was saddened when he told me that he and Flo had divorced in 1961.

Fox had made a career in the Air Force and then worked six years at Mohawk Data Corporation in Utica. Then, he "hit the road to see the world." His travels included most of the United States, Canada, and Mexico, and he had biked through most of Ireland. Even after settling in Florida in 1980, he had continued to travel from there.

Fox was quick to embrace the idea of a reunion, "no matter where." His wanderlust was still alive.

He hadn't changed much. His upbeat personality gives him a unique outlook on life.

He told me he'd had prostate cancer and then, almost within the same breath, added, "But that's all under control! Say, have you heard this one?"

What his jokes lacked in quality, he made up for in quantity.

"Were you aiming at the bird you killed with the rifle?" I asked.

It was a question for which he hadn't supplied a satisfactory answer forty years before.

All I got now was a chuckle and a change of subject.

"Remember the big grizzly? He stood up and swatted the air at us after my bullet kicked up the dirt around his feet."

I was pleased with having found three survivors. Two to go! It was late February. An idea I had entertained earlier began to develop. It had started when I found a stack of envelopes among my mother's things. She had traded letters with the parents of LaDuke, Montgomery, and Olson after the crash. I spent hours pouring over the letters. Catherin Montgomery gave vivid descriptions of their farm in Eldridge, Alabama. Ada Olson's letters sparkled with family matters. The letters from each of the women spanned several years.

Mother had, to my surprise, also written to the parents of some of the men who had died. Mary Knapp's letters showed her family's struggle for meaning in Ed's death. There were a few letters from Grace Betscher, the pilot's mother. They also covered a period of several years. There were a couple from Ella Mae Sparrow, Don McDonough's mother. Her distinctive name and handwriting brought back memories. I had often picked up mail for Knapp and McDonough while we were in Fairbanks and Anchorage, and I remembered handling her letters.

So why not invite the family members of men who had died to our reunion? The idea seemed logical. But might there be some unresolved resentment toward those of us who had survived? Maybe—but with such a great passage of time, it might not be a major problem. However, I'd consult with the other survivors before taking any action.

Newspaper clippings refreshed my memory for the names of Earl Betscher, James Hill, Richard Knickerbocker, Edmund McMahon, Alvi Raymer, Jacob Siplivy, and W. West-Watson. Of course, I needed no memory jog for my friends Ed Knapp and Don McDonough. Only the identity of the copilot remained a mystery. It would be a big task getting in touch with so many people. I wasn't shying away from the work, but first I had to find the other two survivors.

I went to work on Ed Olson. I wasted some time, because I'd copied his name from a newspaper article incorrectly, spelling it "O-l-s-e-n." How I did finally find him is an interesting story, bolstering my feelings that there might be some "unseen hands" involved in my searches.

On the evening of February 27, I typed in "Olsen" and "Iowa." I had tried that before, but had discarded the results because they hadn't seemed to lead anywhere. Now, I looked more closely at the list. There were only a dozen names, with ten from Iowa City and two from Iowa Falls. I pulled out a map and found the two cities. Both were some distance from Elkader, but Iowa Falls looked a little closer. I dialed the first Iowa Falls "Olsen" on my list. A woman answered and listened to my usual introduction.

She seemed interested.

"My name is Swartz, and I just moved in here," she said. "The Olsens, who did live here, have left the area. Funny thing, though—my maiden name is Olson, with an 'o,' not an 'e.'"

She obviously wanted to help, but didn't know anything about the Elkader "Olsen" family.

We were about to hang up when she said, "Say—could you be misspelling his name? Might it be O-l-s-o-n, like mine? I've heard of some 'Olsons' in Elkader."

Stubborn to the end, I said, "I think I'm spelling it correctly—but I'd like any information you can give me."

"I know someone over there in the historical society. I'll give them a call, and then I'll call you back."

I didn't really expect a return call that night, but the phone rang five minutes later.

"Hello, Pratt. This is Ed Olson!"

I was flabbergasted, and I'm sure I stammered as I said, "I was expecting a lady to call back."

Olson chuckled.

"Elkader's a small place. It didn't take long for your number to get to me. I guess we've got some catching up to do."

We did catch up, talking for nearly an hour. Olson had never strayed far from Elkader after his Air Force service. I hadn't talked long with him before realizing he and his wife Ruth had made a career of serving their community. I didn't find out everything about Olson that night, but over the next few months, I learned a great deal.

Edward William Olson, son of Gustav G. and Ada J. Olson, was the youngest of three children. He had two older sisters, Eleanor and Lillian. As he was telling me of Elkader, I could envision the town as a friendly time-forgotten oasis in our desert of modern commercialism.

He went to Iowa State Teachers College (now the University of Northern Iowa), with a dream of becoming a teacher. That dream was cut short when he enlisted in the Air Force. His training as a radio operator set him on course toward St. Lawrence Island, where he was headed when our C-47 crashed. After getting out of the hospital, Olson had requested to remain at Elmendorf, and there, in September 1954, he married Ruth Mary Wayne of Waterloo, Iowa. Their first child, Melissa, was born in Alaska in 1955.

Back in Elkader after his discharge, he managed the family business for a time. In 1956 a daughter, Cynthia, was born. Olson soon entered the political world, taking the position of deputy county treasurer for several years until he was approached to become editor and advertising manager of *The Clayton County Register*. During the next eleven years, the newspaper duties expanded to other things and

Ed became involved in community development. Throughout that period, and throughout his career, he juggled many part-time interests, foremost being artwork and design. In 1971, he and Ruth Mary opened a Sears catalog store, an endeavor that lasted nineteen years. Another child, Jennifer, was born during that period.

Olson was elected to city council, and after one term was asked to run for mayor. He was mayor of Elkader for four terms, eight years altogether. In 1990, the Olsons sold the Sears franchise and opened a small shop, selling office and art supplies and Mary Ruth's crafts. That ended when Olson experienced a heart attack and had to spend months recuperating. After his recovery, he took over as program manager for the Main Street and Elkader Development programs.[51]

Olson offered his help with planning a reunion for that summer. As for the matter of inviting families of men killed in the crash, he thought it was a good idea. His suggestions showed mature wisdom, a quality I saw in him many times afterward. We should, he said, be up-front about our reason for having the reunion. We were going to celebrate the sparing of our lives.

"We're going to be talking about the crash," he said. "I know I have many unanswered questions that have bothered me. I want to be free to talk about it without wondering if I'm hurting someone who was caught unaware. We should tell them we're going to discuss *all* the details. Then they can decide if they want to attend."

We promised to talk again soon. He'd give some thought to where we should have the reunion. Because of Olson's heart problem, he felt as if he might have trouble traveling long distances.

Millie had been standing in the doorway, listening to my side of the conversation. She had been extremely interested in the project from the beginning and had given me encouragement.

"You've really got something going here," she said.

"I've got Greg to thank for it. He gave me the disks."

"I'm going to call him to tell him what you're doing," she said.

Greg was, at the time, a student at the Rochester Institute of Technology in Rochester, New York.

I was getting excited, too. Now, if I could just find Huey Montgomery, our survivor circle would be complete.

Chapter Twenty-three

Late the following morning, Olson called again.

"I've got some news," he said.

A Cedar Rapids reporter, Rita Seymour, had overheard him telling a friend about our conversation.

"She wants to do a story about our upcoming reunion, so I gave her an interview. It's going to be in the *Cedar Rapids Gazette*."

"Save me a copy."

"She wants to interview you, too. I gave her your number. I hope that's all right."

"Of course. When is she calling?"

"Any time now. I wanted to get to you first, so you'd be expecting it."

The call came a few minutes later. Ms. Seymour wanted "my deeper feelings." That was difficult for me. I had shared my emotions with close friends over the years, but opening up for a newspaper article was a new experience. I'd given an interview to the Huntington paper in 1955, but I was young then and still close to the tragedy. My testimony to Air Force officials right after the crash involved only the cold facts. She was gentle with her probing, however, and the interview went smoothly.

I gave her the names and phone numbers of the other survivors with whom I'd been in touch, with her promise that she wouldn't intrude on their privacy should they not want to talk. I called Fox, Sallis, and LaDuke when I got off the phone to warn them.

The February 29 newspaper arrived three days later, compliments of Olson. The bold title said, "Crash survivors planning reunion—Ex-Elkader mayor hopes for answers 42 years later." It was a well-written article, with quotes from each of us, a good mix of descriptions of the crash and our present feelings about it. I guess everyone enjoys having something positive written about them, so I reread the article a few times, and then put it away, thinking that was the end of it.

Finding Montgomery was now my highest priority. I found only two "Huey Montgomerys" on the southeast disk, but neither of them was from Eldridge, Alabama. I tried both numbers. One didn't answer and the other couldn't help me.

I went to my computer maps and copied the names of towns close to Eldridge. Then, in a moment of inspiration, I did a computer search for area churches, knowing from Catherin Montgomery's letters that they were churchgoing people. Churches close together often have strong ties. Maybe someone could give me information to set me on the right path.

On my first try, the pastor answered the phone.

"No," he said, "I don't know any Montgomerys personally, but I know of a family related to the Montgomerys over in the next town. Hold on and I'll get their phone number."

The woman who answered said, "I'm a cousin. Huey moved away from here a few years ago. I don't know where he lives, but I'll give you his brother's number in Texas."

Within minutes, I was talking to Louis Jackson Montgomery.

"He and his wife Minnie are living in Evansville, Indiana," he told me. "Huey's not in very good health. He has emphysema and a lot of other problems."

"Do you think he'd like to talk to me?"

"I'm sure he would, but it would be a good idea if you talked to his son, Huey, Jr., first. Huey gets a little confused on the phone and it would be best if Huey Jr. prepared him for your call."

I dialed the Evansville number and got right to the point.

"Are you the son of the Huey Montgomery who was in an airplane crash in Alaska in 1954?"

"Yes, I am. Who is this?"

After I'd explained, I said, "I want very much to talk to your father."

"He'll want to speak with you, too. I'm going to call him and explain who you are. Wait half an hour before you call him to give me time."

He gave me Huey's number, and I waited nervously. I didn't know what to expect. The way his family was handling it made me suspect that Huey was in a precarious state of health. I would soon know.

A woman answered the phone.

"I'm Minnie, Huey's wife," she said. Her voice was pleasant. "Huey's right here."

"You want to know about that airplane crash up in Alaska?" he asked, speaking loudly.

"No, Huey. I know about the crash. I was there—the same place you were. I'm Rupert Pratt."

"Pratt . . . Pratt. Yes—I remember. I was with LaDuke and Sallis."

"Yes, you were. You were with the airplane. Fox, Olson, and I were around the mountain from you. We were all together in the hospital."

"Right! I've got it now, Pratt."

As we talked, I realized that the abundance of humor I remembered from our hospital days was still there. His memory surrounding the accident was excellent, too. During our reminiscing, he brought up several points I had forgotten.

After a good long talk, I mentioned our reunion plans.

"Well—I'd like to be there," he said.

"And I'm sure the others will be thrilled to see you, Huey."

"Minnie would like to talk to you, Pratt. Thank you for calling!"

Minnie told me she wasn't sure Huey could make it to a reunion unless it was close to Evansville, and maybe not even then. I assured her that we would keep that in mind as we made plans.

I went to bed that night feeling a great deal of satisfaction. I'd finally found all the survivors—*all still alive after forty-two years.*

I answered the phone on a morning in early March.

"You won't believe this," Olson said, laughing. "You're going to get a letter—or a call—from a couple in Chicago. They're in the film-making business and they want to do a documentary about the crash and our reunion. I just talked to them."

"How did *that* come about?"

"A friend of theirs saw the *Cedar Rapids Gazette* newspaper article and sent them a copy. They're very interested. His name is Duncan Campbell and hers is Karen Lautens. I gave them your address and phone number. I hope that's all right."

"Sure. Did you give them information on the others?"

By that time, the survivors had been calling one another regularly and we'd had a considerable dialogue going among us.

"I did. I didn't think anybody would mind. But they're going to call you first." There was a short pause. "Do you think this is a good idea? It certainly puts an entirely different spin on the reunion ball."

"That it does! I don't know, Ed. Let's all talk to these people before we make any decisions."

"Our reunion is going to be a special event and we're talking about major publicity here." Olson said. "We have to take that into account. It might spoil things."

"Why don't we call the others and let them know what's going on? If there are any serious objections, we can tell them we don't want them there."

The other men had no objections about talking to the filmmakers, but we agreed to delay our decision for the time being.

Karen Lautens called a couple of days later. She was young, I could tell. They were just starting Drummer Boy Productions. There were actually four in the group, the other two being Paul Boese and Carrie Clifford.

"This is our first venture," Karen said. "Duncan has had a lot of film experience, as has Carrie and Paul, but most of my experience has been as a director, behind the scenes. I work for the *Jenny Jones Show*."

I told her of my discussions with the others.

"You have nothing to worry about," she said. "We'll have our camera crew there for the reunion, but we won't interfere in any way with the proceedings. We wouldn't do that."

"We haven't decided yet where we're going to hold it, but we will soon," I told her.

"When you decide, we'll start making plans for reserving rooms and the like. We'd like to choose the lodgings and, of course, we'll pick up the tab for the survivors and their families. Is that okay?"

"I have no objections to that arrangement, should we decide to let you do our story. What else will be involved in planning this?"

She said that they'd send out a letter of introduction to each of us and then call us for interviews. There would also be a contract to sign. Then they'd visit each of us at our homes for extensive interviews and camera sessions. Depending on their budget, they'd probably want to take some of us to Alaska. I was frankly surprised at the scope of their proposed project and told her so.

"We feel that your story is important and needs telling," she said.

"I'll see if we can speed up the process of deciding where to have the reunion," I said. Then I added, to make sure she understood, "I'll discuss this with the other men to make sure we're all okay with it."

Their letter, dated March 21, soon arrived. They believed our story was "a wonderful one to share with people." They gave their assurance they "wouldn't disrupt the natural course of the event." Near the end of the letter they stated, "We also understand that most of you have never flown again. We'd like to go back to the crash site, so if any of you are willing to do that, please let us know."

On March 26, I got a letter off to the men, stressing how important it was that they express their opinions.

"This certainly has changed from what we started out to do," I said. "It could be a very rewarding experience or it could have so many strings attached that we'd lose control of it. I'll be a clearing-house, but I don't want to be in the position of making decisions for all of us."

I had told the others several times that I didn't want the reunion to be *my* show. But as time went on, I had to accept the fact that I had, in spite of my objections, become "organizer" for the group. I grumbled some, but took the job seriously.

Bobby Sallis said, as if to make a point, "You started all this."

To bring our ideas into a central place, I decided that a newsletter was necessary. On April 1, I sent out two pages with a photo of the mountain ridge. My biggest concern was for us to agree on a location. There were several things to consider.

"I can travel anywhere, so don't factor me in when thinking of a central location," I wrote. "Some of us have health problems. In particular, I'm thinking of Huey, who has emphysema and may be limited to making a shorter trip. Ed Olson also has some responsibilities that could make long trips difficult."

Olson suggested Dayton, Ohio, as a good central spot. It was near Wright Patterson Air Force Base, within a day's drive for him, and close enough to Evansville to allow Montgomery to attend. After a few phone calls, we had a consensus on Dayton for July 12, 13, and 14. There were no objections to inviting the filmmakers. After I informed Karen Lautens of our decision, she arranged for us to stay at a Best Western in Fairborn, near Wright Patterson AFB.

About that time, I took on another self-imposed job. I wanted a booklet of some kind to take to the reunion. We should, I concluded, have information about the survivors and about the men who had died. Such information could only come from their families.

I had told Karen we were going to try to find families of the victims. We'd explain to them what we were doing and invite then to the reunion. In addition, several people had played a part in our rescue, and if possible, we'd like them to attend. She liked both ideas.

Chapter Twenty-four

Although many reunion details were undecided, I felt good enough about our progress to begin concentrating on finding the relatives of the victims. Not knowing what their reaction would be, I approached the job with some trepidation. The old newspaper articles contained bits of information about those families. Also, the letters my mother had received proved useful. There was one from Grace Betscher, the pilot's mother, and three from Ed Knapp's mother. The Knapp envelopes had Dunbar, Pennsylvania, postmarks. As soon as I saw them, I remembered Ed telling me stories about growing up there.

I tried "Dunbar" on my phone CD. Up came a lone name, "Andrew J. Knapp," with a rural address. I knew Ed had brothers, but I couldn't remember their names.

"Ed was my brother," Andy said.

We chatted awhile before he said it would be better if I called his brother, John, in nearby Uniontown. John and his wife, Betty, had documents he thought I might be interested in.

Betty answered the phone. She knew right away who I was.

"I'm delighted to hear from you!" she said.

Edward J. Knapp, 1953
*Photo supplied by
the Knapp family*

Betty hadn't married John until 1956, but had known the family and had shared their grief.

"The Knapps are a close-knit family," she said. "Ed's death was a blow to all who knew him. His mother died in 1968 and his father in 1975. They were never the same after Ed's death. It was too much for them."

"Who else is left in the family?"

"Ed had four sisters and three brothers. His sister, Margaret Williams, still lives here. And, of course, there's John and Andy, his brothers. There are also numerous nieces and nephews."

"You wrote to me from Alaska after the crash," John said after Betty gave him the phone. "That was a terrible time, wasn't it?"

"Yes, it certainly was."

I'd forgotten about writing to him, but it came back to me then. Actually, he'd written to me first, requesting my personal account of events of that time. I had no recollection of what I'd written, except that I remembered trying to be honest and helpful. John and Betty had saved the letter and later gave me a copy.

When I mentioned the reunion in Dayton to which the victim's families were invited, there was no hesitation in giving it their blessings.

"The only thing is," John said, "we're getting along in years and I'm not sure we can make it—but we'll try."

Donald R.
McDonough,
circa 1952
*Photo supplied by
Ella Mae Sparrow*

"We'll make it!" Betty said after grabbing the phone from John. "We have three children. Ed—who's named after his uncle—and John and Paula. I can't wait to tell them about your call. They've been hearing this story all their lives. Now, maybe it will have more meaning for them."

Betty gave me another useful bit of information. Don McDonough's mother, Ella Mae Sparrow, had corresponded with them for many years. She was living in Florida. I wrote her a letter right away. An answer came in a few days with a picture of Don enclosed. The photograph showed age, with torn edges. It brought back a rush of memories. Don, quite handsome, tall, with black hair and a fair complexion, had always stood out in my mind. I could almost hear his soft and husky voice. Don had been the only child of Ella Mae Sparrow.

I began a search for the family of Earl Betscher, the pilot. There were twenty-four Betschers listed for Ohio, three from Cincinnati. I printed the page and then dialed one of the Cincinnati numbers, that of Sherman Betscher.

"Well," Sherman said, "I know who you mean. He was a distant cousin of mine, but I don't know much about the family. There's a Keith Betscher, though, who lives up in West Chester, who does some genealogical work. He might be able to lead you to the family you're looking for."

"I have his number right here," I said, looking at the sheet I'd printed.

Keith's wife, Jan, answered and quickly gave the phone to Keith.

"You were referred to me by Sherman Betscher in Cincinnati, who said you know something of the Betscher families," I explained. "I'm looking specifically for the family of Earl L. Betscher who was killed in a plane crash in Alaska in 1954. Can you help me?"

Earl Lewis "Bob" Betscher, circa 1952
Photo supplied by the Betscher family

There was a long pause, and then Keith said, "*He was my father.*"

Such quick success continued to surprise me, although by then it shouldn't have. We talked well into the evening. Keith was twenty-two months old when his father died. He didn't remember him. He was, however, well-versed on his family's history and gave me many details.

Earl Lewis "Bob" Betscher, born April 30, 1925, was the son of Earl Louis Betscher and Grace Lewis Betscher. Bob graduated in 1943 from Withrow High School in Cincinnati. After active military duty from June 1943 to December 1945, he had remained in an air reserve unit while attending the University of Ohio and the University of Cincinnati. He married Maudie Burton on Valentine's Day, 1948.

In April 1951, Betscher was recalled to active duty. He served at Langley Air Force Base in Virginia, and Chanute Air Force Base in Illinois, where Keith Lowery Betscher was born on April 21, 1952. Betscher was finally shipped to Elmendorf Air Force Base in August 1952. Holle Lynn Betscher was born October 2, 1954, eight months after Bob's death.

First Lt. Betscher was promoted to Captain posthumously. His tombstone was already in place at the time, so his father, Earl Louis, experimented until he found a way to cut over the rank on the stone to made it read "Capt." Such an endeavor must have required a great deal of love and patience.

Keith's mother had married John A. "Jack" Humphries, Jr., another Air Force officer, when Keith and Holle were very young.

"Jack was a wonderful father," Keith said with affection. "It seems strange to be talking now about my biological father."

He had often wondered about him, he said, and was thrilled to talk to me. His grandmother, Grace, was still alive, but not in good health.

"Dayton is nearby," Keith said. "Jan and I will be there for the reunion. We'll help in any way we can with the arrangements."

Karen Lautens called in mid-April for our one-hour conference. She expertly drew details of the crash from me, along with my memories of the events before and after, some of which I hadn't thought about in many years.

"We'll get similar statements from all of you," she said. "It's been a long time and you've no doubt forgotten some things. There'll be inconsistencies. By putting your statements together, we can construct a truer story."

I continued to be amazed at how well things were coming together. Finding people had been relatively painless. It wasn't that I hadn't expected to find them—I just hadn't expected to find them so quickly. It wasn't dozens of calls I'd had to make; it was usually only one or two. Maybe they were just sitting by their phones waiting for me to call. Eventually, I'd have to hit some snags. Not yet, however.

Finding Richard Knickerbocker's widow, Loretta Shelton, was another jaw-dropper. I knew Richard came from the Rochester, Michigan area. My CD gave me one hundred forty-two Knickerbocker phone numbers in Michigan, but not one was in Rochester.

I went to my *Street Atlas USA* CD and zoomed in to the street level mode. One old newspaper clipping had given a street address for Richard's parents. There had to be someone there who remembered the Knickerbocker family. I typed in the street name and got forty-four names and addresses. I randomly chose a name and dialed the number.

The woman who answered said, "Yes, I know the family—and I know Loretta. We go to the same church. She married Robert Shelton and they live near here."

Glancing at the map, I quickly found the name of the street she gave me.

I was soon talking to Loretta Shelton.

"Oh—I can't believe this!" she said. "So long ago—so many memories. Did you know we'd only been married for four months?"

"I'm sorry," I told her. "I didn't know him. But I remember him from that day. He had blond hair."

"Yes, he did. He was so handsome—such a good young man."

There was a pause then, and I waited for her to regain her composure.

"I'd like any information about Richard and his family that you can give me," I said.

There were no Knickerbocker family members still living in the area. Richard's father, Floyd L. Knickerbocker, was deceased. His mother, Evelyn Jacobson Knickerbocker, was in a nursing home in the south. Richard had been the middle child of five children. George and Floyd were older. Shirley and Jean were younger. George was deceased. Floyd lived in Texas. Shirley lived in, of all places, Alaska. She was the wife of retired General Ed Belyea. Loretta wasn't sure where Jean lived.

She sent a package a few days later that contained useful information. Richard had graduated from Rochester High School in 1951 and had enlisted that same summer. After basic at Sampson AFB and Aircraft Engine Mechanics School at Boston University, he was sent to Alaska. He made a trip home to marry Loretta Jean Hecht in October 1953.

Richard
Knickerbocker, 1951
Photo supplied by
Loretta Shelton

There were several pictures in the packet. It felt strange to be studying the photograph of a young man I barely remembered. He'd been younger than my sons when he died, yet our lives had touched briefly. I had a sudden sense of profound sadness. In days to come, I had cause to wonder about such feelings, because they came again each time I received information about one of the men. I hadn't known them, yet I felt a strong bond between us. I was surprised that such emotions were surfacing now.

During April, I continued to search for the families of the remaining men, although the old clippings gave few addresses and clues were meager. I remembered that there had been three or four from western Pennsylvania; I was quite certain that besides Don McDonough and Ed Knapp, Jacob Siplivy was another. W. West-Watson, a British subject, presented special search difficulties. Alvi Raymer and Edmund McMahon were mysteries. None of us knew the copilot's name. All the clippings said his name wasn't being released because of family illness. Capt. James Hill's only address was Ft. Benning, Georgia. His name was quite common, so I thought I might have to go to military records.

My phone CD gave me five Siplivys in Pennsylvania. I dialed the number at the top of the list, that of Charles Siplivy from South Fork. A woman answered.

"Charles is Jacob's brother," she said, after I'd explained.

"Could I talk to him?"

"He's outside, but he's hard of hearing and has trouble with the phone. We'll try to send you something. His brother, John, lives in Arizona. I don't have his number handy, but we'll try to send it, too."

I was delighted with finding the Siplivy family so quickly, but a little disappointed that I hadn't gotten more information. At least I had a promise of information to come.

Alvi Raymer and Edmund McMahon were from somewhere in the west. I wasn't sure how I knew that. Perhaps we'd talked about them while in the hospital. Resurrected memory is elusive, but often strangely accurate. I went with my gut feeling and loaded up the disk that contained the western states, excluding the Pacific ones. I got hundreds of Raymers. When I typed in "McMahon," the name turned out to be even more common.

Reluctantly, I decided to give that search a brief rest. There was soon a lucky break, however. Among the material I received from the other survivors, an old newspaper clipping revealed that Edmund McMahon was from Butte, Montana.

Acting on the new information, I checked the phone CD. Although Butte came up blank, there were far too many names for Montana. I went to the street atlas CD and brought up the Butte area. I wasn't sure how far out that area code extended, so I copied down names of a few outlying towns. Walkersville, Rocker, Ramsay, and Janney yielded no names. I moved out farther on the map to Crackerville, Opportunity, Anaconda, Warm Springs, Divide, Wise River, Waterloo, and Whitehall. There were three McMahons in Anaconda. I dialed one of the numbers.

"Do you know the McMahons in Butte?" I asked the man on the other end of the line.

"Well, no—I don't know them, although they may have been distant relatives. I don't think any of them are there anymore."

"Can you give me any information about the family?"

"I believe someone went to Helena. Became a doctor, I think."

Helena produced only a handful of names, but one stood out. Dr. Jack W. McMahon, Jr., Obstetrician, was the only physician listed with that name.

He was quite willing to help. Edmund had been a cousin, he said, and Edmund's sister, Joanie Hautzinger, was the only surviving member of that family.

"She lives in Omaha," he said. "I have her phone number."

Joanie Hautzinger was pleased to talk to me. She quickly filled me in on their family history and cried briefly when talking about her brother.

"He was special," she said. "His death just about destroyed our parents. Dad was a doctor and Eddie was going to go to medical school when he got out of the service."

"I'm sorry to bring this up again," I said. "I can see it's still very painful for you."

"Oh—but it's good to remember, too," she said.

A large envelope arrived a few days later with photographs and facts about her brother and their family. Their parents were Dr. Stephen and Nellie McMahon. Edmund Stephen McMahon was born May 9, 1929, in Butte, Montana, the third of six children. "Eddie" was considered a "special gift from God," since his three-year-old sister, Mary

Edmund Stephen
McMahon, circa 1952
*Photo supplied by
Joanie Hautzinger*

Helen, had died two months before his birth. His brother, Brandon, was four years older. Joanie was nearly two years younger, and his baby brother, Joe, was six years younger. Another boy, Patrick, had died a few months after his birth. Edmund was, according to Joanie, "always the peacemaker, very gentle and quiet, with a great sense of humor."

He had attended Immaculate Conception Grade School, Boys Central High School, Carroll College in Helena, and Montana University. He enlisted in 1951, going to Lackland Air Force Base for basic training. His other duties were at Kessler Air Force Base, McClellan Air Force Base, and Guam. He was in Guam only a short time before receiving a transfer to Fairbanks, where he was going when he was killed.

Joanie said sadly, "It was twelve days before they found his body. He was a wonderful son, brother, and friend."

She couldn't attend the reunion, but gave it her blessing.

I felt it was important to find the men responsible for our rescue. I knew that Don Sheldon had died. He'd become famous, and I'd followed his life through magazine articles and his biography. I knew nothing of Dr. Carl Russell or Cliff Hudson. It turned out that both were easy to locate.

I tried the mid-Atlantic disk first and struck pay dirt. There were eighteen Carl Russells listed, but only one was a physician. He lived in Salem, Virginia. He was out, but I talked to Nancy, his wife. A couple of hours later, he called me back and was "gung ho" for a reunion. We spent several minutes reminiscing and talking about our families.

There was only one Cliff Hudson listed in Alaska. I called his Talkeetna number, being careful of the four-hour difference, but got no answer. I tried again the next day without results. Going to the Internet, I found a Talkeetna home page. There I located a link to Hudson Air Service. I fired off a message asking if he remembered the incident. The next day I had an answer:

Mr. Pratt,

Yes, I have thought about you three and also the other three that I found by the remains of the aircraft and that they about shot me out of the sky with parachute flares on the first pass with my plane. Then I left them and wrote a message and flew over them again and dropped the note with a streamer on it. They fired one more flare, darn near got me, oh well. Anyway, when the weather cleared I rode the chopper up to the crash site and helped the other three get to the chopper one at a time, four trips. I rode back to Curry on the last trip.

It is nice to hear all six persons are still around this long. That is very good. I have a small Air Taxi Service with six planes at Talkeetna about twenty miles south of Curry. My brother Glenn started the Air Service in 1946, 50 years ago.

If things work out I might be able to make [it] to your reunion. Please keep in touch.

Cliff Hudson

Chapter Twenty-five

I'd been having frequent correspondence with Karen Lautens, and the motel accommodations were set. I started searching for restaurants that would be suitable for the Saturday evening dinner and large enough for the film crew. I was feeling overworked and was quite happy when Millie stepped in and took over the reunion arrangements.

Olson called one day.

"Alvi Raymer is originally from Iowa," he said. "I have a clipping. He was born in Audubon, but they moved somewhere else."

"Would you like to work on finding his family?" I asked.

"I'd be glad to."

A couple of days later, he called again to say he had located Arlene Keltner, the sister of Alvi Raymer. She lived in Weaubleau, Missouri. The family had moved to Missouri while Alvi was in high school.

Through Arlene, we learned about Staff Sergeant Alvi Roy Raymer. He was born August 30, 1930, at Audubon, Iowa. Alvi was the son of Alfred William Raymer and Bertha Lake Raymer. As the oldest child in the family, he'd had to look after his younger siblings, Arlene and Bill, a job he took seriously and performed cheerfully. Alvi's parents were merchants with a grocery and feed store, and he soon learned the business inside and out.

"Alvi accepted Christ at an early age and read the whole Bible while in grade school," Arlene told us.

She empathized his good nature and willingness to help with any job in the family. His hobby was stamp collecting, which took many hours of his leisure time. She told us of the little one-room Old Memory School, the New Market School in Iowa, and Maple Wood School near Sedalia, Missouri, where Alvi had spent his elementary school years. From there, he'd gone to Tonganoxie High School in

Alvi Roy Raymer
*Photo supplied by
Arlene Keltner*

Kansas, playing baseball, basketball, and football. He was cocaptain of the football team his junior year. Then, during that year, the family moved to Cross Timbers, Missouri.

He went to Kansas University at Lawrence for two years, then to Southwest Missouri State at Springfield. After entering the service, he continued to work toward his accounting degree near the bases where he was assigned. He may have finished that degree, according to Arlene.

Alvi joined the Air Force in 1951, where he worked as an auditor. Ladd AFB was to have been his duty station for two years. He was buried March 6, 1954, at Cross Timbers Cemetery.

On the reunion track, things were moving swiftly. Shirley Belyea, the sister of Richard Knickerbocker, called from Alaska. Loretta Shelton had informed her of the reunion. She might be able to attend, she said.

Shirley added interesting details about her brother. Richard had been philosophical about the dangers of flying, passing it off as of little consequence. He'd been an active young man. Before the Air Force, he was a Sunday school teacher and was active in Boy Scouts. He loved to surprise his family. According to Shirley, he came home once without telling anyone. When he landed at Detroit Airport, he happened onto the mother of a friend who drove him home, but at his insistence, she dropped him off a block from home so he could sneak up and surprise the family.

His mother sent him a loaf of homemade bread every week. Some time after the accident, someone told her that she was lucky to have four other children. Her bittersweet response was that she "had no children to lose."

Fox called to tell me that a newspaper in his area had featured him in an article about the upcoming reunion. As a result, he had received a call from Col. Gene Pickel, Ret., who had been an officer at Elmendorf at the time of the crash. Pickel, a friend of Betscher's, had originally been scheduled to ride on the airplane that crashed, but had shown up without his arctic gear, so Betscher had refused to take him. Pickel had always called himself 'the seventh survivor." Several days after the crash, he had flown above the site and used his 8mm camera to capture the scene. He promised Fox that he'd edit it and send us a copy.

Olson had already heard from a former jet fighter pilot. Dr. Stan Nelson from Shawnee-Mission, Kansas, also had film he'd taken of the area soon after the crash. He was going to send a copy to Olson.

About mid-May, I wrote to an army historical society in England in hopes that they might help me find information about West-Watson. I also sent letters to several military record offices in the United States asking about Capt. Hill. At that point, there were still no clues about the identity of the copilot. I felt as if I'd done all I could to locate the three missing families, and decided to give it a break.

Karen informed me that *People* magazine was interested in our story. The film crew had begun their circuit of the survivors. Karen and Duncan went to Iowa to interview Olson. They set a date for me in late June.

By that time, we had twenty-seven people committed to attend. I expected there would be four from my family. Greg would be on summer break from RIT and our younger son, Jonathan, would be home from a two-year stint as a Campus Crusade for Christ missionary in Bulgaria.

Tom and Nancy DeVito were going with us. They'd been following events closely. Tom, of course, had ties to Ed Knapp and Don McDonough, since we'd all attended tech school together. Millie and I had remained close friends with Tom and Nancy all through the years. Tom had entered Hudson Valley Technical Institute after leaving the Air Force and wound up working at the Knolls Atomic Power Laboratory, which was run by General Electric. He had retired a few years ahead of me. Nancy had been a medical laboratory technician in an area hospital before their children were born. We'd shared many meals, but in the early nineties we started having breakfast together almost every Saturday. It was during these breakfasts in early spring of 1996 that I began to talk to them about the accident and the progress I was making in finding the other survivors.

I'd also been telling a few other friends about what we were doing. One couple, Clarence and Jackie Mosher, were especially interested.

"What a story," Clarence kept saying. One day he called to say he hoped I didn't mind, but he had spoken to a reporter at the *Schenectady Gazette*. "I think you just might get a call," he said sheepishly.

Sure enough, the next day, *Gazette* reporter Cheryl Clark called to make an appointment. We met at the Empire State Aerosciences Museum, in the town of Glenville, only two miles from our house. That wasn't just for my convenience. She wanted my photo with the C-47 they had there.

With photographer Mark Schultz, we spent about an hour in and around the big two-engine airplane. It was the first time I'd been inside a C-47 since leaving the service, and it was a strange feeling. The article appeared on Memorial Day. For a few days, friends and acquaintances called to tell me how much they had enjoyed it. Most hadn't known of the accident.

I had found most of the families, and Millie had taken over the reunion planning, so I had time to work on the booklet I'd promised to produce. Most people had responded by sending the materials I needed. I carefully cataloged everything I received, scanning photographs and documents for eventual transfer into my desktop publishing program.

There had been nothing from the Army Records Division about Capt. Hill, and I had a negative reply from England about West-Watson. However, I lucked out on the identity of the copilot because of material sent by one of the families. I found a small clipping taken from an Anchorage paper. It had been in the February 13, 1954 edition and identified him as Col. Edward L. Burge, son of Emma Longfellow Burge from Indian River City, Florida. With time growing short, I wasn't able to follow through with meaningful research. However, I did find Social Security records that showed an Edward Burge born October 23, 1917 and dying in February 1954.

Social Security records also showed an Emma Burge from Florida dying in December 1966, in Leesville, South Carolina. A quick CD tour produced no more useful material.

I called the Siplivys for the second time. I was anxious to get something from them. Again, I talked to Charles Siplivy's wife. She apologized for not sending anything. There wasn't much information anyway, she said. She was able to give me the phone number of her husband's brother in Arizona. John Siplivy told me that Jacob had been on his second hitch in the Army. Their father had been very ill, and Jacob had left the Army to care for him. He worked in a coal mine to support himself during that time. After their father died, Jacob reenlisted.

Jonathan came home from Bulgaria. We hadn't seen him for almost a year. Meanwhile, Greg had told us he wouldn't make it to the reunion. He'd taken a lab assistant job for the summer.

Paul Boese and Carrie Clifford showed up in Scotia on a beautiful day in late June. They had hired a local photographer to "do the shoot." They set up under the apple tree outside our study window. It was an ideal place, despite some traffic noise. We also spent several hours shooting inside our house before going over to the Empire State Aerosciences Museum to get scenes in and around the C-47—the same one I had visited with the *Schenectady Gazette* people. Darkness was approaching when Paul and Carrie left. Karen emailed me in a few days to say *People* would definitely be at the reunion. The news made me realize for the first time how big our "simple" reunion had become.

Huey Montgomery's family confirmed that they'd be there. That had been in doubt for a time, because Huey had been sick. It was important to me that he make it. I wanted us all there, just as we'd been together at Elmendorf in 1954.

About thirty people had committed to attend. It was pleasing to see that many Knapp family members were going, as was Alvi Raymer's sister. There was a possibility that either the wife or sister of Richard Knickerbocker would attend. With Keith Betscher going, there would be three, and possibly four, families representing men who had died.

To add icing to the reunion cake, Dr. Carl Russell was attending, and Cliff Hudson called to say he'd bought his tickets. The project was actually coming together.

Although I didn't feel as pressured about the booklet, I was still having difficulty getting it finished. I found myself working longer hours as the reunion approached. Ed Olson volunteered to do the cover, which he delivered soon afterward. I got the copy to the printer just days before we would start for Dayton. The day before our departure, I had the pages all stacked up, ready to put together. I was doing last-minute errands in the afternoon and worrying that the assembly job would take more time than I had. When I got home, Millie and Nancy, bless them, had not only assembled the booklets, but they also had them boxed and ready to go.

I sat, exhausted, thinking about all that had happened in the past few months. The whirlwind of preparation was finally over. I was ready for Dayton.

Chapter Twenty-six

On July 11, we stayed overnight at Medina, south of Cleveland, just off Interstate 77. It would be an easy half-day drive to Dayton. Millie did most of the driving the next morning, giving me time to contemplate upcoming events. Questions had gnawed at me the last few days. Who else might attend besides the film people and a magazine writer? What was it going to be like seeing the other five men again? Would the families of the dead men feel comfortable with us? Would the film people be in the way?

I worried about my role. All along, I had tried to play down the fact that I had initiated the reunion. "This is for all of us, it's not just my show," I had repeated several times. I resisted being "in charge," as others seemed to be convinced I was. Nevertheless, it was to me that people kept turning. Okay, if I had to run it, then it would be with a light hand. Just get things going and let it happen, was my thought.

In my heart, I knew that what I really wanted was for the six of us to sit together and talk, a simple conversation among men who had once shared a bad time and wanted some answers. That kind of simplicity might be difficult. We may have, by our own consent, let the event become too big.

It was after twelve o'clock when we pulled into the Best Western at Fairborn. Millie suggested lunch, but I declined.

"I want to go to our room and rest awhile," I said.

We were scheduled to meet at three o'clock and I preferred not to see anyone before then. Millie entered the office area to register while I sat in the car. A few minutes later, she returned.

"Guess who's in the lobby?" she said.

Before I had time to respond, Ed Fox bounded through the door. I jumped from the car and we threw our arms around each other. It seemed fitting to see Fox first. Our parting at the Fairbanks Airport in 1955 had seemed like another lifetime. Now, suddenly, it was only yesterday.

"This is my friend, Joyce," Fox said, turning me to face her.

Joyce Klodnicki, pretty, with a broad smile and pleasant manner, pumped my hand.

"Ed has told me all about you," she said.

I would have recognized Fox, even without introduction. To be sure, he was heavier and things hung down more, but it was vintage Fox. He had a ponytail, reminiscent, I suppose, of his vagabond days. For several minutes, we talked of times old and new. Finally, we excused ourselves in order to register Jon at the Comfort Inn next door.

Back at the Best Western, I plopped down on the bed. I wanted an hour to myself. Millie went out to find the DeVitos, who had arrived ahead of us. The phone rang just as I was getting comfortable. It was Nancy.

"I've been talking to Karen and Duncan," she said. "They want to see you right away. We're in the lobby."

Karen was a petite blonde with freckles. Duncan had dark hair and masculine good looks. They seemed genuinely happy to see me.

"We're sorry to disturb you," Duncan said, "but we need to settle some things so our film crew can set up."

Nancy, Millie, and I walked with them to the room where we were to meet at three o'clock. It was also the site for our dinner, scheduled for six o'clock. The room was smaller than I'd hoped for, but adequate. Tables were already arranged in a tight rectangle, facing one another. I had requested a large TV with a VCR, which was already set up at one end of the room.

"We'd like to make a suggestion," Karen said. She pointed to the pool area outside the sliding glass doors. "It's a beautiful day. If we meet out there first, we can take advantage of the light and people can move around. I've already checked with the management. It's not a problem."

It was an excellent idea. We'd be in the room a long time, as it was. Outside, we could get reacquainted. Then inside, we could go over available documents before dinner and have conversation afterward. I expected it to go well into the night.

As we walked back toward the lobby, Karen asked, "Are you going to emcee?"

I felt my anxiety level rise.

"I thought we'd just let conversation carry things along."

"We think it would go smoother if someone orchestrated it," Duncan said. "We'd like you to do it. Is that all right?"

I wanted to say something about the promise of non-interference at our reunion, but controlled myself. I hated giving up the freedom of just going with the flow, but I recognized the logic of their request. Reluctantly, I agreed.

I sneaked back to our room. I can't say why I was hesitant to see people. That, after all, was why I was there. There was much to say to them and to hear from them. Maybe I wanted to save it all for the one big moment when we'd all be together.

My mind was active and I couldn't rest. Just before three o'clock, I got all my materials together and sat waiting. Millie, Tom, and Nancy came in to help carry things. Jon joined us in the lobby.

This is it, I thought, as we approached the big glass door to the pool area. I could actually hear my heart beating.

My first impression was surprise at the number of people, and at the volume of noise due to conversation. A cameraman approached me in a crouched position, filming as he came. I saw Fox first as he walked toward me. To one side, I saw another figure approach. I knew in an instant it was Ed Olson. The three of us came together at once, hugging, yelling, and pounding one another on the back. Again, it seemed fitting. We'd been together on the mountain.

We all talked at once, telling one another obvious things, such as how great it was to be together again. Olson didn't look like a man who'd survived a massive heart attack. His mature years couldn't hide the same wide smile and pleasant demeanor I remembered.

"Are the others here yet?" I asked.

"Sallis is in the building," Fox said.

No sooner were the words out of his mouth than Olson yelled, "Here he comes!"

Bobby Sallis came through the door, a big smile on his face. Again, we rushed together like a football team huddling up before a big game. We pounded one another some more.

In a few minutes, I caught sight of a slender man standing by himself near the entrance. He appeared to be taking it all in through his dark glasses. It took a few moments before I recognized Eli LaDuke. Somehow, he'd arrived without us spotting him. We rushed him and repeated the shouting and pounding ritual.

Things settled down after a few minutes. In all the excitement, I'd lost contact with my family and the DeVitos. I spotted Nancy in the background, talking with a couple I had noticed earlier at the Comfort Inn. They had looked intently at us but hadn't said anything. They had to be the Keltners, I concluded. Millie was close by—no doubt she had been all the time. I threw her a kiss. Jon was watching at a little more distance, a grin on his face. Tom, not far away, was smiling broadly. We must have made quite a sight in our exuberance.

Where was Huey? It was almost three-thirty. What if he couldn't make it? Maybe he was sick again.

"Lord," I prayed silently, "let him make it."

Olson introduced us to his wife, Ruth, and to their daughter, Melissa Patrick, and her husband, Ed. Sallis led us over to meet his wife, Ramona, and his grandson, Jonathan, who was about twelve years old. LaDuke had come alone.

I sought out John and Betty Knapp. It was a strangely poignant moment as I hugged John, the brother of my friend. They introduced the younger man and woman with them.

"This is our daughter, Paula, and our son, Ed," Betty said. "Their brother, John, couldn't make it, though he really wanted to."

A photographer had been snapping shots all around us as we talked. I would have liked to talk to the Knapps longer, but any lengthy conversations in that atmosphere seemed doomed to failure.

The photographer introduced himself as Taro Yamasaki from *People*.

"I'd like to get a group picture of the survivors," he said.

"We're still missing a man."

He assured me that he'd get more photos later.

"I'll try to get us together," I promised him.

Just then, I spotted two men standing next to the pool, drinks in their hands. I wasn't sure whether they'd been there all the time or if they'd just arrived. I recognized Dr. Carl Russell from the photographs he'd recently sent. The other man stuck out his hand.

"Cliff Hudson," he said.

I hadn't seen a recent photograph of the aviator, but the youthful Hudson was still there in the face of the older man. For a brief moment, I saw, in my mind's eye, the younger version, with wire-rimmed glasses, kneeling to fasten my snowshoes.

Despite a knot in my throat, I managed to say, "So we meet again."

The words seemed empty, but it was all I could think of.

"Yep. It's a little warmer today, though."

Hudson's distinct, clipped speaking style was something I'd forgotten until a phone conversation the month before. He'd been rather quiet during our stay in the Susitna Valley.

"And you know this fellow," Hudson said, nodding toward Dr. Russell.

"Indeed, I do. It's good to have you here for this event. I owe you both a great deal." Then I said specifically to Hudson, "You risked your life flying up there in bad weather to find us."

"Oh, it wasn't so bad. It was a lucky thing I'd just filled my gas tanks."

"Cliff, I remember very well what the weather was like that day," I said, laughing.

I felt some guilt in their presence. Why had I waited forty-two years to find these men? Had I just been insensitive? On the other hand, might it have been an involuntary effort to put the accident out of my mind? It was unforgivable neglect, in any event. There was still time to make it up to Hudson and Russell, but Don Sheldon had been dead for many years. It was a lost opportunity that I regretted.

After reminiscing with Russell and Hudson for several minutes, I moved off to talk to the Keltners. Arlene and Ken seemed glad to meet me. Olson had worried that Arlene might be uncomfortable in our presence. I was relieved that, as with the Knapps, that didn't seem to be the case.

A man with a notepad approached. I'd seen him earlier as he talked to Olson and Fox.

"I'm Tom Beyerluin of the *Dayton Daily News*," he told me.

He asked questions about the crash and the reunion. Then I remembered I was supposed to be getting the survivors together for a picture.

Still no Montgomery. It was almost four o'clock. What could have happened?

Nancy stopped me to say that Kate Klice from *People* was there.

"I'm really impressed with her," Nancy said.

Yamasaki asked Hudson and Dr. Russell to join us. The photographer spent several minutes arranging us for different poses. In one, Ed Fox held up a copy of Sheldon's biography, *Wager with the Wind*.[52] That photo would accompany the *Dayton Daily News* article.

There was a commotion by the doorway.

"Huey's coming!" Olson called out.

A wave of bodies suddenly stampeded toward the doorway. Montgomery burst through the opening, followed closely by other family members. Montgomery was still one of the biggest men I knew. Among some of his shorter family members, he seemed gigantic.

Olson, Fox, LaDuke, Sallis, and I leaped out to greet him. We all grabbed him about the same time, pounding him on the back and screeching loudly. It was a glorious moment—*the six of us together again after forty-two years.*

Chapter Twenty-seven

The reuniting of the crash survivors had been an emotional and satisfying event. Eventually, we regained a degree of order. Montgomery was something of a surprise for me. I had expected a frail man who'd need help getting around. Instead, I saw an apparently robust man, greeting people all around him, much into the spirit of our reunion.

Holding up my hand to his in a high five, I had to laugh at the difference. Montgomery's hands made mine look like a child's. Minnie Montgomery introduced us to their son and his wife. Huey, Jr. was tall and handsome, and Sherri was strikingly beautiful. Later, I would talk at length with Huey, Jr. and get to know him as a quiet, intelligent man. He was the minister of a small church near Evansville.

Taro Yamasaki called the survivors together again. He had a stepladder set up next to the pool. He explained that he'd take photographs from the ladder with us looking up at him.

Fox laughed and said, "So our jowls don't show!"

Jon ran to get the box with my memorabilia from our banquet room. The six of us held up the faded parachute remnant I'd saved all those years. Sallis held the D-ring cut from my parachute in 1955 when Fox and I had visited the crash site. That photograph would be the lead picture in a two-page article in *People*.

A man and woman I had noticed earlier approached me, almost shyly. He stuck out his hand.

"Keith Betscher," he said. "And this is Jan."

I apologized for not speaking to them earlier.

"You've been pretty busy," Keith said. "We just wanted to thank you for making all this possible."

I'd been impressed by Keith from the beginning, when we'd had long phone conversations. I appreciated his energy. Now, in person, he made me feel like an old friend. Jan was quieter, but the same friendliness was apparent.

"Keith," I said, "having you here is very meaningful for me. I thank you both for coming."

Millie reminded me that it was time to get everyone into the banquet room. We spread the word and made our way there in a somewhat orderly fashion. The camera crew quickly moved inside. Reporters and documentary people staked out places on one side of the room. Our group settled in around tables, facing one another. As chaotic as it had been outside, now it was silent, and everyone seemed focused. I went to the podium at the end of the room, with little idea of what I would say.

I managed, nevertheless, formally greeting the survivors, their families, and families of the men who had died in 1954. I made note of the schedule for the evening and for the next two days. From that point, things just seemed to fall into place. I went to the table with my family. We all introduced ourselves again, mainly for the benefit of those new to the group. Any formality dissolved quickly.

The survivors took turns telling their own stories about the crash, and about related events. There was something magical about the time of sharing, so much so that I forgot there were cameras rolling. I hardly noticed the dining crew setting up for dinner.

I listened with great attention as each survivor related his own experience. I had, no doubt, heard their stories during our hospital time together, but now it seemed as if I was hearing them for the first time. When it was my turn, I realized that my own telling had new dimensions. The passage of time had brought new perspective, and maturity had brought more understanding. I noticed some inconsistencies in our memories of the events. Had we, over the years, dramatized certain details more than others until they took on new proportions? That was possible, I concluded.

As I listened, the stories prompted many memories and fuzzy details became clearer. Little bits of information resting in my brain for forty-two years popped out like treasures from a forgotten chest, as new and fresh as the day I had experienced them.

Olson had vivid memories of the sign on the door of the C-47 that stated "STOP—LOOK ME OVER—ALASKA HAS BEEN ROUGH ON ME." I'd later notice a photograph sent to me by Loretta Shelton, showing Richard Knickerbocker in the doorway of that same airplane. When I blew up the photograph, it showed that Olson's memory about the wording was perfect.

Fox talked about finding some junk mail and stuffing it into his pocket, thinking it would make a good fire-starter. He also revealed that Air Force hearing officers had later given him a hard time about it. Their insinuation was pointed. How dare he even think about burning U.S. mail?

Since Fox, Olson, and I had been separated from Montgomery, Sallis, and LaDuke, many details of their stories were new to us. LaDuke and Sallis recalled their escape from the disintegrating aircraft and their efforts to get together at the crash site. Their descriptions of the weather conditions brought vivid recollections to me. Even on that hot summer night, I could remember the bone-chilling cold of the mountain ridge. Watching the faces of the other men, I believed they were experiencing similar thoughts.

Of all the accounts, Huey Montgomery's did the most to stir my emotions. I suspect the other survivors exercised some degree of caution in their words to the group. I know that I didn't want to say anything that might upset family members of the dead men or to embarrass myself. Montgomery, however, spoke simply and elegantly, apparently without regard for what any of us might think. He was graphic in his description of the crash site and his feelings at the time, but his story was tempered by his characteristic humor.

"If my daddy had known I was up there on that mountain, he'd've got in his pickup truck and gone up there to get me," he said.

Huey revealed, and LaDuke confirmed, that LaDuke had unzipped Huey's pants so that he could urinate. Huey's hands had been too cold to manipulate the zippers and buttons. Eli looked embarrassed by the revelation, but Huey continued, unperturbed.

"I needed help. I was just too cold," he said.

I remembered things apparently not recalled by anyone else. Vivid in my mind were the words of Capt. James Hill during our preflight briefing outside the airplane.

"Just grab the D-ring and throw it away," he had said.

Those words had prompted me to open my parachute. I told the story to the group and expressed my disappointment that we'd been unable to find the family of James Hill.

Dr. Russell, as flight surgeon at Elmendorf, was called to duty soon after the C-47 was reported missing. He retold the story I remembered him telling in 1954—of having to climb out and swing the tail of his airplane around so they could take off in the deep snow.

We learned a lot from Cliff Hudson—and a lot about him. There had been several blank spots in our knowledge of the rescue events. The survivors had been in two groups and we hadn't had much contact with Hudson after our rescue. We knew that he'd been first to spot the downed airplane. We also knew that he'd been on the helicopter that first reached the crash site. Still, we hadn't understood the full significance of his role. Now, as his story unfolded and with our combined recollections, pieces fell into place. Hudson's actions had truly been the major factor leading to our rescue. Had he not acted as quickly and as bravely as he had, I'm convinced that it would have taken several more days to find us. That might have made a big difference, since severe weather had arrived soon afterward.

The first edition of Don Sheldon's biography, *Wager with the Wind*, written by James Greiner and published by Rand McNally and Company, had appeared in 1974. Sheldon died not long after that. I didn't know of the book's existence until the mid-eighties. Of course, I knew Sheldon had become quite famous. Articles in *Life* and *Reader's Digest* had made him well-known. The *Life* article mentioned our crash without much detail. *Wager with the Wind* devoted five pages to it.

I was puzzled and troubled by that account. It wasn't so much the inaccuracies, of which there were several, but the absence of Cliff Hudson's name that bewildered me. Hudson had been dropped off by Sheldon and was the first person to meet Fox, Olson, and me as we came down from the ridge. He had told us then of finding the remains of the airplane the day before. The survivors there had shot off flares at his airplane not long after the crash. Then, he'd been on the helicopter that went to their rescue on Sunday. Yet, there was no mention of Hudson in the rescue account in Sheldon's biography. It certainly begged some questions.

Don Sheldon had played a crucial part in our rescue. He was a superb pilot. He had landed his airplane in a place most pilots wouldn't consider going. I still remembered the takeoff "roll" as his Super Cub swerved to avoid small trees, and the abrupt climb to clear taller trees at the end of the clearing. Nevertheless, he hadn't been the lone rescuer. Hudson seemed to have been a forgotten element in the story.

Now, as I listened to Hudson talk, the truth began to emerge. That he was bitter toward Sheldon became apparent. He wasn't vicious, but he took advantage of several opportunities to zing the other pilot. From the things Hudson said, unrelated to our story, it was obvious that they had enmity toward each other. It made me sad. Two men to whom I owed so much, and to whom I had paid verbal homage for so many years, had disliked each other. I wished I could do something to make things right, but I had no idea what that might be.

Dinner was a pleasant time. The group cohesiveness that would define us in years ahead was forming. Fox had brought wine. We toasted our survival, and the lives we had been fortunate to live.

Ed Olson, Cliff Hudson, Huey Montgomery, Ed Fox,
Rupert Pratt, Eli LaDuke, Bob Sallis, July 1996

I had insisted that our tables be placed so that we could face one another, making it easier to hear. I'd also feared that there might be several conversations going on at once. That didn't happen. No one wanted to miss anything.

After dinner, we watched the film segment that Stan Nelson had taken of the accident scene. That initiated a discussion of what might have caused the plane to crash. The lively debate lasted nearly an hour.

Gene Pickel,[53] true to his word, had put together a videotape of film footage he had taken after the crash and had delivered it personally to Fox in Florida. He'd even added a commentary. We started the video and were only a few minutes into it when there was a commotion at the door.

"It's Gene!" Fox said.

Pickel stepped through the door in such a timely entrance that it appeared almost to be choreographed. His wife and several family members accompanied him. We temporarily shut down the video to greet them and make introductions. Pickel was kind enough to guide us through the rest the video. It was stirring to see shots of the scattered wreckage and the recovery team's camp, which was situated on top of the ridge.

We shared family photographs and other materials. Before the group broke up for the evening, Keith Betscher gave us directions and a verbal preview of the Air Force Museum trip scheduled for the next day. The documentary people had arranged with museum officials to film at a C-47 exhibit. When I crawled into bed that night, I should have been exhausted. Instead, I felt invigorated. I couldn't wait for the next day.

Chapter Twenty-eight

Even with all the clarifying detail that our conversations had contributed, no clear ideas about the cause of the crash emerged. I had heard bits and pieces of information while in the hospital at Elmendorf, some of which I'd written home about, and some of which was still in my memory. I don't remember their names, but several people involved in the investigation came to the hospital to tell me what they knew. However, in the summer of 1996, none of us had ever seen an official accident report, or even knew one was available. John Knapp, the nephew of my friend Ed Knapp, would later inform me that he had discovered the report and had a copy. I ordered a microfilm copy for myself.

I had sometimes been asked about the cause of the crash. I always gave the short answer, and still do, that "the airplane hit a downdraft and got into an attitude from which it couldn't recover. It exceeded stress limits and broke apart."

The fact is, there were varying opinions about the cause of the crash, and even after studying the report, I think my explanation is as good as any—but for the record, excerpts from some of the individual reports from within the larger report can be found in the endnotes. Those reports are by the following individuals: Charles Casner,[54] Major Rupert E. Lawrence,[55] T/Sgt. Robert McFarlen,[56] Capt. John H. Walther,[57] and Major Delbert H. Ellis.[58]

Almost everyone showed up for the continental breakfast in the lobby. Fox had bought and passed out several copies of the *Dayton Daily News*. Our story was short, but in a conspicuous front-page position.

Huey Montgomery was in a talkative mood and moved me alternately between tears and laughter. He had displayed the same innocent power at Elmendorf in 1954. Now he told of his years in the coal mines, and of a mine fire that nearly took his life. He spoke of his and Minnie's early life together and the struggles they'd overcome. Both smiled knowingly when he mentioned the little house they'd first moved into.

"We didn't have anything—and I mean *anything*," Minnie said.

Huey laughed and added, "We lived on love."

It was a ten-minute ride to the Air Force Museum, which was housed in two large hangars. When we arrived at the main building, the filmmakers were waiting for us. They wanted shots of us entering. At their request, the six survivors retreated several hundred feet toward the parking lot to wait for their cue to walk toward them. We sat on benches for several minutes, talking. It turned out to be the only time during the reunion that all six of us were together without anyone else present. We didn't know it then, but it would also be the last time.

After the outside filming, we entered the building. A large television monitor near the entrance said "Welcome to the 1954 C-47 crash survivors."

"Keep together, men," Karen said as she directed our progress through the corridors.

A middle-aged man, who'd been matching us stride for stride, moved over beside me.

"I read the article in the paper," he said. "I came over here just to say hello. That was some experience you guys had. I'm glad you're getting some recognition."

That made me feel good, although I was tempted to tell him that we weren't together for recognition, but to renew old friendships.

The C-47 seemed larger than life inside the museum. It was brown, in contrast to the silver and red of the Alaska Air Command. We were there about an hour with the film crew taking shots inside and outside. Taro Yamasaki spent considerable time lining us up for still shots in front of the aircraft. We had a great time laughing and joking with one another.

After the photo shoot, we were on our own to explore the huge museum. Jon met with a missionary friend, Dan Knapke, with whom he had served in Bulgaria and who lived in the area. Kate Klice, the charming *People* writer, found me and we talked at some length. It was early afternoon before the Pratts and DeVitos headed back to the motel for a rest.

Too keyed up to stay long in the room, I went for a walk down the main street. The summer heat soon forced me to return to the comfort of air conditioning. I knocked softly at the Montgomerys' door, not wanting to wake them if they were napping. They were awake, and Minnie invited me in. We spent nearly an hour talking. During that hour, Huey and Minnie revealed much about their background and their life together.

Huey T. Montgomery was a native of Eldridge, Alabama, the third of nine children who grew up on their family farm in Fayette County. In a February 5, 1958, letter to my mother, Catherin Montgomery said of their farm, "A pretty good one . . . I guess altogether about 90 some acres . . . We have a little lake and fish in it. We have fun going fishing, especially in the summer. We live on a hill." The farm is still in the family, Montgomery told me.

Montgomery's brother, Flossye Lee, was killed in an automobile accident in 1955 while home on military leave. The oldest son, Louis, is now a Church of Christ minister in Texas. He is the brother from whom I had obtained their telephone number.

Montgomery was discharged from the Air Force in 1955. He married Minnie Johnson on May 5, 1956. They moved to Worcester, Massachusetts, that year, where he worked on an assembly line, making Buicks, Oldsmobiles, and Pontiacs. Their daughter, Terry Rosemary, was born in 1957.

In 1959, after they left Massachusetts, Montgomery worked in airport construction in Cleveland, Ohio, for six months. They then moved back to Alabama. Huey, Jr. was born July 6, 1959.

Montgomery was a logger for a time, then a strip miner at two different companies for twelve years at each. He was also an underground miner at another company. I asked Montgomery to tell me more about the mine accident in which he'd been involved. He said his crew had been about a mile underground when an exiting mine car had gotten tangled in electrical cables and started a fire. Smoke filled the shaft and the area where the men had taken refuge. Huey was able to breathe by dipping his T-shirt in water from the mine floor and holding it to his face until another mine car got in to take them out.

That period in their lives was hard, but they agreed that there were good times, too. They lived in a small cottage.

But then, according to Montgomery, "You don't need much room when you're in love."

They had five more children: Judy Ann, Katherine Elizabeth, Christopher Troy, Dunn Napoleon, and Flossye Lee. A peaceful look came over Montgomery's face as he talked of his children.

"We loved to go hiking together," he said, "and we once took them to Orlando and SeaWorld."

The Montgomerys have fourteen grandchildren. Huey and Minnie moved to Evansville in 1995.

Montgomery held up his end of the conversation, but I could see that he was getting tired. After leaving them, I made my way back to our room to wait until it was time for us to leave for Dayton.

The Saturday evening dinner had been planned as the highlight of our reunion. We would dine in grand style at the Crowne Plaza in downtown Dayton. Decisions about our future status as a group would occupy some of our time, but mostly we just intended to be together and enjoy one another's company. Seated at individual tables, we were a bit more isolated from one another than we'd been the night before, making conversation more fragmented. Everyone in the room seemed touched by the reading of the names of those men who had died in the crash.

We discussed plans for our future. There was a solid consensus that we'd meet again the following summer. Dayton had worked so well that we decided to return. The Betschers volunteered to host the event. Olson volunteered to publish a newsletter.

With business out of the way, we turned to more lighthearted things. During the planning stages of the reunion, the filmmakers had called Richard Switlik, parachute-maker and executive secretary

The 1996 C-47 Survivors' Reunion group. *Kneeling*; Melissa Patrick, Ed Patrick, Paula Knapp, Jonathan Pratt, Keith Betscher, Jan Betscher, Sherri Montgomery, Huey Montgomery, Jr. *In back as heads appear:* Thomas DeVito, Cliff Hudson, Nancy DeVito, Ed Olson, Ruth Olson, Huey Montgomery, Minnie Montgomery, Joyce Klodnicki, Ed Fox, Rupert Pratt, Millie Pratt, Eli LaDuke, Jonathan Sallis, Lisa LaDuke, Bobby Sallis, Ramona Sallis, Betty Knapp, John Knapp, Ed Knapp. Missing from the picture is Dr. Carl Russell.

of the Caterpillar Club, who, in turn, called me. The club's members are people who have had their lives saved by parachutes. Soon after the accident, the survivors had been invited to join. Mr. Switlik told me that he had looked up our old records, had made copies, and was sending them to me to use as we saw fit. He sent new certificates, pins (some of us had lost ours), and a copy of our original application with our handwritten descriptions of the accident.

Before dinner, I had connived with Dr. Russell to hold a ceremony to present the new pins and certificates to the survivors. The other men didn't know about it. I called them all up front and lined us up in military formation.

"Is there an officer present?" I called out.

Smiling broadly, Dr. Russell came forward. I called the group to attention.

"On behalf of the Switlik Parachute Company and the Caterpillar Club," Russell said, "I hereby give you these packets commemorating your having been saved by using a parachute on February 5, 1954."

We each saluted smartly as we received the packets. It was great fun.

Toward the end of the evening, I introduced each of the film people and gave them a chance to tell us something about themselves. It was late when we left the Crowne Plaza, but everyone was in high spirits.

Sunday promised to be clear and hot again. Brunch, at a Marriott Inn several miles south of Dayton, was to be the finale for our reunion. We were pleasantly surprised at the spacious area they had set aside for us. As usual, the film people were there ahead of us. After the meal, they put us in groups and used lighting to get their footage. We took advantage of the situation to get our own photographs. Dr. Russell was first to leave. He had to catch a plane in Dayton. Finally, departure time came. There were tears, hugs, and promises to meet the following year—and then it was over.

Hudson was going to visit with a relative in a nearby state, so we took him to the bus station.

"Cliff," I said, just before we left him, "the documentary people want me to go to Alaska with them later this summer. Even if that falls through, I'm going to come and visit you soon. I love Alaska and I've always wanted to get back."

His reply sounded familiar.

"You're welcome in Talkeetna any time," he said. "I'll show you around."

The reunion had brought me a sense of fulfillment. What I had set out to do was get together with a group of people who had shared a common moment in time. True, that moment had brought sorrow to many of them and joy at having survived to others. Somehow, and happily, the emotions aroused by those two extremes had been synchronized. The bond formed at Dayton seemed to have given our group a life of its own; I could feel it for weeks afterward.

I wasn't alone in that observation. Some reunion attendees sent letters to Ed Olson for the first formal newsletter, published in August. John and Betty Knapp said:

> The weekend of July 12 to 14, 1996, was truly a heartwarm- ing experience for the Knapp family. After all the years of reading names in the news clippings, we were finally able to add faces to those names. The survivors were most cordial, as were their families. To be able to meet those individuals who shared the final flight with Edward was most impressive. We lost him in February of 1954 and on a weekend in July of 1996, we gained a host of friends because of him. He must be pleased.
>
> Thank you! This has proven to be a healing process that we only imagined prior to this time.

Melissa Patrick wrote:

> . . . we wondered if we could put in words our feelings we had about the trip. The high point was Friday night around the big table, listening to the survivors and the rescuers of the survivors of the plane crash retelling their stories of the event. Growing up, I heard bits and pieces of the crash, but I never knew the importance the crash played in my dad's life. I feel a closer bond to my father, and we both feel honored to have been able to share his moment in Dayton. We hope the second generation of the survivors can keep their father's and uncle's stories alive, after they are gone, by keeping in touch with one another.

In addition, Nancy DeVito said:

Having been in on the planning of this reunion since nearly its beginning, it was our great pleasure to be able to participate. Observing the proceedings from Friday where there was a certain tension to what to expect, to Sunday, when there was a reluctance to leave including tears, hugs, and kisses, I feel a great healing was experienced by many. It was obvious to us that God had a hand in all of this and it was something that had to happen.

Something that had to happen. That expressed it for me, too.

Chapter Twenty-nine

Karen called soon after the reunion. She got right to the point.

"We want to go to Alaska in September—if you're willing."

I'd have to arrange my own transportation and lodging. They'd handle all expenses associated with filming.

"Are any of the other men going?"

"We haven't formally asked them yet, but I gathered from our conversations at the reunion that none of them is inclined to go."

"Are you thinking of going to the crash site?"

"Not on the ground. We don't have budget or time for that. We've talked to Cliff Hudson and he's volunteered to fly us over, close enough to get good shots."

I had known the question was coming and had already made up my mind. Alaska had never been far from my thoughts, and I'd often envisioned going back. During the first few years of our marriage, I'd thought of taking Millie. My secret hope had been that she'd like it enough to consider living there. However, our resources were meager and our schedules were always full. After our children were born, they became a part of my "return visit" fantasy, but time and resources were even more strained. Now, Greg and Jon were doing their own things, and Millie was still teaching. At last, my dream of returning to "Jack London Land" was about to be realized, but it looked as if I was destined to travel alone.

Final plans were made. I'd be away from home about a week. The Campbells (Duncan and Karen had recently married) and I would meet in Anchorage or Talkeetna. There would be interviews with Cliff Hudson on his home ground and two flyovers of the ridge. If weather permitted, we'd land on a glacier to create a "winter atmosphere" in part of the video. I worked a couple of extra days into my schedule so I could visit with Hudson and make a quick trip to Fairbanks.

Millie would have liked to go along, but didn't feel it was prudent for her to leave her classes in the hands of a substitute so early in the school year. However, she did make all the arrangements for me. She booked my flight, reserved my rooms, and rented a car. All I had to do was pack my bags and go.

On Tuesday afternoon, September 10, I boarded a Delta flight at Albany Airport. It was my first flight since my trip from Fairbanks to Seattle in 1955. I'd often told myself (and others as well) that I really had no fear of flying. I'd fly if the need arose. Somehow, the need never arose.

"You'll be fine," Millie said, her hand pressing my arm reassuringly.

I was nonchalant.

"Nothing to it," I said as I kissed her goodbye.

However, when I took my aisle seat, I began to feel anxious. We taxied out to the runway and lined up for takeoff. People around me seemed relaxed, even distracted. We started the roll and gradually picked up speed until I thought we would surely plow into Troy Road. To my relief, we lifted off and climbed at a steep angle. I caught a glimpse of the Hudson River on the right. After a few minutes, I began to feel better.

The airplane was only partially filled on the leg to Cincinnati, and I had three seats to myself. After we reached altitude and cruising speed, I decided to take the window seat. I unfastened my seat belt and started to move over, but then hesitated. I had an almost overwhelming sensation that I was somehow going to upset the balance of the aircraft, much like the feeling of caution one would have in a canoe. I fought the fear down and gradually slid into the seat beside the window. It was disconcerting. Obviously, there were still some demons at my elbow.

On final approach to Anchorage International Airport, I could see, in the fading light of day, the black outline of the Chugach Mountains east of Anchorage. They confirmed that, at last, I was back in Alaska.

Sara Mooney, a teacher friend from New York State who had been in Anchorage for nearly twenty years, met me at the airport. We found the Hertz rental area and I picked up the car Millie had reserved. Sara led me to the downtown Day's Inn, where I collapsed into bed after thirteen hours of travel.

Up early next morning, I found a message under my door to call Duncan and Karen at the Super 8. They had arrived there the evening before. We made plans to meet in Talkeetna at the Roadhouse where they'd be staying. They had to take care of some business in Anchorage first.

I aimed the car north on Route 1 at about 9 AM. As I passed the entrances to Elmendorf and Fort Richardson, strong memories prevailed. The sun was shining, illuminating the tops of the mountains. One of those peaks was the one Knapp, McDonough, Hyek, and I had scaled on a Christmas Eve long ago. There were more houses now, and I couldn't remember the lay of the land well enough to figure out which mountain it was.

About an hour later, I connected with the George Parks Highway (Route 3), going north. I could no longer see mountains except in my rearview mirror. The fall foliage was a brilliant yellow and beautiful in its own way, although the familiar reds of the Northeast were absent.

I passed through Wasilla, a community with banks, restaurants, and fast food places, then on through tiny Nancy and Willow. Eventually, I reached the Talkeetna Spur turnoff, a dead-end side road fourteen miles long that leads to the town. It was a good road, with occasional buildings and side roads that presumably led to residences. As I crested a hill approaching Talkeetna, I could see mountains again and realized that I was looking at the Alaska Range with Denali (Mt. McKinley) in the background. The top and base of the big mountain were cloud-covered, but recognizable. It was nearly noon.

I checked in at Chinook Wind Cabins and then drove to the airport to find Cliff Hudson. His hangar had big letters saying "Hudson Air

Service." Five of his six aircraft were lined up on one side. He had informed me while we were in Dayton that he continued to run the business, but had "lots of help." There were still many hard-to-reach places in Alaska, he had said. I already knew Hudson Air Service was well-known for flying members of mountain-climbing expeditions to the base of Denali. In addition, part of their summer business is flying tourists around the area. Hudson personally took James A. Michener around Denali when he was gathering material for his book *Alaska*.

The hangar door was open and I noticed several stacks of goods on the floor, apparently to be flown out to folks in the bush. It looked to be mostly groceries and other staples, although I saw items such as sinks and small machinery. I was glad to see Hudson Air was still looking out for the homesteaders. Of Hudson's four sons, two fly for him; the other two are commercial fishermen.

Cliff greeted me warmly and introduced me around. Jay Hudson had just landed and was refueling in front of the hangar. Jay had a firm handshake and a "look you in the eye" demeanor. In the lobby, a Native American family sat waiting. Jay was taking them home as soon as he got the aircraft ready, Cliff said. A bearded man, who looked to be in his late thirties, was behind the counter. He stuck out his hand.

"Don Bowers. I've heard all about what happened up on the ridge."

Bowers explained that he was a retired Air Force flyer who now had two jobs he loved, one as a substitute teacher and the other as one of Hudson's pilots. He handed me a card that had his picture and information about his being an Iditarod musher.

"Mr. Pratt's here with some people to do some filming for a documentary," Hudson said.

"Well, it'll make a good story."

That gave me opportunity to bring up a subject I had discussed with only a few people.

"I've started writing some of this down, Cliff. Would you mind if I ask you some questions while I'm in Talkeetna?"

"Ask away. We'll get together. Maybe tomorrow, over at the house."

"Doing a book?" Bowers asked.

"Just writing it down . . . we'll see."

Hudson went into the hangar. While he was gone, Bowers motioned toward the hangar door.

"There's enough material right there for several books. The man's a legend."

Bowers went on to tell me that he was writing his own book about the Iditarod.

"When I was still in the Air Force, I helped out by flying supplies out to rest stop areas. I got interested and decided to get my own dogs and enter the race. I've finished several times, but always way back. I'm titling my book *Back of the Pack*."

When Cliff returned, he and I got into his truck and went to the restaurant at the Talkeetna Motel for soup and pie. From there, we checked the Roadhouse to see whether the Campbells had arrived. They hadn't, so Hudson took me for a tour down along the Talkeetna River. When we returned to the Roadhouse an hour later, the Campbells were there. They were anxious to go up to the crash site to get an idea of the terrain and conditions for filming. The four of us sat around a table in the dining room talking, looking at maps, and trying to decide whether we should go then or wait until the next day.

"Today!" Duncan finally said. "The weather's good. Let's do it!"

It was a lucky choice, because it was to rain the next two days.

Hudson's son Chuck met us at the hangar a few minutes later. He'd be our pilot.

"Chuck's our mechanic," Hudson had explained earlier. "He flies part-time."

Chuck was an agreeable sort with a ready smile, much like his father's.

"Do you know where the wreckage is?" he asked.

"I'll know the spot when I see it," I replied. I had studied maps carefully over the past few months. "If we go up around Gold Creek, I'm sure I'll be able to find it from there."

"Let's go flying, then," Chuck said.

We piled into the Cessna 172 with me in the front right seat. We wasted little time getting out to the runway. Strangely, I felt perfectly at ease, nothing like my feelings on the larger airplanes. We took off and headed north, following the railroad. Chuck pointed out a moose on one ridge.

From Gold Creek, I could see the pass in the ridge to the west.

"It's there," I said, pointing, and Chuck brought the Cessna around.

I began to feel a little uneasy, not because of flying, but because I didn't quite know what to expect. Would the trip all be for nothing? Would there be anything to see? After all, what could be left of the wreckage after more than forty years?

We flew right up to the ridge. The east side was as I remembered, with fat fingers reaching down and gripping the forest. Olson, Fox, and I had pushed, slid, and fallen down one of those fingers to reach safety in the wooded area.

The altimeter read forty-five hundred feet. There was no snow on top and everything looked windswept and barren, except for ground vegetation that had turned rust-colored. It looked bleak and conjured up images I'd encountered when Fox and I had returned in 1955. Chuck gained some altitude and then began to fly tight circles over an area that I thought looked promising.

"I don't see anything," Duncan said after a while.

"I can get down closer," Chuck replied.

We had been a thousand feet over the peaks. He circled down until we were five hundred feet over a section of the ridge that resembled a saddle.

Duncan and I had been taking photographs. Between shots, I strained my eyes to make out details. I wasn't exactly sure what I was looking at, since I'd never viewed it from that altitude. I did know from studying maps and from my memories of the summer of 1955 that the wreckage lay in a little valley between a high peak to the north and lower hills to the south. That saddle-shaped landscape looked like what I remembered, and I was suddenly sure it was the place.

Chuck was looking at me quizzically.

"Do you see anything? Maybe we're not in the right spot."

"Oh, it's here, all right. Can you get closer?"

"Maybe a little."

He throttled back slightly and we gave up some more altitude.

In my focused searching, I lost my awareness of flying. I scanned the rotating earth under us, knowing what I was looking for was surely there, but not knowing whether it was possible to see it.

A sudden turbulence caught us and lifted the nose. The engine sound changed as the Cessna fought gravity. Chuck quickly pushed the nose down again and we leveled out. I sat upright, suddenly feeling nauseous. We'd been going in circles for several minutes, during which time I'd hardly looked up. I glanced back at Karen and she was ashen. I closed my eyes for half a minute until feeling steady enough to focus on the ground again.

I'd been noticing flashes of light at one point in our circuitous route. Then, for the first time, I caught sight of something that violated the randomness of nature. A small silver object stood out starkly against the darkness of the terrain. I quickly raised my camera and got off a shot.

"That's it," I announced, unable to control my excitement.

As we continued to circle, we began to see other small pieces of wreckage reflecting the sunlight. Spots our eyes had hastily scanned before now had our full attention, and we quickly sighted new objects. One was rectangular and looked like a wing flap. Another was triangular and hard to identify. It was only when we spotted a barrel that we had any perspective on their size. The barrel was on the eastern side of the saddle between the peaks. The recovery team must have left it there.

"We need to start back now," Chuck said a little later, and then added, "I think I can get us in closer when we come back."

The plan was to do one more flyover with a professional photographer and with Duncan and me providing a narrative. We regained altitude and turned southwest. I watched the receding mountain ridge with interest. Long and narrow, it combined Kesugi Ridge to the north and Curry Ridge farther south. I had only recently heard the word "Kesugi." I'd always referred to it as "the mountain," or the "mountain ridge." I'm not sure it was commonly called Kesugi in the fifties. The name was used in the 1992 Delorme Mapping *Alaska Atlas & Gazetteer*, although misspelled.

The Chilitna River side of the ridge wasn't as steep as the Susitna River side and presented a friendlier face. Although frost had visited the higher elevations, greenery was still evident in many places. It was obvious that the vegetation was more abundant than I had imagined. The ridge's rugged beauty stirred my feelings. It was a molehill compared with some peaks to the west, but it commanded my respect if for no other reason than its dominating position between the two river valleys. My mood had been alternating between melancholy and appreciation. Uppermost in my mind was the knowledge that my two friends had died there, as had members of other families that I now knew, but balancing that was the awareness of having been given my life back. The peaks were suddenly illuminated in light. I grabbed my camera and took a couple more pictures to preserve the moment.

Chapter Thirty

The rain on Thursday and Friday was a mixed blessing. Not being able to fly bought quality time with Cliff Hudson on Thursday. He showed up at my cabin about ten o'clock with slides and a projector. The slides covered most of his years in Alaska. We passed several pleasant hours going through them.

I went to his house that afternoon. The warm brown two-story structure on Main Street had a sign on the front that said "Hudson Air Service." Their living quarters took up the entire second floor. Ollie Hudson is dark-haired and pretty. Cliff and I sat at their dining room table drinking beer and nibbling at various goodies Ollie kept setting before us. That visit was only one of several I had with Hudson that week. He spoke freely, almost eagerly. I tried to take notes, but eventually just sat back and listened. His colorful stories wouldn't be easily forgotten.

Hudson knows many people and didn't shrink from telling about his friends and neighbors—even his own family. He was never judgmental, whether speaking about himself or others. There was one exception, however. As he'd done in Dayton, he found opportunities to take jabs at Don Sheldon.

I listened, not encouraging him, but doing little to steer conversation to another topic. I had a sense of loyalty to both men, yet I was fascinated by the rivalry between them. It seemed much like the time-worn western plot where the town was "just not big enough for both of them." There had always been scuffles between air services for work. Times could get pretty hard, and Sheldon and Hudson did many things to survive. As a result, their competition sometimes moved into non-flying arenas.

The day before, down by the Talkeetna River, Hudson had shown me the remains of an old boat and told me its story. In the late fifties, times were especially hard. Talkeetna had been inundated with home-steaders who wanted to settle across the river. He had bought the boat to carry them and their goods. Sheldon had done the same, and rivalry was fierce. Hudson's boat, propelled by a twenty-five horse-power Evinrude, was large enough to transport small animals easily, and larger ones with caution. Large animals had to be tied and held down by their owners to prevent capsizing the craft.

"Sheldon had a big boat," Hudson said, "and two real powerful engines. Only thing was—he didn't know how to operate it." He chuckled. "Got caught out there in the current more than once. Don't know how he kept from drowning somebody."

I'd come to recognize Hudson as a curious mixture of serious-mindedness and what might be termed "a character." Important things, business, flying, family responsibility, all represented faces he could present to the world in a sober, even pragmatic manner. Nevertheless—and happily—a thinly concealed humor surfaced regularly and unexpectedly. It was sometimes hard for me to decide when he was playing the "character" and when he was being serious. Talkeetna seems to be fertile ground for characters—both attracting and cultivating them. I learned from listening to him and to some of his neighbors that he did his part to uphold his character image.

As we sat on a log next to the rotting remains of the boat, Hudson continued his story, saying, "I needed money then, and people some-times tried to outdo me."

One settler was looking for the best deal. He asked Hudson how much it would cost to ferry his cow across.

"Today it's free," Hudson said.

"You mean that?"

"Sure—unless she shits in the boat. If she shits in the boat, then it's fifteen dollars."

"Well, it's worth a chance," the homesteader said after some consideration.

About midstream, the cow's bowels purged, as of course Hudson had expected. His early farm experience had given him considerable insight into the nature of cows.

"Sheldon and me fought once," Hudson said, handing me another beer across the big kitchen table.

"A fistfight?"

"Yep—right out there in front of the house. I bloodied his nose and he got in a couple of licks. Busted my lip."

According to Hudson, Sheldon often used the Talkeetna Spur Road to take off.

"Didn't think the airstrip was safe," he added.

On that particular day, two things had connived to force the incident. Hudson was feeling out of sorts and his truck was parked in such a way that it blocked Sheldon from taxiing past it in his plane.

"How about moving it a few feet?" Sheldon requested.

"Nope!" Hudson replied firmly. "You can take off on the airstrip like everybody else around here."

Sheldon cut the engine and jumped out of his Cub.

"We really went at it for a while, on the road and into the store next door, till somebody pulled us apart," Hudson said, laughing.

He inserted humor into the story, but his emotional attitude bothered me, just as it had at the reunion. I wanted to tell him to let it all go. Sheldon had been dead for many years. The rivalry didn't matter anymore. I wanted to say it, but I didn't. The time didn't seem right.

Later, I talked to Don Bowers about it. He had impressed me with his level-headedness. Bowers was philosophical on the subject.

"Yes, Cliff and Don had some problems," he said. "These pilots around here are very competitive and they go to some lengths to outdo one another. But keep this in mind! When there's a problem of any kind, a crash, a disaster, someone in difficulty, or whatever—it's time out—a whole new ballgame!"

"Yes—I certainly know the truth in that," I conceded.

Although it stopped raining late in the day, the sky was still overcast.

"I'll take you over to see the cemetery," Hudson said.

Such a visit was not high on my priority list, but I climbed into the truck beside him. The cemetery was near the airport. Many of the victims Denali had claimed over the years were buried there. Hudson seemed to know them all. He had, he told me, transported some of them to the base camp for their last climb. We wandered through the well-kept grounds with Hudson pointing out friends and neighbors and telling a little story about each. We weren't far from the gate when he pointed to a headstone.

"That's Sheldon's grave," he said. The gray stone had the dates 1921 and 1975 across the top, with a cross in between. Below that was "Donald E. Sheldon" and at the bottom was the inscription: "He wagered with the wind and won. His wife and children loved him."

The inscription was obviously a play on the clever and apt title of Sheldon's biography, *Wager with the Wind*. I had learned many facts about Sheldon's life from the book, from other written stories, and from Talkeetna people who had known him.

Sheldon was born in Mt. Morrison, Colorado. Orphaned early in life, he was forced to go to work at a tender age, which no doubt contributed to his self-sufficient ways. He made it to Talkeetna in about 1937 and survived by doing odd jobs and prospecting. He got his private pilot's license in 1942 and enrolled in the Civilian Pilot Training Corps in Anchorage. Trained as a gunner and mechanic, he eventually did twenty-six missions out of England during the war, earning him the Distinguished Flying Cross and other air medals. He graduated from Williamsport Technical Institute in 1947 and then returned to Talkeetna.

Sheldon became quite expert on matters concerning Denali, finding and establishing several landing sites. Through the years, he aided in the rescue of many climbers. He was intimately involved in the Cassin expedition, the first to conquer the south peak of Denali.

Then there was our accident on February 5, 1954, where he teamed up with Hudson to rescue Fox, Olson, and me from the woods below Kesugi Ridge. In 1955, Sheldon rescued eight U.S. Army surveyors from the Devil's Canyon section of the Susitna River. He had to perform a series of hair-raising landings and takeoffs to get them to safety.

In 1964, Sheldon married Roberta Reeve, daughter of legendary pilot Bob Reeve. They had three children, Holly, born in 1966, Kate, born in 1968, and Robert, born in 1971.

As I observed Sheldon's headstone, I couldn't but be amazed. Against the odds, it seemed to me, he had died of cancer. His biography was finished shortly before his death.

Roberta Sheldon's book, *The Heritage of Talkeetna*, contains sections about Sheldon and Hudson, giving an unbiased description of the competition between the two men.

I waited to see if Hudson had a story about Sheldon, as he had for the others resting there. He was strangely silent, with a faraway look on his face. We left the cemetery in a rather subdued manner.

I had planned to drive to Fairbanks on Saturday, but at Duncan's suggestion, I went Friday instead, with the idea that I could rush back Saturday if the weather cleared. I left early. George Parks Highway, running through Denali State Park and Denali National Park, has breathtaking scenery, even in damp weather. I stopped often to take photographs, arriving in Fairbanks early in the afternoon.

My feelings were mixed. The frontier mystique of the early fifties was gone. Jack London was hard to find. It was sad, but something I should have expected. Progress brings change, and not always as one would like. A superhighway, short as it was, crisscrossed what were once narrow streets with log cabins. The log cabins were mostly gone. Some had been moved, I was told, to the outskirts to a place called "Alaskaland."

Ladd AFB was now Fort Weinright. I stopped at the "gate," a medium-sized white building. The lights were on, but no one was there, so I drove on and explored, unimpeded. There was much that I recognized, but much had changed. The huge hangars were still there. So were many familiar roads and streets, and there were numerous street additions. There was a ghost town feeling compared to the activity of 1955. Gone were the jet fighters and large cargo planes. Only helicopters and small aircraft were present. The Chena

River was a constant, though, still running its swerving course around both ends of the runways, a major fault that had prevented Ladd from expanding and eventually led to a turnover to the United States Army in 1961. The runways had grass growing in the cracks.

I found the area where the 5001st Supply had been located when we first arrived in 1953. There were no gravel roads now, no Quonset huts, no rambling wooden-framed buildings housing mess halls and offices. There was just a paved road, lined with little trees. A few small modern-looking structures, probably utility buildings, were here and there along the road. By mid-afternoon, I'd seen enough and checked in at the Comfort Inn by the Chena River.

Duncan called early Saturday to tell me the weather had cleared and that they were going to film that day. It might be the last chance. I promised to be there by noon. A light snow had fallen, enough to necessitate wiping it from the windshield, but not enough to stick to the road. The sky had cleared by the time I had gassed up and headed down Parks Highway toward Nenana, some fifty miles away. From there, I began the gradual climb up toward Denali Park. It reminded me of the time Fox, Haab, and I had traveled that way, or closely parallel to it, on the train. Of course, there had been no highway then. The farther I went, the more accumulation of snow I encountered. At first, it was only on bushes and trees. Eventually, it covered the road, forcing me to go slower. At Healy, and south for about thirty miles, it was bad. I slowed to twenty miles per hour. I was glad to reach lower elevations where I could again make good time. I pulled into Talkeetna right at noon.

Karen informed me that Duncan was already up over Kesugi Ridge, filming with a photographer from Anchorage. They weren't expected back for another hour. I drove over to Main Street and had a reindeer sandwich at McKinley Deli. When I returned, they had landed and Duncan and Karen were reviewing film on a monitor set up in the hangar. They seemed pleased, but needed to get more shots. They wanted me to do narration over the site.

Chuck fueled up again. Duncan, the photographer, and I climbed aboard. Things weren't as easy as they had been on Wednesday, or even earlier that day, according to Duncan. There was lots of turbulence, tossing us up and down like a kite in a gale. I tried to narrate, with Duncan asking questions, following a script he had prepared beforehand, but I found it extremely difficult. The main problem was the way the radios were set up. We had to use two channels: one for talking to one another and another for recording. When I was recording, I couldn't hear myself speaking because of the engine noise. Therefore, I hesitated a lot and lost continuity. To complicate matters further, the higher elevations had received a dusting of snow and many of the small wreckage parts we had spotted on Wednesday were no longer visible.

We managed, though not without incident. The photographer, who had insisted on downing several candy bars to "hold him over," threw them up as we circled above the ridge. I fought down my own nausea and, luckily, my reindeer sandwich stayed put.

After the filming was complete, we flew west toward higher mountains.

"Thought I'd give you a little side trip," Chuck said.

It was less turbulent over the Chilitna. That valley had been a vast wilderness in 1954, with settlement being sparse. Wilderness was still in great evidence, but the thin line of Parks Highway sliced through the heart of the valley and civilization was spreading out from the highway like branches of a vine. It looked to be approximately five miles from the highway to the top of the ridge. I had recently talked to Fox about the possibility of sometime returning to the crash site on the ground. I thought of the trip we had made in 1955 up the eastern side. Men in their sixties might have difficulty with that route unless they were in superb physical condition. The west side looked easier.

A few minutes later, we were over Ruth Glacier and had climbed to seven thousand feet. Even so, mountains that were jumbles of rock and ice towered over us. The photographer had long ago given up and Duncan had taken over his camera. The sloping glacier rose beneath us as we flew in. Chuck, having given us a nonstop lecture about the terrain, finally turned the airplane back toward the valley. We'd been up for two hours; it was time to return to Talkeetna.

The rest of the day was occupied by filming at the airport and in various places around town while Hudson and I engaged in conversation at the prompting of the Campbells. Afterward, I spent time getting better acquainted with the young couple. Hudson joined us for dinner at the Latitude 62 Restaurant. Ollie wasn't available, which was disappointing. Hudson is a light eater, ordering mostly salads and skipping dessert.

"I want to keep my girlish figure," he said.

Ollie would later tell me he had become a "health nut."

Duncan and Karen left the following day.

"We'll work on this and prepare a trailer," Duncan said as they were putting their gear in their car.

They informed me that the *People* article would be out in a couple of days.

I stayed in Talkeetna through Sunday to visit with the Hudsons. It was a productive time for strengthening our friendship and for gathering Hudson lore.

Chapter Thirty-one

It fits Hudson's personality, his avoiding the spotlight. Although he seldom brags about himself, it's interesting that others do. He's widely regarded as one of Alaska's premier living bush pilots; one of the last of the old-time breed. I heard numerous complimentary comments from Talkeetna people during the few days I was there.

A clerk at a local gift shop gave it a different twist when she said, "Sure, he's an institution here in South Central Alaska—but more importantly, he'll do anything he can to help folks!"

For the wilderness pilot, "helping folks" isn't just moseying over to a neighbor's to help him hoist a generator into the back of his pickup, although it may be accomplished with the same degree of nonchalance. It often means the risk of life and machinery. Alaska affords ample opportunity for people to get into trouble, and they frequently do. Pilots with small airplanes may be the only ones who can get there in a timely manner.

When I asked him about the "helping" comment, he said, with a slight edge of impatience in his voice, "Doggone it—it's no big deal! There's no reason *not* to help people out."

With the Campbells gone, I spent the rest of Sunday with Hudson. He affectionately held his little dog, Skipper, in his arms as he talked. Ollie was busy stacking canned goods in the cupboard. It was a well used, down-to-earth home where people came and went a lot. Jay and Chuck had been there at different times during the morning. A couple by the name of Betts stopped by. They had just flown in from Schulin Lake. They reminisced about the time they had broken a ski on their airplane and Hudson had come to their aid with a new one. After they left, a neighbor came in to give him some moose sausage.

Hudson cut up some of the sausage and put out crackers to go with it.

I was aware of the brief time I had left in Talkeetna, and became somewhat relentless with my questions. He didn't seem to mind. He snuggled his face up close to Skipper's.

"This is pretty rugged country," I said. "Flying must be hard at times—and exciting."

He laughed and said, "Mostly it's doing dirty jobs—jobs nobody else wants to do—or maybe don't know how to do."

"Like?"

"Tell him about that bear," Ollie said.

She'd been quietly working around the kitchen all afternoon.

Skipper, Cliff, and Ollie Hudson, 1996

He told this story.

"Rangers from up at Healey called me and asked if I'd transport a rogue bear out of the park. They couldn't find anybody up there who would do it. My Cessna 185 was equipped with floats and I was looking for work, so I flew the bird on up there. They had already put the bear under and were busy pulling a bad tooth. I got the door off and took out the right front seat, and a seat in the back, to make room. We wrestled all four hundred pounds of her in, and then the vet got in the back with her.

"We got off and was headed south to a lake just outside Denali Park about seventy-five miles away. Her head was up beside me. I began to watch her real close and could see her blinking. I asked the vet how long the shot lasted. When he told me it starts to wear off after about an hour, some quick arithmetic convinced me we might have a problem.

"It made me a little nervous and I told the vet so. He said he'd like to get there without any further sedation. He reminded me that the two of us would have to get her out into the water and if she was still heavily drugged, she might drown. But in a few minutes, her eyes were fluttering like crazy, so he gave her another shot. We landed and she was limp as a dishrag. I got as close to the bank as I could and we snaked her out into shallow water and dragged her up the bank and through a blueberry patch."

"He had blueberry stains all over his clothes," Ollie said. "Never did get them all out."

I already knew Hudson had an exemplary safety record. I asked him about it.

"You never had a major accident. Was that just luck?"

"I'm careful about everything," he said, "but I did have one incident. Sometimes bad luck just outruns you."

During the summer of 1956, he had made arrangements with "Chick," a uranium prospector, to pick him up at Copper Center.

"We were going to a deserted mining camp at Copper Creek, about forty miles away. I hadn't been there before, so I flew in ahead to check it out. The strip was about six hundred feet long. Pretty much overgrown with weeds and some small shrubbery. In real bad shape. I nearly hit a cottonwood going in."

Hudson hacked the tree down as best as he could with a hatchet, but didn't get the entire root. Then he flew to Copper Center to get Chick. They made the flight back and landed without incident.

"I stayed there several days repairing the strip while Chick prospected," Hudson said. "I figured I'd be taking other people in there and I wanted a decent place to land."

Eventually, with their supplies gone, they prepared to leave.

"I wasn't worried about extra weight. My little Aeronica Chief would get off as soon as the tail came up. Even so, I cut down brush at the end of the runway to tuck her in and give us a little longer run.

"I started full-bore and hadn't gone far when we lurched sideways. There's a little disk about this big in the brake," he said, indicating the size with his thumb and forefinger. "Well, don't you know—it picked that very time to fall out and lock up the brake. I might have gotten her under control, but we hit that cottonwood root I'd tried to chop out and it tore the wheel off. That knocked us over sideways and the right wingtip hit the ground. The nose went down and the prop dug in. Stopped real sudden like!"

The two men climbed out, shaken but unhurt. The airplane was still upright, but the prop was bent out of shape and the right wingtip dangled.

"Well—we were in something of a pickle," Hudson said. "I'd left a flight plan, but my ETA was a little vague, so I knew it might be a while before they started looking for us. I figured the best thing was to go down Copper Creek to the Kotsina River and on south toward Chitina, which was about thirty miles away."

They spent three days building a boat. Some chunks of tar at the deserted camp were used to seal up cracks. All the tools they needed were there, left behind by former residents in 1927.

"With our food gone, our bellies started getting pretty close to our backbones."

They were happy to find a cache of dry beans that looked edible.

"I boiled them for twenty-four hours straight," Hudson said, grinning. "Never did get them to the chewable stage!"

Finally, they loaded the boat and shoved off. They floated down Copper Creek and into the Kotsina.

"It got real rough," Hudson said. "Water ran swift and through boulders. We hit one of them and started to sink. Chick jumped out and got to the bank. I tossed him my rifle and just got clear as the boat went under. It took the rest of our supplies with it."

On foot again, they had to make other plans. The Kotsina, at that point, flows several miles westward before swinging south toward Chitina. They followed it, taking shortcuts wherever they could.

"There was a glacier about two miles wide. It took us all day to get across. The next day, an airplane flew over. I'd saved a smoke bomb just for that purpose. I set it off, but they didn't see it."

They ended up walking to within five miles of Chitina before being spotted by one of Hudson's friends who had started to search for him. The friend dropped C-rations.

"Danged best food I ever had," Hudson declared. "My ankles were raw and bleeding where my boots had chaffed them, so we camped there."

The next day, a boat came to pick them up. Hudson paid the boatman with a gold nugget he'd once received as payment from a client.

Hudson never did recover the Aeronica Chief. He made plans to take parts in for repair, but then it disappeared.

"Somebody got a good airplane," he said. Then he added, "Same bird I flew up there to find you fellows."

It was getting late. I invited the Hudsons to have a last dinner with me at the Talkeetna Motel Restaurant. The food was good and we had a leisurely meal. I couldn't resist pumping Hudson one more time.

"Any other stories you'd like to tell me?"

"Tell him about Queenie," Ollie urged.

I would learn later that the tale was well known around the area and had been written about before, one account being in Roberta Sheldon's book, *The Heritage of Talkeetna*.[59] I tell it again as Hudson told it to me because it differs in minor detail.

"I was hauling supplies out to a homesteader in the Talkeetna Mountains," Hudson said. "He wanted me to bring his dog, Queenie, along too, so I loaded everything in the back and Queenie hopped in and lay on top of the stuff. Well—we took off and at about a thousand feet, we begun to bounce a little. Queenie started to squirm. Probably a little airsick. That didn't bother me much—if she puked, I could clean up later, but when she kept trying to get in the front seat with me, I resisted. I kept shoving her back. She was a big dog. I couldn't fly the airplane with her on my lap.

"She wouldn't give up. Finally, I just gave her a real hard shove back—and I don't know if it was her or me, but one of us hit the right-hand door latch and it came open. Before I knew what had happened—she had jumped out.

"By golly, I figured that was the end of her, but I banked the airplane anyway so I could see where she had hit. I saw her falling.

She didn't tumble or anything. Her legs were stiff in front of her and she went down just like that all the way. I saw her hit the snow. I flew over the spot a few times but didn't see any movement, so I went ahead and delivered the load—and the bad news."

He continued, "Going back the next day, I flew over the spot again. I could see some tracks in the snow that hadn't been there before, so I decided to set down and have a look. I couldn't land close to the site, so I had to walk about a mile in deep snow. When I got there, I found Queenie, alive. She'd been moving around the area. Those were the tracks I'd seen from the air. She was still a little dazed, but nothing else seemed to be wrong with her."

Hudson went on to explain that she had landed in a snowdrift with bushes underneath that had softened the impact. It took a long time to carry her back to the airplane.

"She didn't mind getting in," Hudson said. "That kind of surprised me."

Before we parted that evening, I ventured into murky waters.

"Cliff, Don Sheldon's been dead a long time. Maybe it's time—"

"You coming back here anytime soon?"

"I heard somewhere that holding grudges isn't good for your health."

"June is the best month."

"Don't you think—"

"I might have to steal one of my own airplanes, but we could go fishing at a place I know."

I let it go at that. Maybe there'd be a more opportune time—*or maybe not.*

I left Monday morning, stopping to tour Fort Richardson on the way to Anchorage. I didn't recognize anything. I tried to get onto Elmendorf AFB, but was unsuccessful. I needed someone to vouch for me.

In Anchorage, I visited a mall to get a copy of the September 23 *People* magazine. I sat on a bench reading our article and eating a cup of frozen yogurt. I was pleased with the article. It was only two pages, but well written. Kate Klice had captured the spirit of our reunion. At four o'clock, I turned my car in at the airport and Patrick

Mooney picked me up. I stayed with Pat and Sara that night and left for home early the next morning. I promised myself that I'd return to Alaska—and soon.

Chapter Thirty-two

The television program *Extra* had aired a segment about our reunion shortly before the *People* article appeared, and it brought surprising results. Soon after returning from Alaska, Euphemia "Dolly" Hill, widow of Capt. James Hill, called from California. I was delighted, since I'd been unable to find any of Hill's family. She impressed me immediately by telling me she wasn't long out of the Peace Corps.

"I'm proud I could serve," she said with such enthusiasm that I was stopped from making any reference to age.

She had been "astonished" to see the TV segment about the reunion.

She told Ed Olson in a letter, "I saw the date and knew it was the plane crash of so long ago. For some reason, fate had determined that I should see the show. I called my son at work and found out about *People* magazine."

Through Dolly, I learned that James's younger brother, Eugene, was still alive. I found his phone number and we talked at length. He'd like to attend the next reunion, he said. It was likely that Leslie Lowery, his daughter, would accompany him.

An October call came from Yoncalla, Oregon. Nick Botner, the railroad crewmember who had witnessed our airplane going down, had also seen the *People* article. I realized who he was at once, having recently found his statement in the Air Force accident report. I'd known about him in 1954, but had forgotten the details. Botner, in the report, was credited with spotting the C-47 as it went down. I soon learned through our conversation that he had played an additional role. He'd actually initiated the call to military authorities that led to Cliff Hudson's rush to the crash site. He had left Alaska many years ago and was now owner of an orchard, famous for its antique apples.[60]

"I'm delighted you're all still around," he said.

Keith and Jan Betscher had volunteered to host the second reunion, which was to be held during the summer of 1997. As fall melded into winter, Keith either phoned or emailed every few days to keep me posted on an idea about having a plaque attached to a monument in the Memorial Garden at Wright Patterson Air Force Base. He'd been talking to people there and wanted to know if I thought the families would be willing to share the cost. I told him I was sure it would be well supported.

Early in 1997, Keith mailed me a diagram of what he imagined we'd want to include on the plaque. The names of the crash victims would appear on top, and the names of the survivors would be at the bottom. I encouraged him to make the project a high priority. A few days later, he told me that arrangements had been made with Memorial Park officials to place the plaque alongside others on a granite memorial wall containing similar plaques. Keith found a company that would manufacture a plaque to our specifications and commissioned them to do the job.

He called one day to ask what I thought of having two plaques made, since the expense would be little more. The plaque manufacturer was holding off to see what we wanted to do.

"Why two plaques?"

"Someday, I'd like to get to Alaska and go to the crash site. I thought we might erect a duplicate there."

My desire to go back to Kesugi Ridge had been energized by my recent trip to Alaska, so Keith's words were seed on fertile soil. However, I could see there might be some logistical difficulties with such a plan.

"Kesugi Ridge is now within Denali State Park," I pointed out. "We'd need permission to put up a plaque."

I agreed to gather information about Denali State Park so we could proceed with a plan.

There was one regrettable mistake on the plaques that I discovered later, too late to change. The name of the British officer was spelled incorrectly. All newspaper articles to which I'd had access had spelled his name "W. Wes-Watson."

Keith put an article in *The C-47 Survivors' Sentinel* (the newsletter Olson was producing for our reunion family) for February, explaining everything about the plaque and requesting donations. He also made the first mention of a possible group trip to Alaska and of our desire to go to the crash site.

By early March, the date for the reunion, July 18 through 20, was set. Keith arranged not only to have the plaque erected, but also for a military ceremony by VFW Post 3283.

Duncan Campbell reported in mid-March that the Drummer Boy documentary was nearly ready for shipment to the Learning and Discovery channels.

About that time, Ed Olson received a letter from Dr. Stan Nelson. Dr. Nelson's "home movie," along with Gene Pickel's footage, had been star attractions at the first reunion. The letter from Dr. Nelson was full of detail, included a map, and is of particular interest.

March 22, 1997—It is now 43 years since the C-47 was torn apart by ice and turbulence over the foothills of the Alaska Mountain Range. I circled the crash site a day or two after the accident and made the 8mm film of the crash site that many of you saw at the reunion last summer.

I was only involved in the C-47 rescue operation out of Elmendorf AFB, but some might be interested in how I came to film the scene and what flying in the Alaskan territory was like.

I arrived at Elmendorf AFB in July of 1952 as an all weather jet fighter pilot. We lost many fighters during my two years in the 65th Fighter and it was customary after a series of accidents to ground all aircraft. During one of these groundings, I was eating breakfast with a friend, Tom Disch, from the 10th Rescue Division and he asked if I would fly copilot with him in a twin engine SA-16 amphibian aircraft. The mission was to provide communication between the rescue party at the C-47 crash site north of Talkeetna and Elmendorf AFB. Since our fighters were grounded, I agreed to fly with him. The weather had delayed rescue operations and I believe we went to the crash site on the morning of February 7, 1954.

Our route north was that taken by the ill-fated C-47 and most other aircraft that flew to Fairbanks. The route was based on a Radio Range navigation system diagrammed on a WAC chart carried by pilots flying in this region. I have in my possession the WAC chart used when I was there and I include an enlarged copy of the region of the crash (the original chart is color-coded to depict different altitudes). The procedure was to fly north on a heading of 326 degrees outbound after taking off from Elmendorf. After about an hour at C-47 speeds, the Summit radio would be tuned in and when the radio signal shifted from a Morse code "N" to a solid tone, a right turn was made to 358 degrees. This was just north of Talkeetna. . . . following the solid tone radio signal, or beam, carried the aircraft over the towns of Chase, Curry, Sherman, Gold Creek, and Chulitna; towns along the Alaskan Railroad and near the Susitna River.

Of course I cannot recall the exact position when we circled the crash but from *Wager with the Wind* and comments made in the newsletter, I believe it was between Gold Creek and Chulitna (in the book, Don Sheldon talked of being near Chulitna Pass) just west of the railroad. I have drawn an arrow where I believe the aircraft was found. [He did, indeed, correctly identify the site.]

As we began circling the crash site, I took my 8mm Bell and Howell camera from my flight suit pocket and made the film you have seen. We were several thousand feet high in order to relay messages from the ground party to Elmendorf.

The film shows us after landing in Talkeetna for lunch. We ate at the famous "Roadhouse," then returned to the crash site and circled several more hours.

I have thought of the crash many times during these 43 years. The crash scene segment of my "home movie" always made me think of those lost and those that survived. Little

did I realize that someday I would know [their] . . . names
. . . .

During this period, the Pratts had two exciting family events. The first was Greg's graduation from RIT in late May. His had been a long and circuitous route, started in 1989. He had started in film, took a year off, went back with a computer science major, and then switched to information technology after a year. He had run the gauntlet of requirements and as he walked across the stage to receive his diploma, we were filled with pride.

Jon had moved to Philadelphia in the fall of 1996. After returning from Bulgaria, he had enrolled in classes at the University of Pennsylvania to bring himself up to speed in certain Classics disciplines, pursuant to applying to a doctorate program. He was also teaching Latin part-time in a private school. During Christmas break, he returned to Bulgaria. The object of his visit was Boriana Petkova Stoytcheva, whom he had met a year earlier. He and Bobbi became engaged during that visit, and the wedding date was set for June 21, in Sofia, Bulgaria. We had already concluded that the relationship was a serious one. Bobbi had flown to the United States in August and had been our houseguest for two weeks. We liked her immediately, and then she won my heart by the simple act of helping me harvest our abundant tomato crop.

Jon flew to Bulgaria a week before the wedding and Millie and I followed a few days later. Greg arrived the day before the wedding. Bulgaria was something of a culture shock for us. The country was not long out of communism and still retained semblances of that time.

The wedding, in two languages, was held in a Methodist church situated across the street from the former Communist Party headquarters. The church was practically hidden behind other buildings, a common practice that had been necessary to ensure churches a low profile. We were made welcome by Bobbi's relatives and friends, and friends Jon had made while living there. Some of his Princeton classmates and other friends from the States also attended.

Millie, Greg, and I were guests at the home of Brooke and Corrine Rollins, missionaries from Delaware. We stayed in Sofia a week before leaving for England. Jon and Bobbi would honeymoon in Greece, Switzerland, and Macedonia before going to Philadelphia.

Millie and I had, for years, wanted to visit the British Isles, and it seemed like an opportune time. We had planned a week of travel throughout southern England, doing our own driving.

As much as we enjoyed touring England, I had a less obvious motive for being there. In 1996, before the first reunion, I had begun to search for W. West-Watson. I wrote to several military record repositories in the United States, thinking they might be able to give me information on the British colonel, or at least point me toward other information sources. Finally, in May, I was directed to the Army Records Centre of the Ministry of Defense in Middlesex. I wrote to them and received an answer in early July. They'd been unable to locate a service file, but if I could provide more information, such as an "army number," they'd do another search. The first reunion was only a few days away, so I put it off. Early in 1997, I went back over the information in the accident report and discovered West-Watson's serial number. Armed with the new information, I thought I might have a chance to find his family.

While planning our trip to Europe, it occurred to me that since we were visiting England anyway, why not visit the Ministry of Defense in person? Middlesex wasn't far off the route we had planned.

We had no trouble locating it on Bourne Avenue. After explaining to the guard at the gate what I wanted to do, he directed us to a parking space, and then into a large stone building not far away. After listening coolly but respectfully to my request for specific information about West-Watson, the officer who seemed to be in charge said he didn't see how he could help me.

Somewhat put off by his abrupt manner, I asked, "Well, can you put me in contact with someone who can?"

"The records aren't something we just let people in to look at," he explained.

We postured through a few more exchanges before he finally conceded that I might write a letter he would forward to "proper authorities." He gave me stationery and directed me to a writing table. That I could just as well have written the letter at home, and much more efficiently on my computer, kept entering my mind.

A few weeks after our return home, I received a reply to my hand-written letter.

They did indeed have records for the widow, but stated, "It is not, of course, our practice to disclose the addresses of former members of Her Majesty's Forces."

They did say they'd forward a letter to the last known address. I wrote another letter, addressing it to "The West-Watson Family," detailing recent events, but never received an answer.

Lt. Col. W. West-Watson seemed destined to remain a mystery, as he'd been even at the time of the crash. That bothered me. I hadn't been able to find anyone in Burge's family, either, but at least I knew *something* about him. In West-Watson's case, I felt utter failure. I'd never feel complete closure until I knew something—just some little detail of his life.

The rest of our English tour went quite well. We visited Windsor and Oxford, spent three nights in the Cotswolds, toured Leeds Castle, and enjoyed a day in London.

Reunion time finally came, and we drove to Ohio again. The DeVitos didn't go. They'd been having some excitement of their own. Their daughter, Diane Stuto, had delivered triplets that spring. Otherwise, they would have gone to Bulgaria with us. They were so busy helping Diane and her husband, Pete, take care of Jocelyn, Caroline, and Sam that they decided to forego the reunion. Actually, Tom and Nancy have five grandchildren. Their son Dean and his wife, Kim, have two children, Natalie and Breanna. God had blessed them, Nancy often said.

The reunion was different that year, and in some ways better. There wasn't the high level of excitement, and no incessant cameras rolling. Nevertheless, our bonding continued. The memorial service, with the dedication of the plaque, had its own healing powers. I tried to express it later in the August *Sentinel*:

What a wonderful time we had—again! Our second reunion is over but the memories will remain. Such a touching tribute we had at the Memorial Gardens at the Air Force Museum! The opportunity to speak was, for me, part of the healing process we have talked so much about. Just publicly saying a little about each of the men who died on Kesugi Ridge that day in February of 1954 was something I longed to do, even though I didn't fully realize it until it was all over.

Hudson, Russell, LaDuke, and Sallis were absent. Montgomery looked even healthier than he had the year before. Olson brought extremely detailed model C-47s to distribute. They were obvious labors of love, with Alaska Air Command colors, even having the number of our airplane on the tails. Nancy Humphries, with whom I'd been corresponding, and her husband, Jack, attended. The Rev. Bonnie Nolan, Bob Betscher's younger sister, came with her husband, Jim. Eugene Hill came with his daughter, Leslie Lowery. I learned a lot about James Monroe Hill from them.

James "Bud" Hill—Photo supplied by Leslie Lowery

James "Bud" Hill was born in Johnsonburg, Pennsylvania, on September 11, 1924. A superior athlete in high school, he was a member of a 1941 football team that had a series of seventeen straight victories. His military service covered eleven years. He was a veteran of World War II and the Korean War. As a sergeant in Company B of the 101st Airborne Division, he participated in the Normandy invasion. He was wounded in July 1944 and captured by the Germans in December, at Cherbourg, France. He was liberated eight months later.

Hill reenlisted and was commissioned a lieutenant in 1947. Early in the Korean conflict, he served with Company B, 65th Infantry of the 3rd Division for thirteen months. Near Uijongbu, on April 27, 1951, he led his unit out of an enemy encirclement. For his courage and quick thinking, he was awarded the Silver Star for gallantry. Hill was also awarded several other medals during his service career. At the time of the crash, he was stationed at Fort Benning, Georgia, and was on temporary assignment to Alaska. As I spoke with Eugene, it became obvious that he had loved his brother a great deal.

Floyd Knickerbocker came from Texas, and Shirley Belyea, his sister, came from Alaska bearing a cooler full of Alaska salmon for the group. Absent were the filmmakers, although they did send a telegram with best wishes.

1997 C-47 Survivor' Reunion group—Dayton

Keith and Jan Betscher opened their home for a Saturday afternoon picnic, which went well into the night. Without telling any of us beforehand, Keith had arranged to have a local aviation company fly a C-47 over the house. He had placed a large foil "X" on their back lawn. It was large enough to be seen from several thousand feet. Everything went off perfectly. Keith told us at the last minute what was happening. The airplane flew over the yard five times at a low altitude. Unfortunately, a neighbor complained to the FAA and the pilot was later slapped on the hand.

We decided to have a third reunion in Elkader, Iowa, but not until 1999. That seemed a long time away, but a bright note was that some of us were going to Alaska during the summer of 1998. Keith and I were to do the planning.

We looked forward to the following summer, and the adventures it promised. We would, however, have been devastated had we known that before the end of that summer, the number of living survivors would be reduced from six to five.

Chapter Thirty-three

My enthusiasm for the upcoming Alaska trip prompted me to start planning early that fall. I studied an Alaska atlas[61] and several other maps. I wanted to know the terrain as well as possible.

I knew from my 1996 trip that the ridge was on the eastern edge of Denali State Park, which had been formed in 1970 and expanded in 1976. George Parks Highway extended up the Chilitna Valley, bisecting the park. I was familiar with the highway, since I had traveled over it on my way to and from Fairbanks. I was also aware, from studying my aerial photographs, that there was a trail along the ridge. The atlas showed the northern terminus of the Kesugi Ridge Trail as a section called the Little Coal Creek Trail. It began near the highway and ascended east for about three miles, at the same time gaining nearly three thousand feet in altitude. From there, the trail followed the western slope of the ridge southwest for more than thirty miles before joining the highway again. It appeared to come within a mile of the crash site. If the trail was passable—not always a sure thing for Alaska wilderness trails—it would make the trek much easier. I wanted to avoid the eastern side of the ridge, remembering difficulties Fox and I had there.

The DeVitos were going, too. Our weekly breakfasts and frequent dinners became planning sessions. Tom wanted to go to the crash site with me. That pleased me, since we'd been friends since 1953. Moreover, he had more than a casual interest, for Ed Knapp and Don McDonough had been his friends, too.

Ed Fox was so fired up about the trip that he called every few days to check on the progress of the planning. He was going to drive up the Alcan Highway, he said. He needed to overhaul his truck engine, since it had accumulated over two hundred thousand miles. Joyce would likely go with him. Fox wanted to make the hike. I knew he wasn't in perfect health, so I prayed that he'd be in good enough shape when the time came.

The next step was to talk to someone in the Denali State Park System. I searched Alaska State websites until I came up with the phone number of Dale Bingham, supervisor of Denali State Park. After explaining who I was, I told him about our plans to visit the crash site the following summer and about our wish to erect a memorial plaque on the site.

"That may be against park regulations," he said, "but tell me what you have in mind."

"The wreckage is well off the trail as I see it on maps. Hikers wouldn't stumble across it. You'd have to be looking for it. Anyway, the plaque is fairly small."

"Just where is the wreckage located? I've heard about a crash up there, but no one ever told me anything definitive."

With a map in front of me, I gave him as detailed a description as I could. He knew the area well. He seemed fascinated by the story.

"I really want to help," he finally said. "I can't give a definite answer right now, but maybe we can work something out about the plaque. I can see how it's a special place for you—and it should be for the park, as well. It's part of our history."

"We'd really appreciate any help you could give us," I said.

About a week later, Bingham called.

"I've got an idea!" he said.

His proposal was exciting. A few years earlier, Denali State Park, with cooperation from the state, had opened Veterans Memorial Park at milepost one-forty-seven of Parks Highway, near Byers Creek.

"We want to erect your plaque there," he said. "It would be placed among other memorials. We'd mount it on a boulder along a well-traveled walkway. It would have a high profile, much more than it would have on the ridge. The park is only about twenty-five miles from the crash site."

"Yes—I think it's a perfect solution," I said, "and I can't imagine anyone in our group not agreeing—but I do need to run it by them."

There was complete acceptance of the idea, and Keith took over the planning details with Bingham. By December, it was all worked out. The plaque would be mounted in the spring or early summer and we'd hold a dedication ceremony there on Tuesday, July 28. The following morning, those of us who were willing and able would meet at Little Coal Creek trailhead to begin our hike to the crash site.

Besides the DeVitos and Pratts, several people had expressed an interest in going to Alaska for the ceremony, and some of those people wanted to visit the crash site. Foremost in the latter group was Keith Betscher, who had inspired interest in the trip in the first place. Ed Fox and Joyce Klodnicki were still actively planning to go, although Joyce had no interest in climbing the mountain. The two Knapp brothers, Ed and John, wanted the whole package. I suspected Ed Olson and Huey Montgomery would be unable to go for health reasons, but I was disappointed when Bob Sallis and Eli LaDuke declined.

"There's nothing up there I need to see again," Eli quipped.

Early on, Bingham had noted that both rangers at Denali State Park wanted to go with us. It would be a busy time of the year, so there was a good chance one of them couldn't go. I asked Bingham about equipment.

"There's an outfitter in Wasilla who uses llamas as pack animals," he said. "Her name is Pam Barnes and she's owner of Llama Buddies. You'll have to do one overnight, for sure. I think she's probably your best bet, rather than trying to gather your own equipment."

"Why llamas?"

"Horses and mules aren't allowed in the park. Their hooves cause damage to the trails. Llamas have small, soft feet."

I gave Pam Barnes the details about where we wanted to go. She knew the trail, having taken parties up there in previous summers.

"It's beautiful," she said. "One of my favorite places."

The more I heard, the more I realized it was the best solution. I'd been struggling with the long-range logistics of assembling the equipment we'd need for a group of five to ten people. For $235 each, she'd supply not only tents, but also food, which she'd prepare. We'd have to carry small packs with our own belongings, but the llamas would carry everything else.

"But I can't handle more then ten people," she said. "I only have seven llamas, and I keep the load light for each one."

She mentioned one "small" problem. The llamas could only go up to the head of Little Coal Creek, a distance of about three miles. An ancient rockfall blocked their further progress.

"It's really a pristine place to camp," she said. "We'll set up there and then walk to the crash site and back. From what you tell me, it looks to be only four or five miles farther. The trail pretty much follows the line of the ridge, which is easier than the first part."

Despite her assurances, it worried me. Three miles up, another five along the ridge, and then back—thirteen miles altogether—in one day. Keith and the Knapp brothers should be able to handle that without any difficulty, but for Tom, Fox, and me, it would be a tiring day.

By the middle of March, we had the trip thoroughly planned. We'd meet in Talkeetna on Monday, July 27, and attend the dedication ceremony the next day. We would stay in a bed-and-breakfast at Trapper Creek Tuesday night, and meet at the Little Coal Creek trailhead Wednesday morning. Those not going on the ridge would stay in Trapper Creek to await our return. From there, we'd disperse to follow our own agendas.

Tom and I wanted to be in good physical condition, so we spent a lot of that spring and early summer climbing mountains. We figured if we could handle the High Peaks of New York, we'd be in shape for the Alaska climb, which was no higher. As it turned out, Paradox was our only climb qualifying as a High Peak. The others, Tongue, Paramount, and Buck, were lesser peaks, but good workouts, nevertheless.

I had hoped Greg and Jon, or at least one of them, would be able to go, but Greg had a job in Rochester that he felt he couldn't leave and Jon had recently raised his educational sights a few notches. Berkeley had accepted him for work on a doctorate in the classics, and he and Bobbi were moving from Philadelphia to the West Coast in June. He felt his life would be in too much turmoil for a trip to Alaska.

Not long after Jon and Bobbi left for California, I scratched a chronic itch. My moderate (in my mind) fear of flying couldn't overcome my lifelong fascination for the activity. Long flights to Alaska and Eastern Europe had helped tame my overactive imagination about what can happen to an airplane in flight.

On a warm and sunny day, I was in the backyard, weeding my vegetable garden. A single-engine airplane flew over at about a thousand feet. That wasn't unusual, since we're a couple of miles from the Schenectady County Airport. I followed its flight path until it disappeared behind trees to the rear of our property. I realized then that I did that almost every time an airplane passed over. Then I had one of those rare moments, the kind that happens in everyone's life when they do something entirely unplanned. I got into my car, drove to Richmor Aviation at the Schenectady County Airport, and plunked down sixty dollars for a trial lesson.

"It's practically windless and a perfect day for flying," said Richard Kaylor, flight school director of the Schenectady division of Richmor. He and the secretary were the only ones in the office when I walked in. "All my instructors are up with students right now—but what the heck! I'll take you up myself."

My first shock came when he put me in the left seat of the Cessna 152.

"But—" I tried to protest.

"You're the pilot," he said.

I could feel perspiration beginning to form on my forehead. My palms were sweaty as he climbed in the right-hand side—into a seat so close our shoulders touched.

He fitted me with earphones and explained how to work the radio. After fiddling around with the instruments, he reached across my lap and turned the ignition key. The engine roared to life, vibrating the little airplane while he adjusted the throttle.

"Just like running your lawnmower," he said, smiling, before calling the tower to announce our intentions.

He explained how to work the pedals as we moved out.

"Brakes on the top. Use them to turn. Not too fast. Pull back the throttle just a little."

It felt awkward at first, but by the time we got out to the end of the runway, I was doing quite well. We waited in the holding area while another airplane took off, then Kaylor taxied us out and straddled the centerline. The runway ahead shimmered with heat and receded into the distance.

"Keep your eye on the airspeed indicator as we roll. When we get to about sixty-five knots, just pull back on the yoke—but do it slow and easy."

"You want *me* to take off?" I asked, incredulously.

"You're the pilot. When you're ready, just shove the throttle all the way in and use the peddles to keep us straight."

"I don't think I—"

"I won't let you make a mistake," he said, tapping the dual control yoke.

Okay, I thought. It may be the only time I could ever do it— something I'd wanted all my life. In a decisive moment, and with an attitude approximating glee, I shoved the throttle in as far as it would go and the little Cessna leaped forward. We started rolling to the right, and I overcorrected to the left before managing to find something resembling a straight line down the runway.

"Keep one eye on your speed," Kaylor said, his voice calm as a cat's purr.

We reached sixty-five knots far quicker than I'd expected, and I eased back a little on the yoke. We didn't leave the ground.

"Too timid—a little more," Kaylor said.

That time, I found just the right leverage and we rose quickly. The airplane was much more responsive than I'd imagined it would be. We were actually flying—I was flying—and it felt good. After we'd gained some altitude and headed out toward Great Sacandaga Lake, Kaylor took the controls and showed me several attitudes that could be obtained using different control maneuvers. After each demonstration, he'd let me try it. The controls were responsive, and flying felt natural. I could hardly believe it when he said it was time to head back. Looking at my watch, I could see that we'd been up nearly an hour.

I expected him to take the controls as we approached the airport, but he kept issuing me directions. We reduced speed to about sixty knots and he showed me how to use the trim wheel to keep us at about a thousand feet. He directed me into a landing pattern and told me when and where to turn. When we were lined up with the runway, he lowered the flaps and reduced speed so that we were losing "just the right amount of altitude."

"Just watch the numbers on the end of the runway," he said. "Keep them steady in the windscreen. Just as we get a few feet above the runway, pull back a little on the yoke and I'll cut power."

I followed his instructions and we settled, light as a feather, onto the asphalt.

It was several days before I told Millie what I'd done.

When I got home, all flushed and energized, all I had said when she inquired where I had been was, "I've been slaying some demons."

Pam Barnes had been feeding us details about what we should take to the ridge. With that list in our hands, Tom and I paid a visit to Eastern Mountain Sports store. We bought lightweight jackets and other lightweight clothing that would be easy to layer. The capricious nature of weather in Alaska's mountains, which I knew something about, would require constant changes of clothes. I had to laugh to myself, though, as I sifted through the mass of high-tech gear. In 1955, Fox, Haab, and I had just thrown together pretty much what we had, or could borrow, for our trip to the ridge.

Nancy had a relative who was taking an active interest in our trip, but for different reasons. He had information on a government project somewhere in the wilds of Alaska. There was concern from environmental groups, and he would appreciate any information she could dig up. She accepted his packet of papers, filled with articles he'd pulled from the Internet. Nancy wasn't terribly motivated to become a sleuth, but she promised to take the packet along. She showed the material to me and asked me to look it over.

"I don't see how we can do that," she said. "I can't even find a reference to where it is. If it's a government project, the location is probably secret."

I said I'd look at it. I did, but it was a cursory look. I didn't hold out any hope of us running across a low profile government site in the vast Alaska wilderness. She ended up taking the material along, but I soon forgot all about it and I think she did, too.

The day of departure finally came, and the DeVitos and Pratts boarded a Delta flight at Albany Airport. Twelve hours later, after a stop in Atlanta, we touched down in Anchorage. It was early afternoon. The pilot had introduced the forty-ninth state by threading his way between mountain peaks on the way in. My newfound confidence in flying didn't keep me from being glad to have something solid under my feet.

Patrick and Sara Mooney met us at the airport. We proceeded to the car rental section and had our Ford Explorer in just a few minutes. The Mooneys helped us locate Deals B & B, and after that we followed them to their home in southern Anchorage.

We loafed around there awhile, eating moose and caribou tidbits with crackers. Then we all loaded into their car and went for a tour of Anchorage, which included a stop at Merrill Field to see Patrick's airplane. After dinner that evening at the Regal Hotel Restaurant on Lake Hood, we said goodbye to the Mooneys, with their assurance that they'd be at the memorial ceremony on July 28.

There was a note on our door from the Deals. Someone from the governor's office in Juneau had called and wanted me to return the call. It was late, and we were exhausted. Tomorrow would be soon enough. Dale Bingham had already alerted me that there would be considerable interest in the memorial ceremony.

Next morning, we traveled down Turnagain Arm on Seward Highway, stopping every few miles to take photographs of the scenic bay and mountains. We decided to take a "short" trip over to Homer, but what seemed short on the map turned out to be long enough to put us in Seward at seven in the evening instead of early afternoon as we had planned. It rained off and on all day and was raining when we arrived.

I had tried, several times, to call the number the Deals had given me, but was unable to get through. After a night at Bay Vista, we made our way to the waterfront. We had boat reservations for touring Resurrection Bay and visiting a couple of glaciers. While on the dock, I tried the Juneau number again on our cell phone and was finally successful. The man I talked to was Bill Kiger, Natural Resource Officer of the Division of Parks and Outdoor Recreation. He was going to attend the ceremony. He told me that he'd been working on an exhibition for the park. It was about the crash and was already up, but he thought it would need some revision. He wanted to interview Fox and me, since the crash was part of state history. He wanted to make sure facts were straight. I promised to meet with him.

The Kenai Fjords boat tour was enjoyable. We saw lots of wildlife: whales, otters, eagles, and water birds. Nancy's bird book was her constant companion. We made a stop at Fire Island for a grilled salmon lunch. It was cold and windy on the bay, but we had expected that. It was often difficult to know whether it was raining or whether we were going through mist thrown up by the boat. On the way back into the harbor at Seward, it rained in earnest, and we abandoned the deck to sit inside. Despite the weather, I was struck by the splendor of the area, just as I had been when I was twenty years old and standing on the frozen deck of the *USS Jackson*. Marathon Mountain, unchanged, formed the background.

We stayed another night at Bay Vista before going back to Anchorage. We had registered at Deals for that night. The following morning, Sunday, we started early, connecting with northbound Route 1, and were soon beyond the city limits. We took a side trip over to Palmer, then went back to George Parks Highway and on to Wasilla. There, we took time to attend service at a Presbyterian church, where people greeted us warmly. It was with reluctance that we had to say goodbye to our newfound friends. Back on the main highway, it didn't take us long to pass through Willow and reach the intersection with the Talkeetna Spur Road.

At that point, I had a feeling akin to finishing a journey. It felt like going home from Alaska had in 1955 when I exited the bus at Salt Rock and lugged my duffel bag that last couple hundred yards. It seemed strange now, considering I was going in the other direction.

I understood my anticipation, however. Touring southern Alaska had been delightful, but it wasn't really what I'd come to Alaska for. I was excited at the prospect of seeing the Hudsons again after two years, about the upcoming memorial service, and especially about the climb up to the crash site.

Chapter Thirty-four

Talkeetna challenges description, but I had formed my own opinions over the past two years. Less than I expected, yet more, it's a unique mixture of people and place. Personalities from all over, set down in that particular spot, have produced a peculiar mosaic. I'd read everything I could find about the town. It sits at the convergence of three rivers: the Susitna, flowing from the north, swallows the waters of the Chulitna from the northwest and the Talkeetna from the northeast before continuing its journey south to Cook Inlet. Settled in the late nineteenth century, Talkeetna has a winter population in the hundreds, but swells to several times that in summer. Because of its location, its size has little to do with its importance. It's the jumping-off place for numerous outdoor activities in South Central Alaska, whether mountain climbing, hunting, fishing, prospecting, white water rafting, or just sightseeing. The state airport, with paved runway, is a beehive of activity as pilots ferry people and goods to various places, many of which are inaccessible except by air. The old Village Airstrip, though not officially open, is still used by some private pilots.

Kesugi Ridge had also been much on my mind the past two years. I had gathered information from several sources to supplement what I already knew from the fifties and from the 1996 flyover. The southern end of the ridge starts about thirty miles north of Talkeetna, and the Alaska Railroad points the way. The rails follow a path along the eastern side of the Susitna, through places with such picturesque names as Chase, Lane, Curry, Sherman, and Gold Creek. Some of those places have little population, some none at all. On February 5, 1954, Talkeetna and Curry had become bases of operation for the Air Force in their efforts to rescue us. Mostly deserted today, Curry was then a thriving railroad community with a seventy-five-room hotel that catered to tourists. There was even a bridge across the river and a trail west to the top of Curry Ridge where hikers could get a good view of Denali. The railroad-operated hotel had been built at that location by virtue of being halfway between Seward and Fairbanks. It attracted many tourists until it burned down in 1957, killing three people. I remember the hotel well, having been taken there by Don Sheldon before boarding a caboose for Anchorage. Dog teams had carried ground parties from there and from Gold Creek to the crash site.

Gold Creek sits near a junction of two rivers. The Susitna turns from a northeasterly direction there, and the railroad crosses over it on its way north. The railroad follows the Indian River to Canyon and Chulitna, then on through Chulitna Pass to intersect George Parks Highway.

If you were to proceed north from that point by rail or highway, you'd pass Denali National Park on the way to Fairbanks. If, however, you went south on the highway, you'd follow the Chulitna River down through Denali State Park and eventually intersect Talkeetna Spur Road. The southern Chulitna route runs through sparsely populated country, although the Princess Lodge and roadside shops now serve many tourists in the valley.

Between the Chulitna and the Susitna-Indian River Valleys lies the long narrow mountain ridge where our C-47 crashed. The highest point on Kesugi Ridge is 4,558 feet. The crash site is near the four thousand foot level. The ridge's eastern side is steep and craggy, as if formed to block access to itself and to the foothills of Denali.

The other side isn't as steep and invites ingress from the highway for those willing to expend a little effort. Little Coal Creek Trail, as I'd learned from Bingham and by studying maps, winds upward from the highway. From the head of the creek, the trail skirts along the western slope of the ridge and comes near the crash site.

The ridge, which Fox and I had simply called "the mountain" in 1955, had been a cheerless place for me, associated with wind, rain, swirling fog, snow, and ice. Only in 1996 did I begin to see it differently.

During my first night home following that trip, I woke at 3 AM with images of it on my mind. I felt compelled to get up and write. I believe the resulting poem, which I called *The Other Side of the Mountain*, despite its structural deficiencies, caught something of my transitional feelings:

Toward the mountain on leaden wings,
churning decades of memory.
Through misty perspective,
steep, cold, foreboding, dark,
trapped in a mindset.

Over the peaks, round and round,
searching for light in the gloom.
Fighting back devils of wind and mind,
raging in a vortex of time,
spirits entrapped in somber stone.

Over then to the other side,
a gentler slope presented.
And softer winds whispering,
like angel voices soothing,
urging a new way of perceiving.

Behind lies the mountain,
a panorama of light.
Assuring that all may see,
the other side of the mountain,
with spirits set free.

Through my observation and through the eyes of others, I now saw Kesugi as pristine, a place people embraced and enjoyed. I looked forward not only to seeing it again, but to experiencing it firsthand.

I'd been subscribing to *Alaska* magazine for some time and had been surprised the previous summer by a timely article written by Bill Sherwonit. The August 1997 story, titled "Three Accessible Parks," had one section devoted to Kesugi Ridge. His take on the ridge is interesting and informative:

> Kesugi, a Tanaina word meaning "The Ancient One," is nonetheless considered among south central Alaska's premier backpacking routes. One reason is the view. The Alaska Range dominates the western horizon, a vast kingdom of knife-edged ridges and granite walls larger than Yosemite's. And rising above it all, the snow and ice-capped throne of 20,320-foot Mount McKinley, also known by its Athabascan name, Denali. Many of the same great peaks can be seen from the highway, but the ridgetop shows the full panoramic sweep of mountains, glaciers, tundra-covered foothills, wooded lowlands and glacial rivers.[62]

We reached Talkeetna on Sunday afternoon. Ed Fox and Joyce Klodnicki had already arrived a day or two before. They were weary from the long trip up the Alcan and down George Parks Highway from Fairbanks. Fox had rigged sleeping compartments in his closed-in truck bed. It was cramped and claustrophobic, in my view, but seemed to have served them well.

We had, for some time, been corresponding with the Hudsons about our visit and had made reservations with Hudson Air for a flight over Kesugi. That was scheduled for the next day, weather permitting.

The rest of our group had prearranged to meet in Anchorage and to make the trip up Parks Highway together. We found the four of them having lunch at an outdoor table on Main Street shortly before noon. Keith Betscher had brought his adoptive father, Jack Humphries. Ed Knapp had been at the 1996 reunion, but I hadn't met his brother John in person before, although we'd been communicating for some time.

We sat together awhile, then walked around town, taking photographs and getting to know one another better. In early afternoon, the four of them settled into the Back Door B & B, next to The Whistle Stop, where we were staying. Both were just off Main Street.

Monday morning was rainy, but it cleared by ten o'clock. Hudson took the DeVitos and Pratts sightseeing around the area that morning. Eventually, we found our way over to the airport. Hudson, who had gone on ahead, was in the hangar.

"Weather looks pretty good," he said. "If you still want to fly up there, it's a good time to do it."

"I think we're ready," I said.

We'd already decided that we wanted to go if there were airplanes available.

"Jay and Don have the Cessnas all fueled up. They'll be your pilots."

We weren't all going. Jack had opted out. Joyce had never planned on going, and Ed Fox seemed still to have some issues with flight. Tom would have liked to go, but relinquished a seat because the airplanes could take only three passengers each. Nancy, Keith, and Ed Knapp went with Jay Hudson. John Knapp, Millie, and I climbed in with Don Bowers. John is a pilot, so he sat up front.

We took the lead to the runway, since I knew the way to the crash site. We were soon in the air and following the Susitna north. As we had two years before, we turned northwest from Gold Creek and were soon over Kesugi Ridge at about fifty-five hundred feet. It didn't take me long to locate the wreckage-strewn saddle across the ridge. The communication system was configured in such a way that occupants of both airplanes could hear one another talking. As I was pointing out things on the landscape to Millie, those in the other Cessna were listening and trying to spot the same objects. We could see better than they could, because our airplane was at a lower altitude. At Jay's suggestion, we changed places, and then we could see the other Cessna circling below us. We flew around the ridge for several minutes. It was easy to become disoriented, but it was a calm day, and no one became airsick.

After we pulled away from the crash site, we flew north along the ridge. I tried to locate landmarks that would help us find our way from the trail to the saddle once we were on foot. The trail stretched out for miles ahead, just like the line on the map. In a few minutes, the line turned west toward the highway and I knew I was looking at Little Coal Creek. We dropped to three thousand feet and flew back and forth over the trail going up the creek. It was straight in many places, but was largely a series of switchbacks, indicating the steepness of the landscape at that point. All too soon, it was time to return to Talkeetna.

Alaska 1998—Rupert Pratt, Ed Knapp, Millie Pratt, Tom DeVito, Nancy DeVito, Keith Betscher, Jack Humphries, John Knapp

Several of us ate that evening with the Hudsons at the Latitude 62 Restaurant. We were still high from the exciting activities of the day, but knew we should get some rest. With long hours of daylight, it was easy to forget to go to bed. The memorial service was the next day.

However, when we got back to The Whistle Stop we found a message to call a reporter from the *Anchorage Times*. He wanted to interview Fox and me. Tom found Fox at the Hudsons, and after we were all together, we called the reporter back and talked with him for half an hour. It was after eleven o'clock before we finally got to bed.

Chapter Thirty-five

Next day, about mid-morning, we drove to Veterans Memorial Park on Parks Highway to dedicate our plaque to the victims of the plane crash of 1954. Ed Fox had arrived early on our doorstep with several copies of the *Anchorage Times*. He had cleaned out the box in front of the Roadhouse, he said. The article, displayed prominently, had accurately quoted Fox and me.

I was pleased that I'd finally be meeting all those people with whom I'd been corresponding. They had requested we be there early for a conference. We found them all together outside the main building. Dale Bingham, Department of Natural Resources Superintendent for Mat-Su/Valdez-Copper River Area, who had taken a great interest in our project and had set the wheels in motion to set it up, was there. David Porter, Chief Ranger of Denali State Park, who had directed installation of the plaque, stuck out his hand like an old friend. Dave Johnston, the other area ranger, loomed tall over us all. Pam Barnes, owner of Llama Buddies, and our outfitter, along with Josie, her helper, were present. Pam and the rangers gave us a briefing about what to expect in our trek up the mountain. Dave Johnston would be going with us. David Porter would catch up later.

We were introduced to Tom Moyer, Director of the Governor's Office, and to Charles W. McLeod, Jr., State Coordinator for Veteran Affairs, who was going to assist with the ceremony. Bill Kiger, Natural Resource Officer of the Division of Parks and Outdoor Recreation, with whom I had talked a few days earlier, indicated that he wanted to speak with me.

He led me over to the display he had erected some weeks before. I studied it with mixed feelings. It was colorful, with Alaskan scenery in the background, a C-47, a short description of the crash and rescue, a photograph of Don Sheldon, and an inset map of the area showing the crash site.

"It's a great display. The graphics are superb," I said, trying to gently pave the way for what else I had to tell him.

"Do you see any way we could improve it?" he asked. "I'm open to suggestions."

I was blunt. I didn't know any other way to approach it except to be direct.

"There's a serious omission," I said.

He didn't seem surprised.

"Ed Fox just told me the same thing," Kiger said. "We want to see the story recorded in a historically correct manner. You men were there—so you know what really happened. We're going to fix it."

"Thank you for that," I said.

"I'll need your help, though."

I gave him assurance that I'd help in any way I could. In fact, we'd later correspond and he'd eventually erect a display that gave due credit to both Sheldon and Hudson.

We were astonished at the high visibility our plaque was to receive. The memorial garden is located about fifty yards south of a building housing a state park office and gift shop. A paved path led into a large area of monuments, each dedicated to a branch of the military. Our plaque, covered by a tarp, was situated just to the right of the path. It couldn't have been in a better position.

Patrick and Sara Mooney arrived to give us support. There were several other people I didn't know, a dozen or so, milling around the area. Just before the ceremony began, a couple approached me. They were Galen and Velda Griffin of Elkader, Iowa, neighbors and friends of Ed and Ruth Olson. They spent summers in Alaska and had made time to attend our ceremony. Channel 11 from Anchorage had also arrived to record the proceedings.

A color guard from the Talkeetna VFW posted the colors and the ceremony got underway. Chaplin Rick Cavens opened with a prayer, followed by a talk by Keith Betscher and short speeches from several dignitaries. The ceremony lasted nearly an hour, with me telling the story of the crash again and Tom and Nancy reading biographies of the men who had died. Loretta Shelton, widow of Richard Knickerbocker, had sent a message, as had John and Betty Knapp. John, their son, read the messages.

It was a special moment when Ed Fox and Jack Humphries unveiled the plaque, which was set into a beautiful white five-foot-wide boulder. The combination of shining boulder and pristine setting made an exquisite ending to the memorial event. Channel 11 spent a few minutes interviewing Hudson, Fox, and me.

Jack Humphries and Ed Fox
unveiling the memorial plaque
at Veterans Memorial Park,
July 28, 1998
Photo by Ed Knapp

In the main building, park personnel had prepared a reception. We met Marie Gohr, who had baked a beautiful cake with a C-47 on it.

"I remember the crash," she said as she hugged me.

Ed and Joyce went back to Talkeetna, but the rest of us drove to the North Country B & B at Trapper Creek, since we wanted to be closer to the trailhead. It was a tranquil setting on Scottie Lake, with Denali towering in the background. We talked in the rec room for some time before retiring. We needed rest before our upcoming trek. Even so, I had trouble winding down.

The plaque was in a place where thousands would see it each year. Denali State Park staff had been most gracious in setting things up and in welcoming us.

We arose early. The plan was to take both vehicles. One would be left at the trailhead. Jack, Millie, and Nancy would have the other to use while we were gone. Ed Fox and Joyce were coming from Talkeetna to join us.

We got to the trailhead exactly at seven o'clock to meet Pam and Josie with the llamas. The animals were already unloaded and prancing about at one side of the large parking lot. Fox's truck was there, too. I knew something was wrong as soon as I saw his face.

"I can't go," he said. "I've been up all night with vomiting and diarrhea. I'd hold everybody back."

"What happened?"

My disappointment was keen and I couldn't hide that fact.

"Something I ate, I guess. And it's still with me."

I wanted to fix it somehow. For months, Fox and I had talked about a trip to the crash site and made plans together. We were the only ones from the group of survivors who'd ever been back to the site, that having been a year and a half after the crash. He'd been the real sparkplug of that trip. I'd expected him to go this time, too, and I had trouble letting go of that idea.

"Ed—maybe we could go slow until you feel better."

He was adamant.

"Can't make it!" he said. "You go for me."

Joyce had tears in her eyes. It was a bitter pill, but we had to accept it.

I turned to the business of lining up my gear. Because of mixed patterns of weather conditions in the mountains, we had to take an assortment of clothing. I was wearing layers, but also had extras. In addition, I had two jackets and a poncho. My camera pack took up a lot of room in my backpack.

Ranger Dave Johnston helped Jan and Josie tighten straps and lead the llamas into position. Pam gave us all water bottles to slide into the side pockets of our packs. The Knapp brothers were ready to go. Ed had his camera around his neck. He was an amateur photographer and was looking forward to the hike, voicing his hope for good weather. John, a Gulf War veteran, wore Army gear, a reminder of his reservist status. Tom's face was white with bug repellant. He looked as if he was painted for war—which wasn't far from the truth. The enemy was fierce in the parking lot. As I applied my own repellant, I remembered the ferocious attacks we had endured on the other side of the ridge in 1955. I hoped we could leave the scourge behind as we gained altitude.

Finally, we were ready.

Millie kissed me and cautioned, "Be careful. You've had some problems with this place in the past."

"I've made my peace," I said, hoping it was true.

DeVito, Pratt, and Betscher, Little Coal Creek Trail parking lot before start of Kesugi Ridge hike, July 29, 1998

Pam ordered me up front with Camero, an older and trail-wise white llama. I suspect Pam's reasoning was that putting the oldest and slowest in front would prevent overtaxing them. I quickly made friends with Camero, who seemed as eager as I was to get started.

I whispered into her ear, "Let's show them, old girl. We'll set a blistering pace and leave everybody behind."

I hoped she was of the same mind. It was about seven-thirty when we set out.

Chapter Thirty-six

The lower portion of Little Coal Creek Trail had a moderate grade, winding through birch, spruce, and cottonwood, then past a beaver pond before gradually gaining elevation. I turned several times to see the procession of llamas and people strung out behind me on the narrow trail. After all the planning, we were starting at last. It was a good feeling—except for Ed Fox's absence.

The trail lies north of the creek and runs parallel to it. It skirts along the edge of a gorge in most places, but turns away at points of difficulty or danger. Above us, I could see several switchbacks, no doubt the section I had observed from the Cessna two days earlier. The stream itself isn't large and flows almost straight down the mountain. The gorge, however, seemed abysmal, creating a sense of timelessness and mystery. I wouldn't have been surprised to see a dinosaur head appear over the lip of the crevice. The air was sparklingly clear. I sucked it deeply into my lungs as we pushed on up toward the treeless area. Camero followed me silently, with hardly a tug on the line.

"We're making good time," Johnston called from the rear.

We left the timber behind and entered a section of tall brush. We had spread out, and from my position I had trouble seeing the end of the line, but I could hear constant chatter, indicating that all was well.

We stopped for a break after about an hour. It had been cool when we started, but now I was beginning to sweat and took off my heavier shirt. Others were also doffing outerwear. Because of dense undergrowth in that section, it was impossible to see much of the trail in either direction, but by using the valley and road as reference, I could tell we had climbed a respectable distance.

After we were underway again, Johnston came up front with his camera.

"I'm taking lots of pictures," he said. "They're for the park archives."

After that, he was everywhere. He'd disappear for a while, then pop up to snap a picture. We'd already had an earful about Johnston from other rangers. His six-and-a-half-foot frame is a good start toward describing his "rugged" appearance. I had also heard the word "superman" used on his behalf. He was wearing shorts despite hordes of bugs, and sneakers despite rocky terrain. His backpack was an exceptionally long one, making him look about twelve feet tall. In 1967, this mountaineer extraordinaire had been one of three men to reach the peak of Denali, from a party of eight making the first winter accent.[63] He had since climbed the big mountain several times, not to mention scaling several other peaks in Alaska and around the world.

The trail steepened. We stopped again after half an hour. My shirt was wet with perspiration. Denali, like an unexpected specter, had risen from the clouds obscuring it. I was surprised, as always, at its supremacy. Cloud layers still enshrouded much of it, but its familiar shape was a thrill.

"It's giving us a good view today," Pam said.

After several switchbacks, we stood at the bottom of a foreboding rocky stretch that seemed to go straight up. The high brush was behind us, replaced by low vegetation.

Pam called, loud enough for everyone to hear, "We've just got to get up this part to that rocky pinnacle, and then we'll be able to see the face of the last rise, where we'll camp."

Our "blistering pace" became more of a snail's crawl as we inched up the incline. I tried not to loosen stones that would slide down on the others. Camero seemed to be less inclined to participate. Eventually, she balked. I tried to gently drag her forward, to no avail.

"She's tired," Pam said. "Let's get another leader up there."

Tom, with Cuzco, and Keith, with Suede, passed me to get to the front.

We finally made it up to the outcropping. People and animals were breathing hard. We shed our packs and Pam pulled snacks from a bag on one of the llamas. I gulped down cold water from my bottle and had some trail mix. It was about ten o'clock. We rested awhile before Pam and Johnston lined us up with the llamas for a group photograph.

From there to the campsite, the trail was in the open. We actually meandered downhill for a stretch before starting up a last steep incline. Rested, we made it in less than half an hour. Tom and I congratulated each other that the three-mile climb hadn't been any more difficult than some we'd made in the Adirondacks. We might not have been so cocky had we given thought to the many miles ahead of us.

Denali stood behind us, a few bikini-like clouds trying, in vain, to hide it. When we topped the last rise, we could see a broad caribou moss-carpeted meadow that stretched back and down toward a small lake. The altitude there was about three thousand feet. Behind the lake were bleak, dark peaks, among the highest of Kesugi Ridge.

I was thankful that we wouldn't have to climb up there. What looked like loose shale would probably slide under the weight of a hiker. Instead, we would follow the trail south along the ridge on firmer ground. I could see it across the gulch, winding up and around, and finally disappearing over a distant hill about a mile away. Patches of dirty snow dotted the landscape.

Had we been able to travel with llamas to the crash site, we could have camped near the wreckage, visited the site in the evening, and returned the next day. Below us, however, lay the large boulder field Pam had told me about. It was extensive, made up of stones of various sizes, many half the size of automobiles. Pam, a geologist by profession, called it an "ancient rock flow," deposited there by glaciers eons ago. The mess littering our projected path looked to be about fifty yards across and a hundred in length. Boundaries were well-defined. To the left, the mountain sloped upward, steep enough to prevent access in that direction. To the right, there was a severe drop-off where the creek cascaded down into the canyon.

The boulder field was the only way across, and the llamas couldn't walk through it. We'd have to set up camp there, then walk to the crash site and back before dark. Pam estimated it to be five or six miles away. It wasn't going to be a stroll though a meadow.

Pam and Josie removed the packs from the llamas and then turned the animals loose to graze. Being social, they wouldn't wander away, she said. She'd stake one of them out though, just in case. The rest would stay close. We helped where we could.

Pam was going to accompany us. Josie would stay behind to set up tents and watch the llamas. She'd start preparing the evening meal when she could see us returning on the trail across the gulch.

We were soon ready to leave. We had lightened our packs, but I still ended up taking more than I'd planned, reasoning that weather conditions could change quickly. Darkness shouldn't be a problem since it would be daylight until nearly midnight. Nonetheless, it seemed prudent to assume we might have delays, so I took my flashlight.

We left camp and filed down into the hollow. The stream there was small enough to hop across and we were soon at the edge of the boulder field. It wasn't an easy passage. The younger folks seemed to have little difficulty, but Tom and I had to pick our way carefully. Up close now, I could see that the area was filled with literally millions of rocks, strewn across a wide expanse. We hopped from one large rock to the next, after planning each jump carefully. Several times I almost fell between boulders. To our right, water plunged down the gorge, creating a constant roar. Patches of snow lined the walls where the sun didn't reach. I took out my camera and got some shots.

We finally reached the other side. We could see the trail ahead, winding up a slope. After we got to the top of that rise, the path went down through a swampy area before going up another incline. To our left, parallel to the trail, were high somber peaks, strung out in a southerly direction. To our right was the Chulitna Valley and George Parks Highway, which we had traveled over a few hours before. Beyond that, farther west, was a cascade of dark snow-covered peaks leading up to Denali. There were still some clouds around it, but it dominated the landscape.

The trail along Kesugi Ridge was pretty much like that all the way. There were constant ups and downs, but it was seldom steep. Numerous feet had left much of the trail rutted. The beauty around us seemed unreal. I would have liked to stop and enjoy it in a more leisurely way, but everyone else seemed inclined to press on.

What was the difference, I wondered, between today and the day Fox, Haab, and I had climbed up the other side? It didn't take me long to conclude that it was the weather. With today's high visibility, the land under our feet seemed to mirror the splendor of the far vista.

We passed small ponds and walked through rolling meadows. There were scores of small animals and birds—but no bears. Pam had told us we weren't likely to see any, because the berries weren't yet ripe enough. There were recent reports of sheep in the vicinity, but we saw none. There are many animals in the park, some visible, some not. It's home to moose, grizzly and black bears, red foxes, rabbits, gray wolves, marmots, ermines, and coyotes.

Cairns, which are simply piles of stones stacked as trail markers, stood on nearly every rise. You could often see a series of them stretched out ahead. Pam told us Johnston had laid out the trail soon after the park was formed and had built the cairns himself. Modest almost to a fault, he didn't seem inclined to talk about it. He busied himself taking photographs.

We stopped for lunch at the top of a knoll beside a cairn. Pam brought out sandwiches made with tuna, cucumbers, and bean sprouts. We'd all been hitting our water bottles every few minutes. Mine was only half full, even though we had refilled before leaving camp. We rested about half an hour.

The trail was well worn. It's actually nearly forty miles long, stretching from the Little Coal Creek trailhead south, past Byers Creek and Veterans Memorial Park, before it turns back to the highway.

As we were getting ready to leave, a lone figure with a walking stick approached from the direction we had come.

"It's David Porter," Johnston announced.

Porter had told us the day before that he would leave later and catch up with us. His breathing showed little sign of effort, even though he'd been playing catch-up. My impression of the rangers was already high, and growing by the hour. Neither of these men was a youngster, but both were in top-notch physical condition. Moreover, they seemed to love their work.

We pushed off again. I was glad to get moving. I knew approximately where we were. I had studied the map and could remember much of the terrain from our flyover two days before. Johnston estimated we had at least three miles to go before we'd have to leave the trail. We hiked in earnest then, strung out, with some of our group as much as a quarter mile in front. Keith was leading, followed by John and Ed. Tom and I were in back. Pam would occasionally drop to the rear, where she could check out the entire group. Johnston was everywhere.

As miles fell behind us, our reason for being there came increasingly to my mind, and travel itself became a pattern of just putting one foot in front of the other. Keith was nearly out of sight. Johnston yelled for him to wait up. We needed to get a fix on where we were. Keith was shifting his weight from foot to foot impatiently when we caught up with him.

As we circled together, I told Porter that mountains there looked much like the crash area. Johnston pulled out a tattered old map.

"I think it's right up there," I said, pointing up toward a high peak perpendicular to where we were standing.

Johnston pointed to an "x" on his map.

"It may be just a click farther south," he said.

"What about following this creek up?" I asked, pointing to the small stream coming from the area where I believed the wreckage lay.

Porter presented an alternative, pointing to the next peak south.

"If we go on a little farther, then come back up over that hill, we'll be sure to hit it. It'll add a mile or so, but it's the best way to approach."

"A good plan," Johnston said.

My legs were beginning to feel like dead tree trunks and my back hurt from the weight of my pack. The trail took us higher, and finally we reached a valley that seemed to transverse the ridge in a northeasterly direction.

"This is it!" I said. "If we go up there, and around the mountainside, we're going to find where I spent a long night."

With renewed energy and without waiting for anyone, I started in that direction.

Chapter Thirty-seven

I was so obsessed with reaching my destination that I didn't notice that we'd split into two groups. Tom DeVito and Dave Johnston were following me around the slope, but the others went higher, walking along a narrow ridge toward the area I had earlier identified as the crash site.

I was sure this was where my parachute had dragged me across the snow. I knew I had landed close to the east side of the ridge, which was straight ahead. Dark, irregular shapes against the skyline a few hundred yards away could be the boulders I'd barely managed to miss. Since I'd been dragged at least two hundred yards, I couldn't be far from the place Olson, Fox, and I found one another.

Walking wasn't easy. Rock flows, yards across, stretched down the incline. I was surprised to find a piece of aluminum about six inches wide. I held it up for Dave and Tom to see. It was the first evidence that we were in the right place. The piece had a smooth surface and the luster wasn't much diminished, except for faint dark spotting.

As we continued around the slope, we found many other small pieces. I was amazed. I figured we were almost a half-mile from the main wreckage. The accident report had stated that the airplane "broke up at a high altitude." The scattered debris seemed to confirm that.

"I believe that's where we spent the night," I said, pointing.

Scraggly caribou moss tugged at my boots as I went down the slope with the other two men right behind me.

I wasn't sure which of several rocks we had huddled behind, but I knew it was the same area. The view of the valley glimpsed through clouds the morning after the crash had stayed in my memory. In fact, I had a photograph at home of the landscape that I'd taken in 1955. I wished I had brought it with me. With my Canon AE10, I snapped a couple of shots, framing the background as much like the other long-ago shot as I could remember. The two photographs would turn out to be amazingly similar, although the second shot was from a slightly lower altitude.

I searched for the exact location of the "sleeping rock." It had been one of the larger ones. Fox and I had had no trouble finding it, since it had been only a year and a half since the accident. We'd found the parachutes then, still intact. Now I approached a likely prospect and searched the ground around it. I had hoped there might be some evidence left of the abandoned chutes, some small remaining fabric, but I found nothing. Other rocks in the area, likewise, yielded no clues. Disappointed, I finally gave up. We decided to join the others.

A few minutes later, I caught sight of a large piece of metal higher up the incline. As we got nearer, I could see that it was rectangular. It was about six feet by three feet, and seemed undamaged. It looked as if it might have been a panel from inside the airplane. There were many other smaller scraps in every direction. I remembered that one of the aerial photographs I had taken in 1996 had shown a rectangular shape, and it had been south of the main wreckage. Later, at home, I confirmed it was indeed the same piece.

We took pictures of the panel, then moved on up to find the others. We were walking north now and finally climbed up and over the last knoll. Below us was the pass that extended all the way across the top of the ridge. My 1996 aerial photographs had shown the pass, which was highest in the middle. I'd been calling it "the saddle" ever since.

All the others were down there. The glint of metal was everywhere. There were fragments at our feet, all the way down the slope to the saddle and up the other side of the hill. Parts were everywhere, but especially strewn around the saddle. I called down to Ed Knapp, who was closest. He informed me Keith had found instruments from the cockpit.

I was astonished at the quantity of wreckage there, small as the pieces were. Fox and I hadn't found all that in 1955. It had rained off and on the whole time, and tops of the peaks had been constantly in clouds. It's possible that the saddle had been socked-in, so that we weren't able to explore it extensively.

In the valley to the east, I could see where the Indian River flowed into the Susitna near Gold Creek. Fox, Kenneth Haab, and I had forded the Indian River before walking across the valley and up the steep eastern side of the ridge.

As I moved down into the saddle, I saw an area with some weather-beaten boards and other moldy looking objects. On closer examination, I could see the remains of a parachute. Most of the harness was all but unrecognizable, but coming up from the tangle was one of the risers. It extended over and seemed almost to be a part of a rock on which it lay. Following it back between two other large stones, I could distinguish the shroud of the chute. I didn't want to disturb it, but gently lifted the folds enough to see a tinge of orange. I was surprised it had survived that long, exposed to the elements as it was. There was also part of a seat, the webbing not much deteriorated. For a moment, the thought struck me that it could have been *my* seat. Such speculation was, of course, of little value.

Ed Knapp, like me, was constantly photographing objects around him. We discovered a cargo door with its lettering intact. It was nearly covered by vegetation. Johnston would carry it off the ridge with the idea of making it a part of park archives. In an open area lay parts of an engine with rusty pistons looking as if they were beginning to fossilize. We found part of the tailwheel. Most surprising was a section about four by five feet with a window that still had some glass in it. Above the window were the lower parts of the lettering, "TATES." It didn't take our group long to figure out that it was part of the inscription "UNITED STATES OF AMERICA," which was painted on all military aircraft.

Up to that time, we'd been working our way through the saddle toward the highest part and staying close together. However, as in 1955, I felt the need to be by myself. I walked about fifty yards back and up the slope to where I hadn't seen anyone exploring.

I sat on a flat shale-like stone. I hadn't been there long when I noticed a piece of metal, about a foot square and near enough to reach. Entangled in ground-hugging vegetation, it had at first escaped my attention. Its jagged edges looked sharp enough to remove a finger, but the exposed portions were smooth and shiny. Although it wasn't much different from hundreds of other pieces in the area, the sight of it aroused my interest. It seemed incredible that after forty-four years, the piece looked no older than it might have in 1955.

Most people, I would guess, have experienced an instant when there's the feeling of being a part of the whole—of catching a glimpse of something bigger than oneself. It's only happened to me a few times, but enough that I now recognized its presence. Nevertheless, the feeling was fleeting, fluff blown away by the wind across the ridge. Any divine revelation escaped my detection. It was nothing but a piece of metal, I concluded—just an inanimate object.

I reached to pick it up. It was reluctant to separate from the plants. I tugged harder. It still refused to give up its hold. Determined now and curious, I started digging the vegetation from around it. The roots and stems covering it weren't just loose growth, but were so entwined I had to use both hands to pull them up. I realized that because of slow-growth at that climate and altitude, it would have taken many years to have become so entrenched. Finally, I pried the piece loose and was surprised to see a hole in the ground. How many generations of little animals had used it for shelter? Fifteen, perhaps. In people time, that would be four hundred fifty years. That comparison, though interesting, didn't seem especially useful—just a way of seeing "time" as relative. I was sorry to have disturbed the piece and tried to place it back in the same position.

Then it dawned on me. *Time! It's not always measured in like units.* God's time is flexible and not apt to be understood by us—but our time is different, for us an indispensable tool, a gauge for measuring the events of our lives, even our progress. Time makes a difference. My aching body confirmed it. Despite relentless breaking down of the cells in and around us, time is a gift. God had given me a gift of time—and was reminding me. Kesugi, of course, was the perfect place for the revelation.

Later, I joined the others down lower on the western slope of the saddle. They had found a propeller blade. The paint retained its luster and the numbers were still perfectly readable.

"It's good enough to put back on a C-47," John Knapp said.

Johnston got all eight of us together for a group picture with the blade. We assembled near a rock ledge, where he placed his camera and triggered it for a delayed shot. John and Keith held the blade upright between them while Johnston scrambled to get himself into the picture.

"That blade would make a great addition to the memorial rock," David Porter said. "Too bad it's too heavy to carry down."

We'd been in the area for about two hours. It was nearly five o'clock and the rangers seemed to be getting worried about the time. It would take four or more hours to get back to camp, so we prepared to leave. As planned, I called everyone together for a short service.

I had decided to honor the dead at the crash site by writing a letter to them. When our little group had assembled, I read the letter:

I have some words to say to the men who died here: I know your spirits are not residents here. You are freer and live in a reality more vivid than we can imagine. But, as I have come here one last time, I feel your presence also. The others you left behind would have liked to be here too, but couldn't be. We carry their thoughts and their prayers to this place.

I've often pondered why it was that some of us lived and some had to die, but all my pondering was in vain. We have no answers. God has all the answers, and you, being closer to Him than we, probably know far more than we.

I do know that what happened here has been a moral rudder for me all these years. The rudder has sometimes failed, and I've drifted sinfully at worst and aimlessly at best. But the rudder has always been there, and has taken over before I drifted too far.

I think of you often, Ed and Don, my friends, of the good times we had together, as well as the trials—our Christmas Eve climb of the mountain near Fort Rich—the unauthorized party at the lab.

And, I say to you others whom I never knew in life, but whom I have come to know through your loved ones who still grieve your loss—your lives have touched our lives and enriched them immensely. You: Alvi, Edmund, Richard, Jacob, William, James, Edward, Earl. I believe that you have all had a hand in what has taken place in the last two years, you and us, perhaps fulfilling the will of God. As our lives wind down, we pray that we have done it at least as well as you would have done it. We'll discuss it again when the mirror is not so dark.

The letter probably reflected some of the adjustments I'd made in my thinking over the years. My persistent quest for answers, though still important to me, had become less so, and in the mountain setting seemed practically meaningless. In the few moments of quiet after I read the letter, I experienced the peace of knowing I was a part of something larger, something *safe*. I had written about "a reality more vivid than we can imagine," but the full impact of those words had escaped me until that moment. It came as an insight, perhaps an addendum to, the "time" revelation I'd had a few minutes earlier. It was a happy realization of being within God's plan—a plan I might not understand, but which, like the cosmos itself, was present. My thought then, as now, was that my life would be much different if I could hold that understanding—just a piece of it, in my consciousness.

Tom closed our service with a prayer. His powerful words were a testimony to his faith and to his awe of the moment. I could see quiet emotion in the eyes of the others, too, as we prepared to leave.

Ranger Porter, although sensitive to the sanctify of the site, allowed that we might take some small items with us. I had already picked up a couple of pieces, no larger than my hand. Keith took some gauges from the instrument panel, both for himself and for his sister.

Later, with some emotion, he'd say to me, "Sometime during the flight, my dad touched this gauge."

We elected to return to the trail a different way, one which appeared to be closer. We crossed a little stream formed from a branch behind the peak north of the saddle and a smaller trickle coming from the saddle itself. I noticed the rangers with their heads together.

Porter, in his unhurried way, gave us the essence of their conversation.

"This stream doesn't have a real name," he said. "We thought 'Reunion Creek' might be suitable—for obvious reasons."

We all agreed it was a fine idea.

"Is that official, then?" John Knapp asked.

"No—but we'll work on it."

We walked in a northwesterly direction over a series of meadows. They were huge grass-covered steppes taking us progressively downward toward the trail, which we finally reached at a point about a mile farther north than where we had left it.

The rest of the trip back to camp was trying for me. *Everything* hurt. I tried not to think about how I felt, just putting my mind in neutral and one foot in front of the other, making the miles disappear behind me. There had been a lot of talking and yelling back and forth on the way to the crash site, but now everyone was quiet. The wind had increased and I put on my heavy jacket. Denali was giving us a new look now, with the sun at a different angle.

As we walked, I tried to remember the trail ahead. Would we be able to see the camp over that next rise? There were several disappointments in that respect, but finally we spotted the array of yellow tents on the knoll across Little Coal Creek gorge. Josie would be watching for us and would start dinner. With the boulder field in our way, it would probably be another hour before we got there.

The boulder field was the last barrier in our path and, without doubt, the hardest we had faced. Most of the others crossed ahead of Tom and me. The two of us stayed together, ready to help each other. Ed Knapp brought up the rear, probably to watch over us. Pam had warned that it was a dangerous time. In our state of exhaustion, falling was much more likely than when we were fresh. We struggled from stone to stone like drunken men, exchanging places several times and pointing out to each other where to step.

Pam was coming back to meet us.

"Do you need help?" she called.

We declined. I guess it had become a matter of pride, but we were going to finish under our own power.

Eventually, we made it over the boulders and across the stream. My legs seemed to take on new life as we went up the slope toward camp. Dinner was ready, Josie announced.

She had arranged campstools in a circle. Pam brought out a bottle of Irish Mist, and we toasted our successful day. We ate the rice, vegetable, and meat mixture with gusto and topped it off with pie Josie had baked. Hot coffee washed it all down.

David Porter left us, going back down the trail. He was adding another three miles to what had already been a fifteen-mile hike. He didn't even look tired.

It was ten o'clock when we finished dinner. We talked for a while about the day's events, but exhaustion finally overcame us and, one by one, we headed for our tents. Glancing back, I could see Johnston sitting on the ground, barefoot, eating leftovers from a big pot.

I shared a tent with Tom. We took off our boots and climbed into our sleeping bags. I went to sleep almost immediately. I remember turning over a few times in the darkness, and then it was daylight again. A voice outside brought me fully awake.

"Rupe—you've got to see this!"

I glanced at my watch. It was after six. I crawled out the narrow opening and forced my stiff body to stand erect.

"This is what I woke up to!" Tom said, pointing toward Denali.

The sight was unbelievable. There were no clouds in any part of the sky, a condition some say happens only a half-dozen times a summer. Denali and all the surrounding peaks stood out crisp and clear, absolutely dominating the view to the west.

In a few minutes, everyone was up, ogling the scene and snapping pictures. As breakfast was being prepared, I walked around the lake, getting shots from different angles. Dave Johnston joined me across from the camp.

He put his arm around my shoulder and said, "Isn't it great to be alive?"

After a breakfast of eggs and sausage, we had another photo session and then began to break camp. We rounded up the llamas. Some of them seemed not to want to leave. Then, with packs in place, we began the procession back down the trail. At first, my body hurt all over, but as we walked, I began to feel better.

It was early afternoon when we reached the parking lot. We helped load the llamas into the trailer and tarried awhile, reluctant to say goodbye to Pam and Josie. At last, we had to go back down the highway toward Trapper Creek. My mood was jubilant.

Kesugi Ridge hike group with a propeller blade from the C-47—
Pam Barnes, David Porter, Tom DeVito, Ed Knapp, John Knapp,
Keith Betscher, Rupert Pratt, Dave Johnston
Photo by Dave Johnston

These two photos were taken by Rupert Pratt from nearly the same spot, the left one in August 1955, the right one on July 29, 1998. In the background is the Susitna River Valley in the Gold Creek area.

Pratt and DeVito on the Kesugi Ridge Trail
with the Alaska Range in the background
Photo by Dave Johnston

Camp in sight at the head of Little Coal Creek
Photo by Dave Johnston

Chapter Thirty-eight

Next morning, we said our goodbyes. Keith, Jack, and the Knapp brothers left for Anchorage. The Pratts and DeVitos drove north toward Denali National Park. We located our Healy bed and breakfast and registered for a two-night stay.

The following day, we took a bus tour into the park. The weather remained good, giving us an unobstructed view of the north face of Denali. As extraordinary as that scenery was, the early-morning panorama seen from Kesugi reigned as my ultimate Denali sighting.

It was August 2, Tom and Nancy's anniversary. After returning from the park, we enjoyed a leisurely dinner at a restaurant high over Parks Highway. The date and setting put us in a celebratory mood. We were especially conscious of our long friendship.

Two days at Fairbanks pacified my spirit. I was able to share with Millie the space I had occupied in the fifties. Having her at my side filled a void. I told her again of the good times, but didn't mention the bad.

We took a ride on the riverboat *Discovery*, motoring over the Chena River into the Tanana and stopping at several sites along the way. Later that day, we visited Alaskaland, which was commercial, but historically interesting. The Farmers Market in Fairbanks drew us with its foods, arts and crafts, and garden produce. It was raining, and we spent the better part of two hours inside the large building housing the market. Nancy and Millie bought several items, mostly artwork, to take home. I reminded Millie that our luggage had been full coming, and we might not be able to get these new things into our bags.

"Not to worry," was the answer. "We can mail them if we have to."

We left Fairbanks and the Frogpond B & B behind with some reluctance, although we knew we had to be on our way. It was a long drive down Richardson Highway to Big Delta and then south to Gakona on the Copper River. In the section between Fairbanks and Big Delta, we saw a sign for Birch Lake, reminding me of the long-ago trip Ken Haab and I had made in the rickety old oil truck. In 1996, when I was gathering information about survivors and other families, I'd found Haab's phone number and called him. We talked about that trip and many other things. He has a large family, and has retired from a teaching career.

In Gakona, after a stop at the Carriage House restaurant, we registered at the Riverview B & B on the banks of the Copper River. The log house was huge, with a living room that would swallow some homes. Owners Homer and Carol Neil are retired teachers. They intrigued us with their subsistence living lifestyle. Two large greenhouses supplied them with fruits and vegetables not otherwise grown in Alaska. They listened eagerly to accounts of our recent adventures and shared many of their own. The only other guest wouldn't arrive until about eight o'clock. We'd find him interesting, they told us.

That evening, as the seven of us gathered in a small corner of the spacious living area, the Neils introduced William Gordon from Rice University. He was in his eighties, but looked much younger. He was there to take part in an "open house" for area people to help put their minds at ease about a government project ten miles up the road.

"Dr. Gordon has been involved in several large projects," our host said. "He oversaw the one in Puerto Rico some people call 'the big ear.' That's where they listen in on outer space."

"That was in the movie *Contact*. I just saw that," I said.

"What is your project here, Dr. Gordon?" Tom asked.

"It's called HAARP, or High Frequency Auroral Research Program. We have large banks of antennae to observe the aurora borealis and weather phenomenon."

"Now wait a minute!" Nancy said, her voice rising. "I think I know what this is!"

An embarrassed silence pervaded the room for a few moments. I suddenly realized what she was talking about—the project her relative had wanted her to investigate. It was the first time I had thought about it since leaving home. It seemed we had stumbled onto it, despite the improbability.

Nancy proceeded to explain her outburst to Dr. Gordon. He smiled understandingly and then looked over the material she had retrieved from her suitcase.

"There's really a lot of misunderstanding about this project," he said with a sigh. "It has extended to the residents of this valley, too. That's what this meeting will be about tomorrow. Perhaps you'll attend and can carry back the information to your relative."

"Oh—I wish we could," Nancy said.

Tom explained that we were flying home the following night and needed the next day to travel.

"Tell you what!" Dr. Gordon said. "I'll give you my email address and you can have your relative contact me. Not only that—if you have time, come on up to HAARP early in the morning and I'll show you around. We don't have any secrets. You can take pictures wherever you want."

"Invitation accepted," Nancy said quickly. She looked at me as if to say, "Can you believe this?"

Dr. William Gordon was faithful to his word. After an early morning goodbye to the Neils, we toured the HAARP facility, which was located a few hundred yards off the main highway. An ever-green-lined road led up to a large plain where, enclosed within a huge fenced-in area, hundreds of tall antennae were packed close together. Dr. Gordon took us inside the building, where we saw rows of computers that seemed to be conveying information from the cluster of data-collecting constructs outside.

As we walked through the indoor facilities and the grounds outside, Dr. Gordon explained, in layman's terms, what went on there.

"It's under the Air Force and the Navy," he said, "and it's about communication."

Understanding ionospheric processes would, he said, carry us forward in many areas of communication.

"And, yes, in military matters," he admitted at our gentle probing, "but in civilian matters, too."

I remembered from reading the material Nancy's relative had given her that there was much controversy about the damage the site might inadvertently be doing to the ionosphere. I would have liked to ask more questions, but didn't really know what to ask.

"See—we have no big secrets here," Dr. Gordon said as he bid us goodbye.

Later, on the road toward Palmer, I had more time to think about it. What if the doomsayers were right? Was our government on a course with HAARP which appeared on the surface to be firm ground, but which, in reality, was quicksand? Many thoughtful and learned people seemed to think so. In such an issue, it was usually hard to distinguish kooks from rational thinkers. It sometimes seems as if we're all just a step away from Kooksville on some subject. Humans have a checkered record. Much of our time and energy has been spent killing one another or protecting ourselves against being killed. My two years in Alaska in the fifties had been just that, occupying a line of defense against the Russians, who were sitting a few miles west, doing the same thing. Moreover, each of our defensive stances would have become offensive at the slightest provocation. Things didn't always work the way they were supposed to. The Atomic Age wasn't yet the panacea envisioned. What if the reality of HAARP turned out to be quite different from the vision?

Those were dark thoughts, and I made an effort to turn them aside. Positive thinking seemed to me to be the high road.

"Sticking your head in the sand," some might suggest.

"Searching for the best in humankind," I could retort.

Yet, my darker side wondered. I expressed an opinion to the others in the car.

"I don't know about you, but I wouldn't have recognized a secret there if it had jumped up and bit me. He really wasn't taking any chances with anything he showed me."

We rode through territory I'd never seen before. Wild and beautiful scenery threatened to steal our attention from the perilous mountain road. Glaciers and rugged valleys ruled the landscape.

We stopped for lunch at a restaurant perched on a mountainside above the road. They specialized in soup and pie, and we partook of both without restraint. From my seat, I watched a small airplane circle and land somewhere above us. Every small community in Alaska seemed to have an airstrip. If we had lived there, I would have been flying, too. There was some sadness and regret associated with the thought. Life was a tradeoff, I realized. Certainly, we could have had a good life in Alaska, or in West Virginia, or anywhere else, but the truth was that we'd had a good life in upper New York State. The roots we put down found the soil fertile with friendship and caring people. I was thankful for that, and determined not to lament over my years of absence from Alaska and to enjoy every minute I was there.

Stopping in Palmer in mid-afternoon, we spent some time in a gift shop and adjoining flower garden before turning south to Anchorage. Our flight wasn't scheduled to leave until midnight, so we had lots of time to kill. We explored the city and surrounding area, then had dinner at a restaurant in the heart of Anchorage, where Sara Mooney joined us. We went early to the airport to begin the long flight home.

Chapter Thirty-nine

The runway lights of Heaven
shine brighter for us to see,
as the ship of love and friendship
delivers Huey T.
Joining the manifest of Angels
who left us in the sky,
to carry out God's missions
in that reunion up on high.

He staged a valiant effort
while fighting for his health,
his treasure was his family
and friendship was his wealth.
Memories of his yesterdays
can balance out the sorrow,
as we think of him with gladness
and look at our tomorrow.

He joins the list of airmen
which now has reached eleven,
those who left the mountain
and journeyed up to Heaven.
He'll take his place there with them
and we have this hunch,
his positive words and actions
will fit right in the bunch.

We're so glad we got together
after more than forty years,
to share the times of laughter
and possibly some tears.
And when we get to Heaven
we're longing for to see,
a reunion with those airmen,
including Huey T. and me.

Edward Olson, 1998

On the morning of Friday, August 21, 1998, I received a phone call from Minnie Montgomery, informing us that Huey had died the previous evening. It wasn't unexpected. Minnie had called right after our return from Alaska to tell us about the doctors finding cancer in his kidneys. It had spread to other parts of his body. They had taken him to a specialist in St. Louis, who had sent him home. I had talked to Huey briefly on the phone, but I don't think he recognized me.

I called the other survivors and several other families as Millie and I prepared to leave for Evansville to attend the August 26 funeral. It was a pleasant surprise to find Bobby and Ramona Sallis registered at the Hampton Inn.

The Montgomerys, even in their grief, took time to be gracious. The Tuesday evening wake had a large turnout, with many out-of-town Montgomery family members attending. Huey, Jr. was to conduct the service the following morning at Boonville, in the church where he was pastor. He asked me to "speak a few words." After breakfast with Ramona and Bobby, we drove out to Boonville, about twenty miles northeast of Evansville.

Huey, Jr. spoke about the time he spent with his father in his final days, of their singing hymns together, and of Huey's faith. When it was my turn, I talked about his way with words, which could make you laugh or make you cry, of how we were all on the earth for a purpose, and how I had only to look at his many wonderful children and grandchildren to see a major purpose of Huey's life.

Huey was buried not far from Evansville. From his gravesite, airplanes can be seen taking off and landing at the Evansville Airport. Somehow, it seemed fitting.

The air crash survivors had been periodically receiving mail informing us of the documentary progress. *On the Wing* would be dedicated to the memory of Huey Montgomery. An October 12, 1998 letter from Carrie Clifford explained what the filmmakers were doing. A "trailer" would be sent out to places such as HBO, PBS, A & E, and The History Channel. An alternative idea was to enter the completed work in various film festivals around the country. We all received a copy of the trailer. Carrie promised to keep us posted.

My trial flight earlier in the year at the Schenectady County Airport hadn't doused the flame within me, but had fanned it instead. In early September, I decided to take more lessons.

I should state up front that my expectations weren't to become a licensed pilot. I just wanted to experience flight—with me at the controls. Since childhood, Hop Harrigan and Jack Armstrong had been lurking somewhere in my brain, prodding me, however gently, to action. Finally, after the better part of a lifetime, I succumbed. Learning the basics of flight would satisfy me, I was sure.

It would be reasonable to believe that I was trying to face down a fear. That I had had some apprehension of flying is a fact. A set of circumstances beyond my control had imposed that on me. My love for flying, however, had been born long before that incident. I had overcome any present-day fear with several commercial flights and an impromptu flying lesson. Now, I was merely reclaiming my boyhood dream.

When I met Mike, my instructor, he looked askance at me. He was, no doubt, used to younger students at Richmor Aviation.

"Can you put up with an old guy?" I asked as we walked out to the flightline toward a C-152 parked in the grass.

"Well—sure—just don't expect any concessions."

"I'd be insulted if you gave me any."

We did a thorough inspection of the airplane and all its systems, which took about fifteen minutes. I learned that I was expected to follow that procedure before each flight. It was my responsibility, but I'd be checked for thoroughness.

As we taxied out to line up at the end of runway two-two, I felt calm. I knew what to expect this time. Mike did everything by the book. *Here's how you do it. Now, do it. Nope, do it again. Better—but do it again, anyway.* In that first hour, I learned about carb heat, mixture control, using the rudder, setting the trim wheel, making gradual controlled turns, slow flight, staying on a heading, and several other things. My head was full.

Later lessons concentrated on maneuvers that were more complicated, such as power-off stalls, landing techniques, and various other intricacies. Flying lessons, one or two a week, were interspersed with ground school sessions. I'd hit the books and then recite back to Mike what I had memorized.

We'd usually fly northwest, up around the Great Sacandaga Lake area, but occasionally went east toward the Hudson River. Mike taught me to stay above two thousand feet there, since I'd be in Albany International Airport space without permission otherwise. Once, I clipped it, and Mike gave me a tongue-lashing. Nevertheless, learning the mechanics of flying seemed to be coming easily to me. I was living my dream, and I loved it.

There was a problem, however: I had trouble with the radio. I couldn't hear the instructions from the control tower. "Not hear" probably isn't the best description. It wasn't a matter of volume or of deciphering the code commonly used in flight control. It was more the speed with which instructions were given and the way ends of words were clipped off. It was also sorting the flight controller's voice out from the noise, much like the trouble I was already having in carrying on a conversation in a crowded room.

We were coming in one day from the northwest. About five miles out, I called the airport.

"Schenectady tower—5394 Bravo, incoming at Charlton water tower."

"94 Bravo . . . Take . . . left . . . runway . . . "

"Say again!"

"Proceed to . . . one–zero . . ."

"Schenectady tower, I can't understand what you're saying!"

At that point, Mike cut me off and proceeded to get our landing instructions himself. In the following days, we tried adjusting volume, changing headsets, even visiting the tower to meet the controllers. Nothing seemed to help.

It reached crisis level for me in mid-November, at the beginning of lesson ten. We were going north that day to practice landings at Saratoga. We had to cross a runway and the tower instructed us to hold. I heard that part. A couple of minutes later, the controller came on the radio with an instruction that seemed totally garbled. I asked for a repeat. I got the same distorted communication. I could see the look of frustration on Mike's face.

"Can *you* understand that?" I asked him.

"Quite clearly—he wants us to proceed across and on to runway two-eight."

The incident bothered me a lot during the next hour. We did a series of touch-and-goes at Saratoga, and some complicated higher altitude maneuvers. I felt as if I did well, but my mind kept going back to the radio problem. I was getting close to solo time. How could I fly alone if I couldn't communicate with the tower? By the time we landed, I had reached a decision.

"I'm hanging it up," I told Mike.

He was disappointed.

"We can overcome the problem," he insisted.

"No," I said, "I don't want to hurt someone—or myself. Anyway, I've accomplished what I set out to do."

I think I'll always regret that I couldn't go further, yet I feel a sense of accomplishment for what I did. I admit to a touch of frustration, too. Even while recognizing my own limitations, it seems to me that the art of flight communication might be improved.

March brought the sad news that Eugene Hill had died while recovering from surgery. I was glad that Capt. Hill's younger brother had been able to attend the 1997 reunion. Leslie Lowery, Eugene's daughter, had been instrumental in bringing that about.

Greg, after a year and a half of moving from job to job in Rochester, decided to go for the real thing. He put his résumé out to several places around the country. There were multiple replies, but most promising was one from the New York branch of the Federal Reserve Bank System. After an interview, he was hired as a computer systems administrator. He was to work in their branch in East Rutherford, New Jersey. He found an apartment near his employment and we helped him move.

On the other coast, Jon and Bobbi had settled into a satisfactory routine. Bobbi had found work at the university and Jon was well into his studies. All was good in our family.

Elkader, Iowa, was site of the 1999 reunion, which was to begin July 28. The DeVitos, having missed the 1997 reunion, were anxious to attend. We decided to travel together in one car. We'd take our time, seeing the sights as we went.

The weather turned hot about the time we left. We drove to Niagara Falls, then the following day went west through southern Canada into Michigan. Next day, we traveled north along the west side of Lake Huron to Mackinaw City, where we stayed two nights. We spent a day touring Mackinac Island—a trip into the past. Horse-drawn vehicles are the main means of transportation, motor vehicles not being allowed on the island. We were amused by a horse-drawn UPS wagon. We had lunch in the large and famous Grand Hotel, which had been the setting for the movie *Somewhere in Time*, starring Christopher Reeve.

From Mackinaw City, we crossed the bridge into the Upper Peninsula, and then down the west side of Lake Michigan to Green Bay, Wisconsin. We arrived there in the early afternoon, allowing Tom and me time to go to the Packers training camp across from the stadium. From the street next to their practice field, we watched them for half an hour. It was brutally hot, and we soon sought shelter in the air-conditioned football museum. With some time left, we toured Packers Stadium before Millie and Nancy picked us up.

The next morning, we went on to Galena, Illinois, a quaint old town where we had lunch and went on a historical bus tour before crossing the Mississippi River into Iowa. After the long distance we'd traveled, it seemed like a short drive to Elkader.

I had imagined the area would be flat with lots of corn. The reality was rolling hills with picturesque villages situated along meandering streams. Olson had already told us it was called "the 'driftless' area, as it was missed by the glaciers that flattened most of Iowa." There was certainly corn, but it mingled artfully with soybeans and other crops, forming a pattern of varying greens and browns against a cloudless, blue sky.

The Turkey River, not wide enough to have to "holler" across, split Elkader in two. Homes with well-kept gardens and lawns were testimonies to pride of ownership. A good-sized business district was made up of old buildings in good repair. The town's lone movie theater had a sign on the marquee saying, "Welcome to the C-47 Survivors."

The Olsons soon found us. They proudly showed us mementos and clothing they had received from the president of Algeria in 1984. While Olson was mayor of Elkader, he learned that the town had been named after Emir Abdel-Kader, the "George Washington" of Algeria. That led to a "sister city twinning," which in turn led to visits back and forth. It became an important public relations exchange and was an exciting time for the Olsons.

Ed Fox, traveling alone, made his appearance the next morning. The Montgomerys arrived mid-afternoon. Unbelievably, Huey, Jr. had brought twelve family members in his large van.

Tree planting at Elkader, July 29, 1999

The Olsons had reserved a large room at a local bank. It overlooked the river and dam. We used that room several times. A Saturday tree-planting ceremony was a highlight of the reunion. Young birch trees were spread out on both sides of a little stream in Elkader City Park. Ten were white birch, for the men who died in the crash, and six were river birch, for the survivors. Each tree had a brass tag attached to it, with the name of an individual. Jeremy Bossard, a Scout working on his Eagle badge, along with three other Scouts, had dug holes and made all the preparations ahead of time. Iowa State Representative Roger Thomas made an opening statement.

Taking in our activities in the background was Ray Farrell. I met him after the ceremony beside a big boulder near the high school athletic complex. He showed me several plaques he had engraved and attached to the boulder. They were all tributes to Elkader events. He said he wanted to engrave a plaque about our group. Olson would later write to say he had indeed "hammered out the plaque on stainless steel" in the shape of Alaska. It contained the same information as our plaques in Dayton and Alaska, plus a short story about the crash and tree planting. Elkader, thanks to Ray Farrell, has another lasting memorial to our visit.

Keith and Jan Betscher got there late Saturday after taking part in the seven-day Ragbrai, a 530-mile grueling bicycle race across Iowa. Most days had been 100 degrees or higher, and the cyclists were exhausted. They arrived just in time to join the whole gang at a local ice cream parlor.

We sat for nearly an hour in the old seats at the restored Opera House, absorbing the mystique that still clings to the walls. The multitalented Montgomery youngsters caught the spirit and gave us an impromptu performance that had us in stitches. People in Elkader have a sense of their history and are doing what they can to preserve it. As might be expected, the Olsons are at the forefront of the movement.

Several people had asked about the status of the documentary being produced by Drummer Boy Productions. In a business session on Saturday, I voiced my concerns about the project. Early in 1999, email from Paul Boese had indicated that they were planning a "premiere," likely to take place in March. A location was to be decided. They were to let me know soon, but I'd heard nothing after that.

"The way I see it," I said, "it's been three years since the first reunion. It's old news now."

Two of our own projects were initiated that day. I was asked by the reunion group to contact Bill Kiger, Alaska Natural Resource Officer for the Division of Parks and Outdoor Recreation. He had been present at the ceremony in Alaska the summer before, and stated that he'd work to see the display at the Veterans Memorial Park made historically correct. Our group wanted an update on the project. I would, soon after my return home, send him a letter. He'd phone in short order to say the changes had been made, and had, in fact, been in place for nearly a year.

Ed Fox suggested the other project.

"We need to get some recognition for Cliff Hudson," he said as we were winding up the business part of our reunion. "Don Sheldon was recognized by the Air Force, according to his book, and I don't understand why Cliff wasn't. He found us, for God's sake!"

The group commissioned Fox and me to investigate and, if possible, to begin the process to honor Hudson. Fox said that he'd write a letter to the Secretary of the Air Force. I wasn't sure, at that point, how I was going to proceed, but promised to give it thought. As it turned out, the project would be one of the things of which I'm most proud. I have no doubt that Fox feels the same way.

Chapter Forty

Later that summer, we had word that Andy Knapp had died. Millie and I had visited the Knapps the year before and had met many family members, including Andy. It had been Andy with whom I'd made initial contact before the first reunion. He had endured a lengthy illness.

By the end of the year, I started looking for ways to honor Cliff Hudson. It was long overdue, something I'd known in my heart but had failed to accept with my head. He needed recognition for his part in the 1954 rescue—more than just a change on a poster. Moreover, it was up to us to do something about it. Fox knew it, too. In his no-nonsense fashion, he had jolted the survivor group into action. Hudson was along in years and not in the best of health. That we shouldn't delay was the unanimous message that night on the banks of the Turkey River. When Fox and I "volunteered" to initiate the process, I didn't have the least idea how to start.

Nevertheless, on January 17, I composed a letter to Alaskan Senator Frank Murkowski. I told the straightforward story of the crash and Hudson's part in the rescue. At the end of the letter, I appealed for help. On January 27, I had an answer from the senator's Alaska office:

Mr. Pratt,
    Your request for recognition for Cliff Hudson was referred to me. It was certainly fascinating and I'm happy to work on it for you on behalf of Senator Murkowski.
    I know the Air Force will be asking for lots of back-up material, as they don't give out awards easily. Do you have anything? Are there other people, especially your fellow sur-

vivors, with whom you have kept in contact that may be able to support your account of the incident? Please send me their names, addresses, and phone numbers . . . If I have the opportunity, I will look up the accident in the newspaper archives and talk to some of the old bush pilots. The Air Force archivist should have information as well.

Patricia Heller, State Director

I quickly supplied her with every bit of supporting evidence I had and assured her that the other survivors would cooperate in any way they could.

About mid-February, a telephone call came from Lt. Col. Mark Avery in the Alaska Command. He asked numerous questions about the accident and about Hudson's part in the rescue. It was encouraging that they had started an investigation. Most such requests, he said, don't get that far. He would exchange information with the senator's office and they'd call me. A couple of weeks later, Pat Heller did call to say there were some final details to iron out, but that it looked good.

On March 16, Col. Avery called again.

"It's been approved by the Alaskan Air Command," he said.

"It's really going to happen, then!"

"It is. It looks as if it's going to be a high award, although that part isn't definite. It still needs approval by higher Air Force officials."

"Can you tell me about the award?"

"If it's approved, it will likely be the Air Force Exceptional Service Award. We won't waste any time. It would be awarded in about thirty days."

"Where?" I asked.

He explained that they'd been talking to the State Park Service. Veterans Memorial Park would be an appropriate place to present the medal.

"I want to be there!" I said.

"I thought you might. I'll let you know as soon as I hear anything."

On March 31, Pat Heller wrote to confirm that General Thomas Case had indeed recommended the Exceptional Service Award for

Hudson and that the recommendation was being sent to higher command. She further stated:

> . . . nothing has been mentioned about this to Cliff or his family, and no plans have been initiated for any kind of ceremony—I welcome your suggestions and I'm sure the Air Force would go along with it. My boss will be in Anchorage June 1 and it would be nice if we could involve him along with General Case . . .

I immediately went to the Internet and searched for something about the Exceptional Service Award. I found that it's awarded to civilians for "exceptional services to the Department of the Air Force or for an act of heroism involving voluntary risk of life." The act had to be "voluntary" and performed as a public service. It's comparable to the Distinguished Service Medal given to Armed Services members.

Pat Heller and I sent messages back and forth for several days to sort out minor details, one of them being a date for the ceremony. Millie was teaching until the end of June and couldn't travel before then. I wasn't sure how much influence I had in suggesting a date, but I did let it be known that I'd like to hold off until July. I didn't hear anything for a long time. Millie was getting anxious about making travel plans, so at the end of May, I emailed Pat. She wrote back to say the secretary of the Air Force had signed the award. She suggested July 7 or 8 for the ceremony. We bought our tickets and made reservations that day. The next day, Pat sent another message to confirm July 7. The senator, however, would be unable to attend.

I soon learned that the plan to have the award ceremony at Veterans Memorial Park had been scrapped and that the Air Force was looking at Talkeetna—especially at a new lodge that had a large terrace with an unobstructed view of Denali.

When our reunion group members learned about the award, several sent congratulatory letters for me to carry to Hudson. Tech Sergeant Angel Newman, from Elmendorf Air Force Base, was helping organize the event at Talkeetna. After she called me, I sent the letters to her to be included in a display case that Hudson could keep.

"We're going to make this a great event for Mr. Hudson," she promised.

Ollie had been informed about the award and was doing a delicate balancing act between keeping it a secret from Hudson and letting the rest of Talkeetna know.

On June 8, Millie and I experienced, for the first time, the joy of being grandparents. Jon and Bobbi had been home for Christmas and had broken the good news of the coming event. Throughout all the planning for the affair in Alaska, we were also anxiously waiting for news from Berkeley. When it finally came, our first thought was that we should head straight west, but we soon realized the optimum plan was to combine a visit there with the Alaska trip. Anyway, the parents probably needed some quality time alone with Elizabeth Milla—or "Lizzie," as they were affectionately calling her.

There were other things happening that extraordinary spring. Millie had decided to retire from teaching. That, with the resultant party and other honors, caused me to gasp. The passage of time since the beginning of our teaching careers seemed extremely short.

We saw quite a bit of Greg that spring, too. A trip to New Jersey usually consisted of a drive down on Friday, dinner out, a ride into New York City on Saturday, and breakfast Sunday morning before the four-hour drive home. He was doing well.

The documentary was dead. I had suspected that for the past year, but it was the lack of an answer to my inquiring letter that extinguished hope. I was disappointed, of course, but more than that, I was saddened by the loss that must have been felt by the filmmakers. They had put enormous time, energy, and love into it. Still, an explanation would have been welcomed.

Tragedy struck without warning. I read about it first on a news website, then had it confirmed by a message from Pat Heller. While taking off from a glacier, Hudson Air Service Chief Pilot Don Bowers had been killed, along with three young park rangers. Pat said that, although "the mood was somber," Ollie wanted to go ahead with the ceremony.

For days, I couldn't stop thinking about Don Bowers. He'd been our pilot in the flyover of the crash site in 1998. I had two copies of his book, *Back of the Pack*,[64] one of them autographed with a personal message. His Iditarod card was stuck on the outside of my filing cabinet. Once again, I had cause to ponder the reality of accidental death. Four people, just doing their jobs, were now gone. Flying in Alaska was still dangerous, and I had great admiration for those with the skill and courage to undertake it.

Chapter Forty-one

When Millie and I arrived in Talkeetna on the morning of July 7, we found Fox eating breakfast at the Roadhouse. He'd arrived the night before. If Hudson thought it strange that both of us should appear without warning, he didn't say anything. Ollie had been able to monitor mail and steer him away from situations where he might find out about the award. It was a masterful job, considering that, at the same time, she had to communicate with the Air Force, Senator Murkowski's office, and us.

Hudson picked up the three of us in his car. The "Hudson tour" was something he insisted on each time we visited. As we inched over the dirt streets for the next hour, he told us about each house, and talked a few minutes with everyone we met. Even the animals received his attention. If a dog barked at Hudson, he barked back. He startled a stray cat down by the river when he stopped the car, stuck his head out the window, and emitted a bloodcurdling screech, sending the feline for cover.

Millie and I looked at each other with amusement. The bed and breakfast owner where we stayed the first night after our arrival had told us a story about Hudson.

"One of his friends out in the bush had had an infestation of rodents and wanted a cat delivered, if that was possible," she said.

She went on to say that there was no landing strip nearby and Hudson always dropped supplies near the cabin. One day, a padded sack landed close to the doorstep. When the man opened it, there were two cats in the bag, a little shook up, but otherwise unhurt.

"The strange thing was," she said, "one of Hudson's neighbors went missing two cats about that time."

The ceremony was scheduled for three o'clock at the Alaskan

Lodge. Ollie, Fox, and I were scheduled to meet some Air Force people at the hangar at about twelve-thirty. We made some excuses to leave Hudson as soon as we got back to their house.

Ollie helped us out.

"Dad," she said. "Don't forget that we have a birthday party to go to up at the lodge this afternoon."

It was the excuse she was using to get him to the ceremony, but she had confided that it was a shaky one at best. Hudson had wanted to know whose birthday it was and she had put him off with "oh, you know—what's his name."

"Guess I'll have to change into something better," Hudson said. "You're all invited. If I'm invited I guess I can bring *my* friends too."

We drove to the hangar with Fox and Ollie, where we met four military personnel: Tech Sergeant Angel Newman, the only one I knew; Chief Master Sergeant Jon Hake, from the 11th Air Force Command; Tech Sergeant Tom Helbling, with the 11th AF Commander's Action Group; and Col. Dan Bonney, Chief of Staff for the Alaskan Command.

They briefed us on the ceremony, its steps, and where we'd be seated. When General Case arrived before the ceremony, he'd go to a room reserved for him. Then, when Hudson came in at two-thirty, he'd be escorted to General Case's room, where he'd be told about the award and briefed on the procedure.

On the way back to our cars, Sergeant Newman showed us the letter exhibit she had prepared for public viewing. She'd made copies for the exhibit and put the originals into a permanent folder for Hudson to keep. Fox and I had been asked to speak, and I'd been asked to read portions of the letters.

Millie and I went to the lobby at two-fifteen. The terrace, just outside, was set up for the ceremony with about a hundred chairs arranged in half-circle rows. Already, a few people were sitting there. It was a clear day with some haze in the background. Denali was a ghost-like image to the northwest.

Several military personnel introduced themselves. Among them was Lt. Col. Mark Avery, the Air Force officer I had talked to several times on the telephone. He introduced us to Major Les A. Kodlick,

Director of Public Affairs, and Staff Sergeant Jerome Tayborn, from the 3rd Communications Squadron. Major Kodlick was to be narrator for the ceremony. Sergeant Tayborn, a military photographer, was already busy snapping pictures. Lt. Col. Sue Stice, Assistant to the Joint Staff Secretariat, news media escort and liaison officer, soon joined us.

We chatted awhile before Col. Avery said, "There's General Case coming in the door right now."

General Thomas Case walked directly to us, flanked by two other high-ranking officers. My awe of high rank wasn't dead and I fought down an impulse to snap-to. I stuck out my hand instead.

"General Case, I'm Rupert Pratt. Thank you, sir, for being here for this event."

His eyes were soft, as was his voice.

"It's my pleasure. I'm honored to meet you," he said.

I introduced Millie and we all talked for a few minutes before he took leave to go to the room prepared for him. We went out onto the terrace, where Ed Fox was talking to Peter Porco, an *Anchorage Daily News* reporter. An Air Force videographer, A1C Demarrio Spence, from the 3rd Communications Squadron, was also there. I took turns with them and gave an interview to Channel 11.

Just after that interview, an attractive woman walked up to me.

"I'm Pat Heller," she said.

I had imagined her being older. I'd been impressed by her competence in dealing with all the issues involved in initiating and coordinating the preparations for the day, and I told her so.

Nearly all the seats were filled by that time. Ollie's communication system had worked superbly. Sergeant Newman started rounding us up. Millie, Ed Fox, and I were led to the front row to sit among the dignitaries. Sergeant Helbling was Ollie Hudson's special escort. I could see the medal lying on a bright purple pillow on the terrace ledge nearby. We arose as Major Kodlick announced General Case. The general came forward to be seated. Then a cheer came from the back, and swelled as Hudson entered the terrace. It took him several minutes to get to the front because so many people wanted to shake his hand. He lingered with each of them to chat a moment. Finally, he and Ollie were seated next to General Case.

Fox was sitting next to me.

He nudged me and said, "I'm getting nervous. I hope I can just say my piece and get through it."

Confidently, I offered advice.

"Just talk to them like you're talking to a group of friends. You'll be all right."

Tech Sergeant Judi Waters, an Air Force Band of the Pacific vocalist, sang the National Anthem and Alaska's state song. Major Kodlick made the opening statements and introductions.

Then it was my turn to speak. When I reached the podium, I caught the expression on Hudson's face. His emotions seemed near the surface. I sensed that he was still in disbelief. For a moment, my knees went weak as the significance of the moment fully dawned on me. I thought of the glib advise I'd just given Fox, and had to take a moment to compose myself.

I gave a brief account of the rescue efforts of February 5–7, 1954. Most of my remarks were for Hudson, and I tried to look directly at him as I talked. Then I read parts of some of the letters from the survivors and paraphrased others. From Eli LaDuke's letter, I read:

> . . . I was the one who shot flares into the sky to catch your attention. We had found some flares and smoke bombs in the wreckage of the plane. I had no idea how high you were or how high the flares would go. I recall you saying that one of the flares almost hit you . . . Why did it take us and/or the military so long to give you this recognition?

From Ed Olson's letter:

> I wish I could be with you to tell you this in person, but I can't. I hope this message will still carry some meaning when we say thanks for being there for us in the mountains when we really needed help. We are privileged to send our warmest congratulations to you for the much-deserved honors that you are receiving from the U.S. Air Force.

Forty-six years have passed since the ill-fated C-47 went down in the foothills of Mt. McKinley and a lot of snow has fallen and melted since you discovered the first survivors there. Hopefully you feel that the lives you saved were dedicated to serving others much like you have done.

I talked about Dr. Russell and his part in the rescue and referred the audience to his letter on the board in the back. I didn't read from my own letter or from Fox's, but mentioned that they were on the board.

I ended by reading a short letter that Jonathan had written to Hudson.

"Not because he's my son," I said, "but because it sums up much of *my* feelings, and, I believe, the feelings of the other survivors."

I suppose that most people don't have the time or the inclination to think through all the effects that their actions might have on the future. Computers can do that, but people don't. And the good ones don't need to: when a need arises, they recognize it and help, without knowing just where their actions will lead.

Yet once in a while we do get to see the fruit of our action. When you got into your plane back in 1954 to look for the wreckage of a downed C-47 you probably had no idea whether you would find any survivors. As it turned out, you helped save my father's life that day. I wasn't to be born for another eighteen years, but here I am now, older than my father was when you rescued him, married and with a newborn child of my own. I can't help but think that what you did that day, whether you realized it or not, was part of God's providence. Thank you, Cliff, for the role you played in it.

Fox spoke next.

Looking directly at Hudson, he said, "I had forty-six years more of life because of you. I wish I could say I did something great with my life. I wish I could say I got a bachelor's degree or invented a cure for cancer. I think what I did with my life was make up for a lack of life for the guys who died. I've been all over the place—and done everything—just had a really, really, happy life."

General Case rose and stated that he was honored to take part in such a special event.

"A celebration of a great American!" he said. Then he added, "A great Alaskan!"

He went on to praise Hudson for spending a lifetime in the air over Alaska, and for "sharing this great wonderful state and serving others in so many, many ways."

His voice took on a special tone of earnestness as he leaned toward Hudson.

"Sometimes events happen that leave an indelible mark—as did the events of that February day in 1954. You gave no thought at all of your personal safety. You saw what needed to be done and went right to it—and got the job done. And because of that, six Americans are alive."

I glanced over at Hudson. His eyes were moist as the General continued.

"I'm pleased to participate in this awarding of the Air Force Exceptional Service Award—and we're going to make that official. Mr. Hudson—I ask you to come and join me here."

We all stood as Hudson went forward to be presented with one of the Air Force's highest awards. I had hoped he'd be asked to speak, and was happy when he moved to the podium. In typical Hudson fashion, he started by addressing the weather issue.

"It wasn't bad, really. I was chopping ice off my wings."

That contradiction brought scattered laughter from the audience, which contained many fellow aviators.

Hudson told how he and Don Sheldon came to ride together the day after the crash.

"He said we might find somebody. He didn't know I'd already spotted the other people. I got in the plane against my better relations, I guess."

That brought more laughter from the crowd. Talkeetnans are well aware of the friction that had existed between Hudson and Sheldon.

General Thomas Case presenting Cliff Hudson with
the Air Force Exceptional Service Award, July 7, 2000
Photograph by Sgt. Jerome Tayborn, 3rd Communications Squadron

Hudson added with a chuckle, "It goes way back!"

He went on to tell about spotting our tracks and reaching us on
the ground, of the doctor arriving, of the night spent at the makeshift
camp, and of our Sunday morning departure. Then he spoke of the
helicopter picking him up.

"We went up on the hill there to get the first three that I'd
found—the ones who dang near set my wing on fire."

His tone became more serious.

"Flying is something I've always loved to do. I'm really amazed—
and thankful—for all the Air Force has done for me and my wife."

After the ceremony, Hudson mingled with the crowd. It was a
time of celebration. I was so busy that I almost missed seeing the cake
before it was cut. Written on the large, white, rectangular dessert was:
"I probably could get more money hauling tourists, but I still have

people out in the bush who need service." I believe the quote was from a magazine article about Hudson from several years before.

I had noticed several familiar faces in the crowd. Jon and Kathy Reynolds, owners of the Gold Pan B & B, had promised to attend—and they did. Dave Johnston was there as the representative of Denali State Park—and as a friend. I looked for Pat Heller. I wanted to talk to her some more—but she had left.

The Air Force people said their goodbyes. Many townspeople lingered on and around the lodge terrace, talking and reminiscing about Hudson and his exploits. We arranged with Fox and the Hudsons to have dinner in the lodge restaurant. I caught Dave Johnston just as he was leaving and invited him to join us—along with his wife, Cari, and son, Galen.

Dinner was pleasant. Cari, pretty and gracious, was an elementary school teacher, so she and I had plenty to share. Galen, an eleven-year-old, full of life and enthusiasm, showed us respect in a manner beyond his years. We talked well into the evening.

The next day was the start of Talkeetna's Moose Dropping Festival weekend. Ed Fox treated Millie, Hudson, and me to breakfast at the Roadhouse. We were momentarily repulsed by round pellets of "too real" moose droppings topping our eggs.

Fox was going to take Hudson over to Veterans Memorial Park later in the morning, since neither of them had seen the new display. We decided to join them, even though it hadn't been in our plans. Once there, we were reluctant to leave. We didn't know when we'd see Hudson again. He was still on a high from the day before, proudly wearing the lapel version of his award on his jacket. We finally said our goodbyes and headed south.

We stayed that night with the Mooneys in their lovely new home overlooking Cook Inlet. The following day, we all toured the nearby village of Eagle River, which was also celebrating the widely revered moose. Pat left at 4 PM for a flying adventure and we spent a good part of that evening with Sara before heading to Anchorage to turn in the car and catch our midnight flight.

We were surprised when Ed Fox appeared at the airport to see us off. He was leaving the following morning. We spent a couple of quality hours together before boarding the airplane that would take us to Berkeley to see our new granddaughter.

Would we see Hudson again? I'd noticed a subtle change in his behavior. He forgot names a lot and seemed to struggle to organize his thoughts. I wanted to be positive, but as we took off, my thoughts on the matter turned as dark as the mountains in the dusk-dawn off our left wingtip.

Chapter Forty-two

Near the end of August, I had an adventure of a different kind, one altogether unfamiliar to me. While in California, I had tried to continue my regular exercise pattern, walking a mile or two every day. I'd walk up Delaware Street each morning to pick up a newspaper near the BART station. It was uphill to the station, but not a steep grade. I had difficulty breathing by the time I reached the top, and each day even more so. Once we got back home, it was discovered that I needed angioplasty. I had little difficulty with the procedure and almost no pain. My recovery was uncomplicated. In six weeks, my cardiologist placed me back on an exercise routine.

Jon, Bobbi, and Lizzie came to Scotia for the two weeks of Jon's Christmas break, bringing Bobbi's parents with them. Petko and Milka were visiting them for three months. Millie and I extended the friendship we'd begun with them in Bulgaria, and although we spoke no more than a half-dozen words of each other's language, we managed quite well with Jon and Bobbi acting as translators. Greg was with us for three days at Christmas, making it a glorious family holiday.

Keith Betscher called us one day in January to say that he and Jan were about to become adoptive parents. I hadn't heard such excitement in his voice since we'd been together on Kesugi Ridge. It was late March when we got word that Nicole had been born on March 11.

With Tom and Nancy assisting, we began preparing early in 2001 for that year's reunion, which was to be in Scotia. In all fairness, Millie did most of the work. She has a knack for that sort of thing and seems to enjoy it. We had decided to hold the reunion in June, instead of July, as had been the custom.

As in the past, most of our time together was during meals. We did make suggestions for area events, museums, and activities. We'd learned to not schedule things too close together. Time for relaxation was important.

The Knapps had missed the Iowa reunion but made this one, all except the younger John. Dr. Russell came from Virginia, accompanied by his wife, Nancy. Eli LaDuke was there with his wife, Ginger. The LaDukes were combining the reunion with a trip to Au Sable Forks. Joyce Klodnicki came with Ed Fox. The Montgomerys had a significant presence, with three teens accompanying Huey, Jr., Sherri, and Minnie. I was pleased that Greg was able to attend a reunion for the first time. Peter Spoor, a longtime friend, was present for some events. Altogether, forty-two people attended.

Our initial meeting took place at Scotia United Methodist Church, where Millie and I are members. Hot weather didn't keep us from enjoying ourselves in the Fellowship Room as we ate lunch and caught up on family news. Some of us even braved the heat that afternoon to visit the Empire State Aerosciences Museum a couple of miles away.

That evening, we had dinner at the Turf Tavern in Scotia. It was our largest gathering, since we'd invited a few of our own friends. Town supervisor Clarence Mosher and his wife, Jackie, officially welcomed the visitors to Scotia and the Town of Glenville. Also present were the Rev. Janice Rowell and her husband, David; Ralph and Sandy Mason; Bill and Ruth Holman; Sid and Doris Brown; and Pat Parisi.

We were honored by the attendance of Clarence Dart and his wife. Dart, a resident of Saratoga Springs, was one of the original

Huey Montgomery, Jr., Rupert Pratt, Ed Fox, Eli LaDuke
2001 reunion in Scotia, New York

Reunion dinner in Scotia—Rupert Pratt, Greg Pratt,
Joyce Klodnicki, Ed Fox

Tuskegee Airmen. He held us spellbound for forty-five minutes with flying stories from World War II.

LaDuke said to me after dinner, "There's a real hero. What happened to us, bad as it was, was an accident. Those men put themselves in harm's way voluntarily."

Breakfast at the Pratts' on Saturday morning was a laid-back affair. We watched a video of Cliff Hudson's medal presentation and then sat around talking. Saturday evening, we ate at the Century House and discussed a possible trip to Alaska in 2004, the fiftieth anniversary of the airplane crash. Several people expressed an interest. The Montgomerys volunteered to host the 2003 reunion in Evansville.

The finale was a Sunday morning brunch at the Gideon Putman Hotel in Saratoga Springs. Most of the DeVito family joined us, including their son, Dean, with his two daughters, Natalie and Breanna. Kim, Dean's wife and the mother of the two girls, was ill and couldn't attend. Tom and Nancy's daughter, Diane Stuto, with husband, Pete, brought their triplets, Jocelyn, Caroline, and Sam. As always, parting was a bittersweet experience, but we immediately began looking forward to Evansville.

For me, a real bonus of the Scotia reunion was getting to know Dr. Carl Russell better. Sheldon and Hudson were recognized as principals in our rescue. Russell, however, also played a vital role in getting us back to "military control."

He had grown up in small towns within a fifty-mile radius of Chattanooga, and was drafted into the Army in 1943. He earned his MD from Yale in 1949, at which time he accepted a commission in the Army.

The Korean War started about the time he finished his internship, and instead of being able to start his residency, Russell was sent there. Due to that circumstance, and other unforeseen events, he wasn't able to return to residency until after his duty in Korea, Japan, Alaska, and Lake Charles, Louisiana. He remained in the service for a full twenty years, retiring in 1966. During his military years, he was variously a general duty officer, flight surgeon, and radiologist.

While serving at Elmendorf as a flight surgeon, Dr. Russell had been on several rescue missions. His wife, Virginia, had sent the big jug of coffee for the three distressed men in the wilds of Alaska, an act that I remember with a great deal of appreciation. Their daughter, Debra, had been born in Alaska.

After retirement from the military, he and Virginia moved to Roanoke, Virginia, where he joined the Lewis-Gale Clinic. He worked there as a radiologist for twenty years. Dr. Russell retired from civilian practice in 1986.

Virginia died of leukemia in 1990, and he later married Nancy, one of her friends. In retirement, Russell has taken up watercolors. Millie and I treasure a print of one of his Roanoke Valley paintings, *Sycamores on a Country Lane*, which hangs in a prominent place in our home.[65]

The two intervening years between reunions were eventful. Millie had to have a kidney stone removed. Just as blocked arteries had sneaked up on me, she too was surprised by her vulnerability. She managed just fine, with few aftereffects. Sitting in the hospital waiting room, however, was more stressful for me than having my own procedure the year before.

As I waited, my thoughts focused on our years together and of the times we'd shared. Our love was meant to be, we figured, and that belief led to our marriage in 1956. Our two years in West Virginia had been a great adventure. We lived in Huntington, where she worked as a billing clerk at Foster-Thornburg, a hardware wholesaler, and took classes at Marshall College.[66] I earned my bachelor's degree, got a teaching position at Peyton School in the Cabell County School District, and took night and summer courses toward my master's degree. We spent many weekends at Salt Rock, enjoying country life. Money was tight. When our 1953 Ford blew its engine, it cost over two hundred dollars to replace, an expense from which it took us months to recover.

Even with those difficulties, we were happy. Our world consisted of each other and a few close friends. It was then, with reluctance, that we decided to move to Schenectady. It was a purely financial decision. I would teach, and Millie would attend the State University of New York at Albany.

Her college years flew by while I immersed myself in my career. In 1964, she also attained a teaching position in the Schenectady City School District. Within a year, she had earned a master's degree.

Desiring to broaden our educational experiences, we decided in 1969 to apply for teaching positions in a foreign country. We traveled to New York City to meet with an administrator from an American school in Iran. We were ready to accept three-year positions there when an unforeseen event changed our plans—and our lives—forever. Millie was pregnant.

We had wanted children, but as the years passed, we had to embrace the notion that we might never be parents. However, on the last day of 1970, Gregory arrived. Less than two years later, Jonathan joined his brother in our household. We then proceeded through the mostly joyful, but sometimes difficult years of raising children and saw them off to college, Greg to the Rochester Institute of Technology, and Jon to Princeton. Our empty nest had some sadness attached to it, but only briefly, for once again she and I had quality time for each other. Our love brought us closer together, as it had in the beginning. When I saw her, groggy, but returned to health, I was profoundly grateful for her life and for our years together.

I went out to California alone near the end of August to take care of Lizzie while her parents worked and studied. They had recently moved from a residential rental home in Berkeley to University Village, the Berkeley graduate housing complex in Albany. I got up early each morning to walk up Marin Street and back before Jon and Bobbi left the apartment. On the morning of September 11, I had just returned when Jon met me at the door. He seemed to be in shock.

"Dad," he said, "come and see this. You won't believe what's happening."

On the TV screen were the burning World Trade Center towers. I watched in horror at what was happening. The announcer was saying something about two airplanes hitting them. My legs started trembling so much I had to sit down. We watched for the next hour as both towers burned and collapsed. Finally, Jon had to leave. He had to teach a class, and to his knowledge, it hadn't been cancelled.

I watched over Lizzie as best I could that day. We went to a little playground, as was our custom. It was usually packed with children, parents, and grandparents. That day, however, we were the only people there. There seemed to be little activity in the whole village. The world seemed to have stopped. I now have trouble recalling exactly what I felt that day. Whatever it was, it was fueled by anger. The needless loss of life stunned me at my soul level. Sitting on a bench, I wanted to pray, but couldn't. Prayer and my anger seemed incompatible.

"Grandpa—" Lizzie said, reaching up to me.

Young as she was, she sensed something was wrong. I picked her up and held her in my arms for a long time.

News came from Alaska in 2002, some bad, some good. I had suspected, even when we were there for Cliff Hudson's award, that he might be experiencing some dementia. Ollie's call confirmed my suspicions. Cliff was going into an assisted living facility in Anchorage. He had Alzheimer's, and it had advanced rapidly.

In November, a 7.9 earthquake hit South Central Alaska. There was little damage, except for some huge craters in roads. Later, a newspaper story said that if the quake had occurred in a metropolitan area, damage would have been extensive and many lives would have been lost.

Another piece of news came through *Alaska* magazine. Dave Johnston had scaled Denali again, taking Cari and Galen with him. Galen became the youngest person to accomplish that feat.

Jon and Bobbi seemed to appreciate our help in caring for Lizzie, so Millie and I took alternate trips to Berkeley for a few months. Millie's father, Floyd Mereness, was in a nursing home in Glenville, near us. He'd lived alone for eighteen years on the Great Sacandaga Lake after Marguerite's death, but at the age of ninety-six, Floyd had grown unable to care for himself. Millie's sister, Marion Kverek, and her husband, Dick, made the trip from Wappenger Falls many times while Millie was away, and I helped however I could. Floyd died in April, 2003. Our second grandchild, Nathan Rupert, was born May 20. Of course, we had to make a trip together to see him.

Reunion time arrived again. The 2003 C-47 Crash Family Reunion in Evansville, Indiana, was another smashing success. The Montgomerys planned and carried it off in grand style. The rest of the large Montgomery clan was there with big hearts and warm smiles.

Millie and I had planned to drive to Evansville with the DeVitos, but as the time approached, the four of us looked at the distance, blinked, and decided to fly. It was a good choice. We left Albany at 6 AM and had breakfast at a Cracker Barrel in Evansville. People started arriving Thursday afternoon. Eli and Ginger LaDuke had stayed overnight in Louisville and had driven over that morning. Ed Fox and Joyce Klodnicki appeared early afternoon. John and Betty Knapp pulled in around three o'clock. By that time, the motel staff had started cooking hamburgers and hot dogs next to the pool, as prearranged by the Montgomerys. At four o'clock, they arrived, four generations of them, along with other friends and relatives, and of course, more food. It was hot outside, so we moved into a conference room around a large table. The evening had a great sense of family, with everyone just talking and catching up. Later, I set up my laptop computer and displayed a slideshow of photographs from the previous reunions. Huey Montgomery III, a student at the University of Evansville and talented young man, showed off some of his outstanding artwork to the group.

Friday morning, Huey and Sherri came to the motel and picked us all up for a tour of the historical Reitz House and Museum in downtown Evansville. Keith, Jan, and Nicole Betscher arrived that afternoon. Keith and Jan had kept us updated on Coley's progress since her birth, but we were unprepared for the charming two-year-old we met that day. In fact, two very young children were present that weekend. Yasmine, Brandi Nagi's daughter, also won our hearts. That evening, we dined at the Homestead Restaurant.

Saturday afternoon, Huey and Sherri had the whole group at their new home. We ate and played games in the spacious backyard. Saturday evening's meal was at the Executive Inn in downtown Evansville. We were pleased that the LaDukes' son, Alan, his wife, LeAnna, and their daughter, Danielle, were able to attend the dinner. They'd been on an Alaskan cruise and were on their way home to Cincinnati. Sixteen-year-old Danielle quickly became friends with the children who were present. At the end of the evening, Brandi Nagi brought tears to our eyes singing "Wind Beneath My Wings" to the three survivors present and surprising us with gifts and roses.

Huey Montgomery gravesite, 2003 reunion at Evansville, Indiana

Sunday morning, we drove out to Huey's church at Boonville. For Millie and me, it was our second time there. From Boonville, our group went caravan-style to the cemetery north of Evansville where Huey, Sr. is buried. We placed flowers on his grave and spent more than an hour remembering Huey and saying our farewells to one another.

A question had been troubling me for some time: What was to be the future of our group? I'd seen a couple of long-standing West Virginia family reunions terminate simply because the older people died and the younger members didn't make an effort to plan events. I realized that would be the eventual fate of all but the most famous of family groups, and probably of our C-47 Survivor family as well. I'd been wondering if there wasn't already an erosion of interest. However, I was delighted by the voices calling for a 2005 reunion. Encouraged by Eli and Ginger, Alan and LeAnna volunteered to be hosts for a gathering in Cincinnati. The Betschers said they'd help in any way they could.

We also continued discussion of the upcoming fiftieth anniversary-year Alaska trip and proposed trek to the crash site. The number of people wanting to go exceeded my expectations.

Chapter Forty-three

It was near the end of the year when I started serious planning for the Alaska trip. I sent letters to Dale Bingham, David Porter, and Dave Johnston, informing them of our plans to visit the crash site on July 28, 2004, and inviting them to go along. I also left messages on Pam Barnes's answering machine, since I wanted to explore the possibility of using her llamas again.

In March, I received a note from David Porter. He informed me that there had been a change in the guard. He and Bingham had retired. Dave Johnston was already retired when Millie and I were in Alaska in 2000, but I knew he still volunteered some of his time to the park. Porter and Bingham had passed along my letters to the new supervisor, Dennis Heikes, and to the new head ranger, Ryan Gosse.

I talked to Heikes first. He was supportive of our plan and said he would have a ranger accompany us. He would talk to Gosse, who'd deal with the particulars. Ryan called a few days later. He was ready to give his support in any way he could and would certainly like to go along. He also suggested an alternative—the use of a helicopter. Choppers are normally forbidden in the park, but they'd make an exception for us. I told him it was an idea I'd have to consider, partly because of expense, but mainly because he had informed me that we'd be limited to one hour on the ground at the site. I worried that it wasn't enough time.

I learned from Ryan that the old Ermine Hill Trail, some fifteen miles south of Little Coal Creek Trail, had been upgraded. It was little used in 1998 at the time of our first hike, largely due to a dangerously steep grade near the bottom. As I studied newer maps of the area, I noticed that Ermine Hill trailhead looked to be no farther from the crash site than Little Coal Creek trailhead. We'd had a good trip with

Pam and her llamas on that trail, but it had been problematic because the llamas could go no farther than the head of the creek. Looking at the Ermine Hill Trail map, it seemed as if we might be able to walk most of the way to the crash site in one day and back the next day, thereby evening out the distance. Even more tantalizing was the thought that the whole hike might be doable in one long day.

When Pam Barnes called back, I discussed all the options with her. As for her having a part, she agreed to look into that possibility, even though she'd scaled down her outfitting and guiding business. Getting her llamas up Ermine Hill Trail was a big question mark. A few days later, she called again to say that she'd decided not to contract with us. There were just too many expenses involved to make it practical. She had, however, made inquiries about a helicopter. That idea wouldn't go away, it seemed. The flight company, Era, had quoted a price of $265 per person, providing there were six passengers. Again, we'd have only one hour at the crash site. I relayed that information to the people who had expressed interest in the trip, asking their opinions. I had only one positive response, and decided not to pursue it.

A few days later, I received another call from Ryan Gosse. He was full of enthusiasm for the venture. I asked whether having a two-day window to allow for good weather conditions and for beginning the hike would be a problem. He assured me it wouldn't.

I also had a conversation with Dave Johnston. He estimated the distance from the Ermine Hill trailhead to the crash site to be only six miles. I suggested, hopefully, that we might be able to walk up and back the same day. He didn't sound optimistic about that, but promised to investigate trail conditions once the snow cleared out— and to give us his expert opinion.

I let it rest there, confident it would all work out. Should we have to stay overnight, we'd surely be able to acquire sleeping bags and tents in Alaska. The smell of spring was in the air before I sent Ed Olson a letter for the *Sentinel*, detailing possible scenarios.

There's no escaping the realization of our own vulnerability as we reach three score and ten years. Minor ills, at the least, are already plaguing many of us, even after decades of glowing health. Still, it comes as a solid blow to the spirit when one of our own is summoned home.

Eli LaDuke's son, Alan, called late on the evening of April 3, 2004. There was pain in his voice that radiated to my heart with the immediate and clear meaning of the call.

"Dad died this evening," he said. "I just got word from Mom a few minutes ago. I don't know any of the details yet."

"I'm sorry, Alan."

My mind raced to find other words, but they were too elusive.

"I'll send you email when I know about the arrangements."

Two days later, Alan wrote to say there would be a private service in Florida, but plans were also being made for a memorial service on May 29, in Peru, New York. Peru is between Plattsburg and Au Sable Forks, where Eli grew up. I promised to be there.

The DeVitos wanted to go, too, and we planned to make it a three-day trip, even though it was only a four-hour drive on the Northway. Tom and I had hiked the eight-mile Tongue Mountain trail a week before, with thoughts of increasing our endurance for the Kesugi Ridge hike coming up in July. We knew, however, that we needed more time on the trail to get in shape. If we left early Thursday morning on our way to the memorial service, we could get in a hike that day, stay overnight in Lake Placid, and leisurely continue on to Plattsburg on Friday. We'd have only a short drive to Peru Saturday morning. Knowing Eli, we felt that he'd approve of the plan.

It worked out pretty much that way. Tom and I climbed Prospect Mountain, following a six-mile round-trip trail out of Lake George Village. We were lost once while descending, due to inadequate trail markings, but eventually found our way down. Millie and Nancy, who'd been shopping to kill time, picked us up below the footbridge that crosses the Northway.

The weather was beautiful that day and the next. After we left Lake Placid, we passed through Au Sable Forks. In Peru, we stopped to see if we could find St. Patrick's Church. A waitress gave us directions. It seemed that the church wasn't really in Peru, but about ten miles out in the country. We found it without trouble, a small country church on a scenic road, a serene spot, suitable for the occasion.

The following morning, when we returned to the church, a large crowd of friends and family members had already gathered. The service was simple, but dignified. Eli's spirit seemed, literally, to permeate the sanctuary. I would liked to have had Fox, Olson, and Sallis in the pew with me. I knew they would have been there if they could have made it.

I had a particular feeling of gratitude that Eli and I had become closer over the past two years. We had, on the telephone, conversed at length about my writing of the crash. I had enlisted his help in putting together details of the ordeal of the three men at the crash site, since I hadn't been in that group. He had, in 1996, at our first reunion, shown some reluctance to speak about it. Now, he answered all my questions without hesitation. In addition, Eli and Ginger had for many years made an annual trip to New York to visit relatives. On their previous two trips, they had stayed overnight with us while on their way north. It was during that time that Eli shared the most intimate details about Kesugi Ridge.

After the memorial service, we attended a reception at the home of Ginger's sister in Peru. Friends and relatives shared many interesting and funny Eli stories that I hadn't heard before. Ginger candidly related circumstances of Eli's death. Being a retiree who couldn't really let go, he had worked part-time as a guard at a gated community. He also looked after the homes of residents who were away. It was in one of those homes that he collapsed and died. When he didn't show up for dinner, Ginger retraced his regimented steps until she found him. It had been quick, she said. She still had hurt in her eyes as we left, but there was a resolve there, too, and a promise that she'd keep in touch.

Although this isn't a book about my spiritual beliefs, the topic runs through it like an underground river. I don't intend to give a summary of my theological understandings, but I'd like to bring one thing to the surface for a brief examination—my urge to question.

I had questioned God in 1954 concerning the deaths of my friends, and I now had questions concerning Huey and Eli. Early in life, I'd been discouraged from questioning, a restriction I always had trouble with. My path had led me through doubts about God's relevance in my life, into a searching process that included some "alternative" groups and ideas, and finally back to the kind of simple faith I had experienced on the Johnnie Porter Hill. That faith was more mature now, and God was friendlier—and desirous of answering questions.

The "insights" I experienced on Kesugi Ridge in 1998 strengthened my faith and increased my conviction that we're a part of something much larger than is readily apparent. That belief helped me when Huey Montgomery and other friends died. Now, Eli's death was fresh on my mind. Therefore, the questions came again—and I suppose they are really questions of the ages: *What had their lives meant? Where were they? Were they aware?*

My faith requires me to believe that God always answers prayers—*and questions.* Nevertheless, that belief must be tempered with the realization that He doesn't reveal all (we couldn't begin to understand everything, anyway). The answer to my questions, given to me at my present level of understanding, is this: love—our love for Huey and Eli, and others, and theirs for us, is the meaning of their lives; and they have stepped through a door from our world into God's bigger reality—the same reality where I expect to find friends and relatives—and eventually the crew and passengers of a C-47 with the tail number 5895.

On June 1, Millie and I flew to Berkeley for a three-week visit with Jon and his family. I wanted to continue hiking while there, so Jon and I planned a trip to Mt. Diablo, which is out of the Bay Area and beyond the city of Walnut Creek. We underestimated the time it would take to get to Diablo State Park and ended up doing only a two-mile section of the trail; we failed to reach the peak. That was disappointing, but the experience was exhilarating, nonetheless. Unlike Adirondack hiking, where trees, more often than not, obscured the view, Mt. Diablo provided a panoramic vista. Nathan, too, enjoyed the hike from his father's back.

That day also provided an answer to a question. Since Jon had been in California, I had wanted to visit the site of Parks Air Force Base where I had embarked for Alaska in 1953. The only problem was that I hadn't been able to locate it. I did remember it being thirty or forty miles out of San Francisco and being near hills. A friend of Jon gave us a good clue, and we finally found it near Pleasanton, across the hills and south of Oakland off Interstate 680. It's now Parks Reserve Forces Training Area for the United States Army Reserve. We didn't try to go inside, but I did get a picture at Gate Four.

We planned another hike for our last week in California. Temperatures near the bay seemed to be perpetually moderate, but a few miles inland, it was a different thing entirely. With the mercury well into the nineties on our hike day, we called it off.

On returning to New York, we found Tom was undergoing physical therapy. He had complained of back pains on our previous hikes, but had seemed confident that he could work through the discomfort.

Now he said, "Rupe, I don't believe I'm going to be able to do it."

"Don't worry about it," I said, trying hard not to show my disappointment. Tom's presence on the 1998 hike had been such a positive thing that I hadn't imagined doing it again without him.

"You went with me the last time. It's not necessary to do it again. We'll still enjoy ourselves in Alaska."

I had thought the 1998 trip to Kesugi Ridge would be my last, but now, the "fifty-year itch" had infected me and I was looking forward to the *real* last return.

Therefore, I was disappointed when plans began to fall apart. One by one, those who had wanted to go were, for various good reasons, forced to cancel. A couple of weeks before our departure, I knew with certainty it would be only Tom and Nancy DeVito, Jon, Millie, and me going to Alaska. Greg was one of the casualties. That had been disappointing, but at least one of our sons would be accompanying us. Equally disappointing was Ed Fox's cancellation. In my mind's eye, I'd been imagining the two of us standing on top of the ridge, surveying the two great river valleys. Joyce was in the hospital, and commitment to the trip would be impossible for Ed.

Tom's back problem didn't improve. His doctor strongly suggested that he not climb any mountains. He was packing his hiking boots for the trip, anyway.

"Just in case," he said with a familiar, obstinate twinkle in his eye.

Nevertheless, I knew the likelihood was that it would just be Jon, the Denali Park ranger, and me going up the ridge. At first, I had thoughts of canceling the hike. We could go to Alaska with the DeVitos, meet Jon in Anchorage as planned, and tour around the state. After all, we had enjoyed perfect weather the last time. Why do it again, even if it was the fiftieth year? However, after giving it consideration, I concluded that I desperately wanted Jon to experience Kesugi Ridge. With Greg out of it for now, it fell to my younger son; he would, by default, become "keeper of the history," at least for that particular part of our family saga. I talked to Jon about the hike and it seemed important to him to see the site. That settled it for me, and plans went forward.

On July 7, I sent an email to Ryan Gosse, explaining the reduction in the number of participants. I asked about trail conditions. Would we be able to do the hike in one day? Ryan's answer was quick: an overnight would be necessary. He'd provide a tent and cooking gear. We'd only need to take sleeping bags and backpacks. I quickly agreed, relieved that the decision had been made.

That, however, didn't spare me from having some anxiety. I had tried to get into good shape. Tom and I had climbed two peaks and Millie had just recently hiked Buck Mountain with me. I noticed some deterioration in my walking, especially with balance. I had difficulty walking across logs and stepping from stone to stone in creeks.

A True Story of Tragedy and Reunion* *341*

I remembered that Kesugi Ridge trail had rock flows that had given us minor problems. Six years later, at age seventy-one, would I be able to handle that? Aerobically, I should have little difficulty. I could still climb at a steady pace. Angioplasty in 2000 seemed to have helped with that. Most of the time I felt confident, but on certain days when I closely analyzed my abilities, doubt assailed me.

On Sunday, July 25, Millie and I flew on United Airlines to Chicago, and from there to Anchorage. The DeVitos would follow the same route the next day. I had time on the flight to reflect on my Alaska experiences and to think about the days ahead. Despite the trauma I'd once experienced there, Alaska had remained for me a land of beauty and fascination. Kesugi Ridge, however, had required a transformation of viewpoint. In the beginning of this book, I mentioned my symbolic connection with hills and mountains. I guess that on some level, I'd come to recognize Kesugi, or "the mountain," as I called it, as a factor in my overall psyche, but I'd failed to examine that connection. My mountain experiences had been mostly pleasant.

Therefore, as a positive mountain experience, Kesugi had trouble measuring up. That, however, started to change in 1996, after our first reunion, when I finally returned to Alaska. On a bright and sunny day, I flew over the crash area, observing subtle fall colors covering what I had long considered barren peaks. Life was evident, even among the clusters of dark volcanic stone and glacier-strewn boulders. It made me start thinking of the ridge in an entirely new way. There, on foot in 1998, with Denali standing majestically in the west, Kesugi took on spiritual significance, giving me a glimpse of the bigger picture, just as the Johnnie Porter hill had many years before. The ridge moved from a dark place in my mind to a bright place in my heart. Now, as our jet took us on the journey toward Alaska, I looked forward to seeing Kesugi again.

Chapter Forty-four

We lodged that night in Anchorage at Lake Hood Inn, where we watched floatplanes begin their takeoff runs, practically under our window. The following day, Monday, we greeted Tom and Nancy at the airport early in the afternoon, and a couple of hours later, we met Jon coming in from San Francisco. After the DeVitos had picked up their rental car, we headed north, stopping only for dinner in Wasilla.

It was a good feeling to be back in Talkeetna, but Cliff Hudson's absence was a keenly felt distraction. His family had moved him from Anchorage to a nursing home in Palmer, which made it easier for them to see him.

Later, Tuesday morning, Ryan Gosse called, as had been prearranged. He wanted to meet with us at our cabin to discuss the trip to the crash site. In person, he lived up to my image of an Alaskan ranger, complete with sidearm. He was younger than I had imagined, twenty-seven, and married just two weeks. Kendra, his wife, was anxious to meet us, he said.

In his own good time, he told us that he had an idea, one to which he'd given lots of thought. He believed it could be the solution to our problem. We listened as he explained.

"The park has an arrangement with Era Helicopters," he said. "Their choppers hold six passengers in addition to the pilot. Tomorrow, if the weather cooperates, we'll take you all up there, courtesy of the State Park System. Maybe we'll be able to stretch out the time on the ground, too."

I mentally cheered as the implications of what Ryan was saying became clear. Tom would be able to make the trip he'd given up on. Nancy had wanted to go, too, but felt unable to make the climb.

Most of all, I had dreamed of having Millie see the site. Hope of that happening had become remote. Moreover, as much as I hated to admit it, it would be easier for me. It was a no-brainer.

"When you say 'if the weather cooperates,' what do you mean?" I inquired.

"Poor enough that the flight service isn't swamped with people wanting to charter flightseeing tours, but good enough to land on the ridge," Ryan said.

He went on to explain that Era had to put business first, and to have a pilot on the ground up there for an hour or two while customers were waiting wouldn't be profitable for them.

"I just want you to know that it's not a done deal, but right now the weather pattern looks favorable."

Later that day, we drove to Veterans Memorial Park. I wanted to get new pictures of the memorial site. The year before, David Porter had removed the propeller (the one we had found in 1998) from the crash site and made it a part of the memorial.

The weather co-operated, and the next morning, through broken clouds, we rode toward the high peaks of Kesugi. It took sixteen minutes from liftoff, a few miles north of Trapper Creek, to the area where most of the wreckage lay. Adrian Strutz, our pilot, asked me to locate the site, which I managed to do after a turn around the peaks. We descended slowly, at the edge of the saddle

Rupert, Millie, and Jonathan Pratt at Veterans Memorial Park, July 27, 2004

and adjacent to a dark wall of barren stones. Small pieces of jagged metal lay all around the chosen landing spot below us.

"I don't want to kick up any of that debris," Adrian said as we hovered, like a giant hummingbird, twenty feet above the surface. His eyes scanned the landscape before he started easing us down. We settled gently to the tundra.

It was unclear just how long we'd have on the ground, so we quickly exited the helicopter. Tom and I knew what to expect, but the others uttered words of surprise at the extent of scattered wreckage.

We moved out in twos and threes, examining bits and pieces of debris. Adrian stayed at my heels awhile, asking questions about the crash, since he'd known nothing about it before. Tom kept his camcorder rolling while Jon and I took photographs.

I was finding things that I hadn't seen on previous visits. One particularly stirring scene was of a deteriorating shoe, with a shoetree still in it. I couldn't help wondering whose baggage it had been torn from.

Eventually we separated, each finding our own points of interest, but generally staying within shouting distance of one another. As in 1998, I discovered things that challenged my idea of the passage of time. A hose, with clamps still on it, looked as if it might have been dropped there the week before. On a mountaintop, exposed to some of North America's harshest weather, one would have expected the deterioration to be more obvious. Jon found a whole window. The aluminum frame around the Plexiglas and the rubber gasket seemed little worn.

Clouds drifted in periodically, but overall, the weather wasn't bad. The wind wasn't much more than a whisper, unusual for there. Without wind, the silence was noticeable. I wondered how many people in today's complex society had ever experienced such quiet. Jon was never far from me.

After about an hour, he called to me, saying, "Do you know where you landed in your parachute?"

"Over in that direction, maybe a quarter mile," I said, indicating a knoll that lay to the south.

"The Saddle," looking north, July 28, 2004. Three
figures can be seen near the center of the picture.
Visible wreckage is on the right side.

We walked over a few rises until we could see a gully below us.
Beyond that, the Susitna Valley loomed through the clouds with the
familiar cut in the mountains near Gold Creek clearly visible. It took
some time, but I finally located a rock that I believed could be the
one behind which Fox, Olson, and I had taken shelter. I dug gingerly
into the soil to see whether I might find evidence of parachutes we'd
left there. Nothing. I wasn't one hundred percent sure we were in the
right place, although we couldn't have been off by much. We took
pictures of each other at the rock, anyway, before heading back up the
slope toward the others.

Adrian had become so engrossed with the fifty-year-old wreckage
that he let us stay on the ground nearly two hours. He finally used his
radio to let his headquarters know departure was imminent.

When it did come time to leave, Jon and I elected to walk down.
It seemed important to us—a macho thing, I guess. We had planned
it that way, and anticipated the challenge it presented. Even more
important to me, I wanted us to have the time together. We had

Pilot Adrian Strutz took this photograph of our group on Kesugi
Ridge, July 28, 2004—Ranger Ryan Gosse, Nancy DeVito, Millie
Pratt, Tom DeVito, Jon Pratt, Rupert Pratt

hiked and camped in Jon's growing up years, and that had brought us close. Now, even though our relationship is fine, I felt as if it was an ideal way to reconnect. I believe Jon felt it, too.

"Whatever you want to do," Ryan said. "We can ride home or hoof it. Either way, I'm with you."

We chose the hard way, and the three of us watched as the chopper climbed up and over the peaks and headed west toward the Chilitna.

I experienced a moment of frustration as I remembered that I had wanted to hold a little ceremony before the others left. In all the excitement, I had forgotten.

I said to Jon and Ryan, "I'd like for us to have a prayer before we start down."

We stood close together and I spoke a few simple words, asking God to bless the site, the survivors, and the families of the men who had died there. I struggled to find other words appropriate to the occasion, but they wouldn't come. Emotions, stronger than words, seemed to lock my tongue. All I could manage was "amen."

The walk down took more effort than I'd anticipated. It rained a couple of times early on and we became pretty well soaked. Daytime valley temperatures in the area had been hovering around seventy degrees, but on the ridge it was cooler, and as the wind began to blow, the mercury dropped several more degrees. We became uncomfortable and dug jackets out of our packs. We ate our lunches while sitting on the tundra.

We had already left the higher elevations and had hooked up with the ridge trail. There was abundant vegetation there. Alpine meadows overflowed with a mosaic of green carpet segments scattered in haphazard patterns and interspersed with clusters of various-sized glacier-dropped rocks.

In the few hours we had been together, I could see that Ryan loved his work. He was master of the domain. I recalled a time in my junior high days when I had wanted to be a forest ranger, a desire inspired by a book I'd read. I might have been happy with a job like Ryan's. It wasn't regret, but merely appreciation of what I saw around me. As we were eating our sandwiches, Ryan pointed toward the mountains on the other side of the Chilitna Valley.

"See that cut there? If you go up that stream, there's a creek that runs into it. I named it. Called it 'Hitch Creek.'"

When Jon and I didn't say anything, he grinned and said, "I took Kendra up there and proposed to her. Then we got *hitched* in Montana."

I felt as if I were living a little bit of history. After all, streams back home are all named and the mountains are all explored.

We finished eating and gulped down some water before setting out again. It was challenging terrain for me. "Down" isn't quite an accurate word to describe the trail's direction. It wound up, down, and around peaks in a general southerly direction. Ryan pointed out our destination, far to the southwest. We seemed to be headed in another direction. I asked why.

"Too steep and rocky," Ryan said. "No trail. Believe me, you wouldn't like it in that direction."

The trail ahead of us went to the top of a peak.

"Couldn't it have gone around it just as well?" I asked.

Ryan laughed.

"Dave Johnston laid out this trail, you know. He had his own way of doing things. He probably liked the view from up there."

I understood better when we reached a hilltop area strewn with huge boulders.

"Dave calls it 'Stonehenge,'" Ryan said.

The aesthetic value more than made up for the extra steps it took to get there. We rested and took pictures. The boulders, glacial erratics, were clustered on the one peak, but we were to see many individual ones in other locations, always looking out of place.

Most of the trail was rough. Ryan usually led the way, and I noticed that he stuck pretty much to the narrow path, following the custom of doing as little harm as possible to the environment. Jon and I tried to do the same. The path itself was worn several inches deep and there were roots growing through it, which made walking difficult. We crossed several small streams. There were fewer rock flows than we'd encountered on the Little Coal Creek Trail section in 1998, but enough to make me uncomfortable. Ryan was considerate, stopping to wait for us to catch up, and pausing often to point out flora and small animals. He kept watching through his binoculars for bears, but we saw none the whole trip.

Eventually, we reached the cutoff where we left the ridge trail and took the Ermine Hill Trail west toward Parks Highway. We started to lose altitude quickly. The Alpine meadows eventually gave way to brush. We skirted the edge of a deep ravine. The trail was so steep that I left it and made my own switchbacks before catching up with Jon and Ryan. They had no difficulty. The trail paralleled the quarter-mile-long Giardia Lake, giving us temporary relief from steep inclines. Below the lake, we could see tall, scraggly, and lonely black spruce scattered hundreds of yards apart. Each seemed to be clinging tenaciously to life, facing marginal altitude and soil conditions. Aspens, cottonwoods, and poplars gradually became more numerous. For the last few miles, we walked through an endless blueberry patch, stopping often to sample the quality of the berries. We had seen berries all over the ridge, even at the crash site, but they were small and bitter. Lower down, they were large and succulent.

Throughout the entire walk, Jon kept a watchful eye on me, seemingly concerned for my safety in the more difficult stretches. In steep descents, he stationed himself below me. He recognized—and rightly so—that I was having some difficulty. About midpoint in our descent, I had a poignant recognition of the role reversal that had taken place in our relationship.

We'd been on the trail a long time, and in spite of my fascination for the landscape, I wanted the hike to be over. Tired to my bones, I had to call for rest times at increasingly closer intervals. Time wasn't a big factor, since it wouldn't be dark until nearly midnight, but I began to fear that I couldn't finish the trek at the current pace. My cell phone couldn't pick up a signal, and I didn't want Millie and the others to worry about us. The younger men were patient, giving me time to sit on a log or rock until I was ready to go again. I had to admit that Ryan's helicopter idea had been a good one. I was embarrassed to think that I had considered going up and back the same day. Even two days would have been troublesome.

350 of 392 Touching the Ancient One

We followed a series of six switchbacks down toward Byers Creek and then paralleled the stream toward the highway before starting a heart-buster of a climb up toward the trailhead.

"Give me your pack," Ryan commanded.

I slipped out of it, thinking he was going to adjust the straps. He took it from me, and in one quick motion, hooked it over his own pack.

"Now take the lead," he said.

I tried to protest, but he'd have none of it. That last twenty minutes, even with my lightened load, was the longest of the whole hike. We had left the crash site at 11 AM and arrived at the trailhead at 8 PM. The trail length turned out to be nine miles.

"You did well," Ryan said as he unlocked the truck one of his helpers had left for us.

"I hope that when you're seventy-one, someone will carry your pack for you," I said.

He just smiled. It was hard, no doubt, for him to imagine being that age.

I was wiped out, of course, but happy. On the ride to Talkeetna, I savored the chance to rest and to put my rear end on something soft, yet, at the same time, I took pride in my body's aches and pains, and even at the rumble of my empty stomach. Badges of accomplishment, I mused, even if known only to myself.

I hung around our cabin Thursday, resting and processing photographs on my laptop. I wasn't as muscle-sore as I'd thought I would be. That evening, we went to dinner at Talkeetna Alaskan Lodge on the hill overlooking the town, the site of Cliff Hudson's award presentation. We invited Ryan and Kendra. She, beautiful and vibrant, added zest to our group. Dave Johnston was with us, as well. Dave was his usual humble, unpretentious self, shrugging off any mention of the mountaineering feats that had made him famous. We had hoped Cari and Galen would be with him, but they were out of the state.

During the evening, we discussed a couple of things I'd talked about with Ryan on the trail. One was naming the stream that flows westward from the peak behind the crash site. David Porter and Dave

Johnston had, in 1998, talked about calling it "Reunion Creek," to honor our reunion group.

The other discussion involved a question Ryan had asked me on the ridge as we were standing near a collection of twisted airplane parts.

"What would you like to see happen to this site?" he'd asked.

It was a question that I'd asked myself often, and one to which I'd given careful thought. His apparent sensitivity to the issue surprised me, though. I had a ready answer.

"This site is a sacred place to me. Men died here. Two of them were my good friends. Others, I feel I know through their families. I'd like to see it somehow set apart from the rest of the park and protected, but to be realistic, that may not be possible. It's less than a mile from the trail and quite accessible."

Now, at the table, Ryan said that he wanted to follow up on both issues—not to initiate them, but to investigate what was possible. Then decisions could be made.

The rest of our trip was less exciting, but excellent, nonetheless. We stayed in Talkeetna until Saturday, when we took Jon to the airport in Anchorage. Then Millie and I drove south to Seward, where we stayed for two nights. From there, we went back north to Palmer and hooked up with Tom and Nancy for an evening to celebrate their forty-fifth wedding anniversary. It was the second time we'd marked their anniversary in Alaska. We had dinner at Hatcher Pass Lodge, an out-of-the-way restaurant where we had to help chase a marmot out of the dining room before we could be seated.

Our hostess at the Iditarod House B & B in Palmer was Donna Gentry, retired Iditarod musher and 1980 Iditarod "Rookie of the Year." She entertained us with numerous dog-racing stories and anecdotes about Cliff Hudson from a time when she had lived in the bush.

We visited Cliff at the Pioneer Nursing Home the morning we left Palmer. Alzheimer's had taken its toll and it hurt to realize that there would probably be no more stories from that source. We were thankful, though, for the time since 1996 that we'd been able to spend with him.

We took leave of the DeVitos, who were going to Vancouver. We traveled toward Fairbanks, staying overnight at Healey in the Dome House B & B. Wednesday we were at Chena Hot Springs, where we soaked in near-boiling (or so it seemed) waters. I thought it might help my arthritis. Not much. We saw numerous moose in the north. Thursday and Friday nights were spent near Fairbanks at the secluded Cloudberry Lookout B & B on a little lake. Sean McGuire, the owner, had used an Alaskan old-growth tree as a center post for his bed and breakfast, with a spiral stairway going up to a lofty lookout tower. Tony Knowles, former two-term governor and U.S. Senate candidate, was also a guest the second night. He was congenial, chatting with Millie and me at some length.

Saturday, we stopped over in Talkeetna for a night, staying at the Latitude 62 Motel. We caught Ollie sitting at a table in front of the Hudson home and had a long talk. Her feelings about Cliff's condition were intense.

"Oh, how I'd like to have him back here the way it was before!" she said.

They had married in 1957. Since first meeting Ollie in 1996, I realized that, despite her modest disposition, she had a great influence on her family and their business. She was a strong woman, but it hurt to see how desperately she missed her husband.

We drove to Anchorage on Sunday, then on Monday started the twelve-hour trip home. Just as I'd had time to anticipate the coming adventure on the flight to Alaska, I now had time to reflect on the reality. Surely, it wouldn't be our last time in Alaska. I refused to let myself think that way. I resolved to start planning a return trip.

I considered the consequences of Jon's and my walk off the ridge instead of riding in the helicopter. Had it been worth it? I had experienced some feelings of accomplishment, even though there'd been some pain involved. Far more important than satisfying my ego, however, was my time with Jon, a reconnection on a level we hadn't experienced for years. We didn't talk a lot; the day itself seemed to make speech insignificant. I could tell he was enjoying himself. I'd hoped it would work out that way.

I was pleased when he pressed my arm at the Ermine Hill trailhead and said, "Dad, this has been a special day."

At the end, I felt that Kesugi Ridge and what had happened there long ago had taken on greater significance for Jon. It would be my last time on the ridge, but maybe he'd go back someday, perhaps with his own children—my grandchildren. Moreover, Greg might make it there, too. Such are an old man's musings.

Chapter Forty-five

On the evening of February 16, 2005, I received a telephone call from Wales.

A male voice with a smooth British accent said, "I'm looking for a man by the name of Rupert Pratt."

"Speaking."

"Are you a survivor of an airplane crash in Alaska in 1954?"

"Yes, I am!"

"Mr. Pratt, I'm David West-Watson, the son of William Ronald West-Watson. My father was aboard that airplane. He died in the crash."

I was stunned into silence for a moment. For nine years, I had periodically searched for W. West-Watson, writing to various military repositories and other organizations. I had even visited England and their Ministry of Defense, searching for a lead to someone in his family. I'd never come close to finding anyone. Now, with those few dynamic words from the United Kingdom, I knew the solution to a mystery was about to be revealed.

"David, I'm thrilled to hear from you!" I said, nearly choking on the words.

"I discovered an Internet picture of the memorial plaque in Alaska and found my father's name on it."

"I'm sorry we spelled it wrong."

I explained how that mistake had come about.

"It's all right. It's just a thrill to know it's there."

We talked at length. He told me that he was a captain in the Merchant Navy and had been only four years old when his father died. He had vague memories of that time.

"My mother is still alive. She is eighty-eight and in good health," he said.

He explained that he didn't know a lot about his father or his family. I was surprised to learn that William Ronald West-Watson had been a medical doctor. He had two brothers, and David was trying to find them.

"He was in the Royal Army Medical Corps on assignment to the American government in Washington," David said. "He was a medical liaison officer, along with other doctors from the United Kingdom."

"Do you know why he was on the flight?" I asked.

"I believe he was supposed to be on another scheduled flight, but the war office delayed making a decision about his agenda, which is why he ended up on the C-47."[67]

We promised to exchange information. I said I'd send him copies of our newsletters. The following day, I received an email that contained the following:

I have read all of the letters that my mother received, after he was killed, and various other documents relating to the crash. . . . We [David, his older sister, and their mother] returned [to the UK] on the *Queen Mary*, with some friends of the family, who were on the same trip, which I am sure is why there was so much haste. . . . He was buried on June 30, 1954.[68]

The following day, I sent copies of David's letter to Fox, Olson, and Sallis, gratified that I was able to relay such good news. Olson immediately sent David a letter, here reproduced in part:

I have some information to share with you about your dad that I hope might be useful to you. At one point, I struck up a conversation with your father, who had moved to the radio operator's position. (They didn't carry radio operators on intra-Alaska flights). Being trained in electronics I showed your father how to tune the radio to the broadcast band where he could listen to music. He was very appreciative and smiled and thanked me. That was the last word I had with him before the plane started breaking apart.

. . . About five years ago while sitting in a local restaurant, I was asked by a friend to tell him about the plane crash. A party sitting at a table next to me overhead what I was saying and came up to me afterward, saying, "Did I hear you mention the name West-Watson?" I said yes, and he went on to tell me that he had been a Colonel in the Army Medical Service in Washington, D.C. and was a close friend of your father. His name was Colonel Harry Powell (retired) and was back living in my hometown of Elkader, Iowa. He said that he drove your dad to the air base and saw him board the plane to take him on the first leg of his trip to Alaska. He was very broken up about the death of your father.

David, that same day, sent an answer to Olson, adding information about himself and his family:

To think that less than ten days ago, I was trying to find out about my father's two brothers on the Internet so that I could learn more about my father, and found unexpectedly "Explorenorth.com." Unfortunately, I have not met my uncles since I was about five years old, and have virtually no knowledge of my father's side of the family. However, I did make contact with a cousin "Andrew West-Watson" last year, once again via the Internet! I must contact him again and tell him about the new friends I have made.

. . . I have recently wanted to know more about my father, as a boy, teenager and young man, rather than the formal character I seem to have had in my mind. I know it must sound strange, but your email will always be special to me, as in one small sentence, you have given me something I have never had before. As I said, I thought of my father as a "formal" person, normally in uniform. I have referred to him as "my father," and heard others refer to him as "your father," but in the one simple sentence, "I have some information to share with you about your dad," you have given me "my *dad.*" I cannot put into words how much that means to me. I know you hardly knew him, but thank you. . . you and Rupert have finally made him human and very real, and for that I thank you both.

David soon let us know that he and his wife, Anne, would attend the upcoming reunion in Cincinnati. They were also planning a trip to Alaska, but hadn't ironed out all the details. David wanted to visit his father's grave at Fort Richardson and go to the crash site on Kesugi Ridge.

It was heartwarming to see an elusive mystery solved, bringing about some closure, not only for David West-Watson, but for us, as well. Now, only the family of copilot Edward Burge remained "unfound."

Maybe the phone will ring again someday, and a voice will say, "Is this Rupert Pratt who was in an airplane crash in Alaska in 1954?"

I would be delighted—but not surprised.

William Ronald West-
Watson, circa 1953
*Photo supplied by
David West-Watson*

June 3, 4, and 5 at Cincinnati turned out to be a reunion with its own flavor—as had been the case with all our reunions. Several LaDuke family members attended, as well as the DeVitos, Betschers, and Montgomerys. Ed Fox and I were the only survivors present. Alan and LeAnna LaDuke kicked things off with a cookout at Pattison Park in Owensville. Alan's culinary skills were extraordinary. The LaDuke family, in hosting the reunion while still grieving their loss, paid a great tribute to Eli. Social time at the Holiday Inn took place around the pool and in the spacious terrace area with its waterfalls.

At our Saturday evening meal at the Boomerang Grill, Alan's sister, Lisa, presented Alan with a homemade quilt that had pictures of both Eli and Alan in Air Force uniform. It contained patterns of stars and stripes, extending the patriotic theme. It was a beautiful work, full of love and caring. Lisa expressed her wish that the quilt might be expanded or that other quilts might be started. Maybe it was the birth of a new tradition for our group.

Minnie Montgomery held a signing party for the book of poetry, *The Mindspot Collective*, which contained several of her poems. I had long been aware of the creative abilities of the Montgomery family, and having known Huey for so long, I had assumed the ability had come through him. I've had to adjust my thinking to give Minnie equal credit.

From the section of the book that introduces her work, it's worth quoting, "At age three she began reciting short stories and continued throughout her school years. Minnie has always had a love for art and written word. Her family is bursting with gifts of artistry in all forms. . . . Now at the age of seventy, she continues to write and indulge in her own poetic legacy."[69]

Minnie honored us with a recitation of an unpublished poem about our reunion group.

An exciting aspect of the reunion was getting to know David and Anne West-Watson. Full of wit and enthusiasm, they added much to the reunion group. They shared their plans with us. On Monday, they'd leave for Alaska, visit the gravesite of David's father, and then tour Alaska in a camper. If the weather permitted, they'd hike to the crash site. Trying to minimize their potential disappointment about the hiking part, I pointed out that early June might be difficult, with still-wet trails and snow not yet melted.

David asked to speak to the group Saturday evening. He gave us a heartwarming and candid account of his attempts to gain information about his father. He spoke of Ed Olson's message that had finally given him "his dad" after so many years. That message had led him to seek out an uncle he hadn't seen for fifty years—as well as others in his father's family.

Cincinnati 2005—*Kneeling*: Nancy DeVito, Millie Pratt, Anne West-Watson. *Standing*: Ed Fox, Tom DeVito, Keith Betscher, David West-Watson, Rupert Pratt.

2005 reunion group—Cincinnati, Ohio

"I didn't know that my father played the piano," he said, obviously moved. "Such a small thing—"

Everyone in the room felt his humble and emotional acceptance of us. There were many wet eyes. Anne was supportive as he spoke, holding his hands tightly with her own.

We voted to meet again in two years. After a playful exchange with the West-Watsons about meeting in Wales, we opted instead for Orlando in February 2007.

After returning home, we waited anxiously for a report about the West-Watsons' Alaska trip. They had been guests of the Betschers while in Cincinnati and had promised to contact them before returning to the United Kingdom. Nine days later, Keith called us to relay the good news. David and Anne had realized every one of their goals. Even the weather had cooperated, and they had hiked to the crash site with little difficulty.

Anne wrote a few days later to say that nothing had prepared them for the "awesome power of Alaska." As for the trip to the crash site, it hadn't been the emotional extreme they had feared, but had seemed "so right." I knew just what she meant. Kesugi, once again, had welcomed us.

I think often about Alaska—and Kesugi Ridge in particular. "The Ancient One" has mystique and symbolism. I've probably pushed that symbolism to its limit at times. I have, nevertheless, spoken from my own perspective, which was shaped by personal images and spiritual beliefs. "Why did some of us live and some of us have to die," is a question I raised, and one pondered by members of our reunion group; it is perhaps a universal question. I desperately wanted to answer it—but could not. I have, however, had a concluding thought: I believe all that has happened to us is buried in the mind of God and will someday be revealed. But for now, we "see" only with peripheral glances. If one of the other crash survivors had told our story, the facts would have remained the same, but the interpretation undoubtedly would have been different, because he would see it through different eyes, and would have filtered it through his own metaphors. My eyes see mountains. They help connect me to the bigger reality—and that pleases me.

Endnotes

1. Salt Rock, West Virginia sits by the Guyandotte River, eighteen miles southeast of Huntington on Route 10. In 1953, it was a community of about two hundred people, made up of families who either farmed for a living or commuted to jobs in the Huntington area. Some did both. In any event, no one was far removed from agriculture. Family vegetable gardens were the rule, and many families kept milk cows on their land or in a common pasture. The community is not much changed today in size and appearance, but agriculture is not as apparent. I grew up there, except for two years during World War II when we lived in South Charleston and Spring Hill.

2. Parks AFB in California, which had opened for basic training in August, 1951, was then phasing out basic training and had become largely a staging area for overseas duty to Alaska and to the Pacific and Asian areas.

3. Non-Commissioned Officer

4. Base Exchange. The Army designated their counterpart as PX, or Post Exchange.

5. Sampson AFB, in the Fingerlakes region of New York State was, according to the HQ POC: AETC History Office Webmaster, one of three large training bases for the United States Air Force. Parks AFB in California and Lackland AFB in Texas were the other two. Sampson had been a training base for the Navy during the Second World War. It became an Air Force training base in November, 1950 when Lackland became overcrowded. Sampson was closed in July 1956, not long after a tragic barracks fire that took a number of lives.

6. The following men were, to the best of my knowledge, members of Sampson AFB Basic Training Flight 2547: Richard L. Boshart, Raymond Burgo, Bruno Caputo, Joseph H. Carlson, Samuel Caudle, Edmund G. Clark, Anthony M. Coppola, Thomas A. DeVito, Jr., David M. Dill, David L. Drake, Hobert W. Easthom, Percival D. Fox, Vincent Geoghegan, Charles W. Hicks, Lewis J. Jackson, John R. Kasha, Edward J. Knapp, James P. Knolly, Eddie Kuryn, Jr., Walter J. Magdalenski, Hermenio Paris, Rupert C. Pratt, Charles E. Sutovich, Edward J. Wadlinger, and James Williamson. The list was taken from June 23, 1953 orders sending members to different tech schools. It is not complete. Some members of the flight were set back because of illness. Sgt. James Gusha was the TI.

7. In the summer of 1953, sixteen Air Force men were in the Petroleum Analysis School at Bayonne, New Jersey: Richard L. Boshart, Andrew M. Breza, John E. Bullers, Samuel Caudle, Samuel W. Churchill, Thomas A. DeVito, Jr., David M. Dill, Paul F. Jackson, John R. Kasha, Edward J. Knapp, Robert A. Marsh, Donald R. McDonough, Frank K. Patterson, Rupert C. Pratt, Joseph A. Russell, and Murray Stolman.

8. Fort Wadsworth, in 1953, was a U.S. Army post located on the northeastern shore of Staten Island. The fort, built in the early nineteenth century, was created to guard the harbor of New York. Fort Wadsworth is now a national park.

9. Ladd AFB, located at Fairbanks in the north central part of the territory, was then "America's Farthest North Air Force Base." Ladd was assigned to the Army in 1961 and was renamed Fort Wainwright.

10. Seward was named for Secretary of State William H. Seward, who was responsible for the purchase of Alaska from Russia. It lies on the Kenai Peninsula at the western end of Resurrection Bay. Settled in 1903, it became a supply base for interior Alaska and the Yukon, largely because it remains ice-free all winter. The winter population is now about three thousand.

11. Top Cover for America, by John Cloe, p.160, states that Elmendorf AFB, built in 1940, is the largest Air Force base in Alaska and is headquarters of the Alaskan Air Command (AAC). It was first named Fort Richardson. In the early 1950s, a new Fort Richardson was built nearby and the old Fort Richardson became Elmendorf. In 1953, the commands of these two installations were still in the process of exchange.

12. Strategic Air Command

13. Distant Early Warning

14. The town of Nenana got its name from an Indian word meaning "a place to camp between the rivers," the rivers being the Tanana and the Nenana. The town is now homeport to a freight-carrying tug and barge fleet.

15. The 440-mile-long Tanana, formed from the joining of the Nabesna and Chisana Rivers near Northway, is basically a northwest flowing river. It empties into the Yukon River somewhat west of Fairbanks.

16. Fairbanks was started as a mining camp in 1902, during the gold rush.

17. The Chena empties into the Tanana River just south of Fairbanks.

18. POL (Petroleum, Oil, and Lubricants).

19. Personal letter from Rupert Pratt to Glenna Morrison, October 30, 1953.

20. The wired head bolt heater took the place of one of the head bolts on the engine block and kept it warm. It could be plugged into any electrical outlet. Many of the buildings on the base and in Fairbanks had banks of receptacles just for this purpose.

21. The air begins to crystallize at around -25 degrees, forming a fog of ice crystals, sometimes so dense that visibility extends only a few yards. Engine exhaust seems to add to the problem.

22. Personal letter from Rupert Pratt to Glenna Morrison, November 23, 1953.

23. Military Occupational Specialty

24. Travel Duty

25. The Douglas C-124 Globemaster II was a huge aircraft with two big doors in the front and a ramp for loading heavy equipment. It could carry 222 fully equipped troops.

26. He really was from Chapmansville, but I've forgotten his name. "Midkiff" is a common name in the Guyandotte River Valley, so I'm borrowing it.

27. I believe, after looking at a modern topographical map, that this was probably Mount Gordon, which is about three thousand feet high.

28. Although some literary license has been taken, this account is based on facts given to me by Nancy Humphries in a letter written on June 7, 1996. Nancy Humphries was the former Maudie Betscher, wife of Earl Betscher. She later married Col. John A. "Jack" Humphries, Jr. Nancy Humphries died in the spring of 2005.

29. I have taken some liberties in speculating about what Col. West-Watson might have been thinking during this time. However, the sequence of events is factual, substantiated by copies of letters recently sent to me.

30. The de Havilland Canada L-20 Beaver was a single engine, high wing utility-liaison aircraft used by the Air Force in arctic conditions.

31. This account is based on personal conversations with Col. Gene Pickel, and on information in the *United States Air Force Aircraft Accident Report #46975*, mainly depositions by other officers who were present.

32. According to the McDonnell-Douglas History Web Site, the Army Air Force first used The Douglas C-47 Skytrain Transport in 1941. The two-engine, 31,000 pound "Gooney Bird" can travel at 160 mph and ascend to 24,000 feet. Its wingspan is ninety-five feet six inches and it is sixty-three feet nine inches long. It could carry 6,000 pounds of cargo or twenty-eight soldiers in full battle gear.

33. The "record" consists of information from interviews, weather reports, checkpoint data, etc., which was printed in the official Air Force accident report.

34. Cliff Hudson's role as a pioneer bush pilot is a matter of record. In addition, he told me many extraordinary stories about his experiences in Alaska. His integrity and helpful nature are qualities attested to by his friends and neighbors, and by my own observations.

35. The material in chapter seven came mainly from three sources: interviews and written reports from the *United States Air Force Aircraft Accident Report #46975*, written statements on application forms from Switlik Parachute Company to become members of the Caterpillar Club, and from my personal interviews with the men involved. My own memories are vivid and consistent with what I had written in 1954.

36. The reason for this second unconscious state was later suggested to have been due to my loosening the parachute leg straps in the airplane. That had caused the crosspiece between the risers to be higher than normal, and when the canopy opened, the crosspiece may have struck me in the face.

37. Based on an Air Force investigative interview with Mr. Thompson and reported in the *United States Air Force Aircraft Accident Report #46975*.

38. Alaska Communication System.

39. Curry, Alaska, at mile 248.5 of the Alaska Railroad, was first a maintenance station for the railroad. Founded in 1922 and being halfway between Seward and Fairbanks, it became a good place to stop overnight. The hotel was built in 1923. Curry became a popular stop for tourists. A 540-foot suspension bridge was built over the Susitna River and a five-mile trail was laid to the top of Curry Ridge, where tourists could get a good view of Mt. McKinley. The Curry Hotel was improved over the years, but in 1957, it burned to the ground, killing three people. There is little there today.

40. I'm not sure if such bravado was meant to relieve her fears after the fact, but it was only partially true. I'd had confidence, as had Fox and Olson, that we would survive. Once we reached the bottom of the mountain and the deeper snow, however, we realized that we could never make it to the railroad. I admit some element of fear at that point.

41. My father, Rupert, was the oldest in a family of eight children. His brothers, Ausley and Maxwell, are also dead. Five sisters, Olga Keesee, Mary Harvey, Emegene Porter, Elizabeth Cremeans, and Lavonia Fry are all still living in the Huntington area. My grandparents were Alie and Hattie Pratt.

42. Lucian and Jenny Adkins had four children. Glenna, my mother, was oldest, followed by Cline, Milo, and Gaynelle.

43. Humphries, Nancy, letter to Rupert Pratt, June 7, 1996.

44. Charge of Quarters—a non-commissioned officer who answers the phone and oversees headquarters, in general, during non-working hours.

45. This list is not intended to be all-inclusive, but the following men were in POL at Ladd AFB December 3, 1954: *Tech Sergeants*: Leslie C. Hoover, James E. Lilly, and John P. Schmelz. *Staff Sergeants*: Ford Bonds, James A. Crawford, Richard M. Dorris, Henry E. Gage, Ray L. Hickman, Francis D. Higdon, Robert J. Seairs, Leo P. Sharon, Pinckney E. Steen, and Felix N. Thomas. *Airmen First Class*: Marvin W. Connell, Willie A. Druesedow, George Malone, Derril E. Pilkington, Eugene Posey, Leo A. Shamka, Theodore D. Souder, and Grover E. Swindle. *Airmen Second Class*: Nathaniel S. Bey, Kenneth L. Black, Carl C. Castle, Ralph Daniel, Harry L. Dellinger, Franklin D. Ehresman, Adam Gathers, Kenneth A. Haab, William N. Lathrem, Arden D. Lawley, James E. Luttrell, Gerald L. Main, Robert W. Metcalf, Eduardo Negron-Orsini, Rupert C. Pratt, James E. Ritchie, Thomas P. Sargent, Jr., Darell S. Weeks, and Lyle F. Whittier. *Airmen Third Class*: Henry B. Hall, Frank E. Stephensen, and James D. Weaver. *Airman Basic*: Robert R. Gilbert.

46. Kitchen Patrol

47. Some of the other men on this team were Speedy Hopson, Jim McClure, John Mills, Ken Crompton, Jim Boone, William Long, Eugene Wardell, Tom Donegan, Tony Elenio, Ase Davis, Joe Bond, and Dave Webb.

48. Less than six months before rotation back to the States.

49. Pro CD "Select Phone."

50. Delorme *Street Atlas USA.*

51. Much of this information about Ed Olson and family is used as he wrote it in a letter to me in 1996. I have, however, taken some liberties in rearranging and paraphrasing.

52. Greiner, James, *Wager with the Wind: The Don Sheldon Story*, 2nd Ed., St. Martin's Press, New York, 1982.

53. I got to know Col. Pickel well in the last few years. He died in January 2003.

54. Charles Casner, Civilian Crew Chief 5025th Maintenance.

I arrived at the scene of the wreckage on the evening of 10 February 1954. . . . The aircraft evidently disintegrated at high altitude and parts fell over an area of approximately four to five hundred yards radius. Both engines tore off in the air, fuselage parted from center section and broke in half over the wing. No evidence of fire was found. Fuel tanks were still intact with the center section. Nothing was found to indicate that a blast had occurred. . . . Rime ice was found on the prop blade, left hand prop, approximately 1/8 inch thickness. . . .

55. Rupert E. Lawrence, Major, USAF, Engineering Officer

Aircraft-C-47-45DK Number 45-895A
Date of Manufacture—July 1945
Total Flight Hours 8769

This aircraft airframe failed while in flight. These failures were apparently due to exceeding the design load limits of the aircraft airframe. The aircraft broke at approximately the bulkhead between the crew compartment and the main cargo compartment and it broke approximately one (1) foot forward of the main cargo door. The main cargo section between these breaks completely disintegrated. The vertical and horizontal stabilizers broke off outboard of the filits. The right wing broke at, but not through, the attach angles; The left wing broke five feet outboard of the attach angles; The left wing tip broke off; and the left wing rurther split lengthwise in several pieces. Both ailerons, both elevators, and the rudder were pulled loose at their hinges, and most control surfaces broke up into smaller pieces.

56. Report of T/Sgt Robert McFarlen

Investigation of the aircraft wreckage of aircraft C-47 895 leaves no doubt in my mind that there was a positive break up of the aircraft in the air. All indications are that the aircraft came all apart like it might [have] from a sharp pull out while the aircraft was in a dive at a high rate of speed. The only indication of any break up on the ground was on the left engine, which landed on the rocks and as it rolled, broke into pieces. . . . The only evidence of weakened or of structure corrosion was at the separation of the lower wing section. Fair flaking of metal was noted in the area adjacent to the exhaust stack. All structures of major importance were facing in a northerly direction and were separated by considerable distance. The overall wreckage was scattered in an area of a thousand yards or better. It is my opinion that the aircraft hit turbulence, severe in nature and upon partial recovery a portion of the left prop or the left engine itself came off and struck the fuselage in the vicinity of the left fuselage radio compartment tearing a large hole and then the aircraft rolling to the right dumping out passengers and cargo and in an effort to right the aircraft as it spiraled down excessive forces tore it apart and pieces fluttered down.

57. Captain John H. Walther, Accident Investigating Officer

I first investigated the wreckage of C-47 5895 on 10 February. I returned and remained on the scene from 11 February until 15 February. During this period I examined all the wreckage at least once and re-examined most of it again. The strong winds which came up on 12 and 13 February blew away a lot of the loose snow and uncovered numerous pieces not previously available.

In none of the wreckage was it possible to find any evidence of fire or explosion, either in the air or on the ground after impact. The tanks in the center section of the wings had fuel in them on my first examination, but the tanks were apparently ruptured on impact, because they were dry two days later.

I believe that the survivors heard the aircraft break up and assumed that there had been an explosion and flash.

58. Report of Major Delbert H. Ellis, Chief Maintenance Engineering Service Division, 22 September, 1954.

[In a closing report] Review of subject aircraft accident report and allied papers indicate the cause of the accident to be the disintegration of the aircraft due to aerodynamics leading beyond the stress limits of the aircraft.

59. Sheldon, Roberta, *The Heritage of Talkeetna*, Talkeetna Editions, Talkeetna, Alaska, 1995.

60. Before completing this book, I learned of an article about Nick Botner in the February–March 2004 *Mother Earth News* magazine, entitled "One Man's Apples: Oregon Orchardist Tends 6,000 Trees." It was written by Kris Wetherbee.

61. *Alaska Atlas and Gazetteer*, DeLorme Mapping, Freeport, Maine, 1992.

62. Sherwonit, Bill, "Three Accessible Parks," *Alaska*, August 1997.

63. Sherwonit, Bill, *Alaska Ascents*, Alaska Northwest Books, Seattle, 1996.

64. Bowers, Don, *Back of the Pack*, Publication Consultants, Anchorage, Alaska, 1998.

65. Russell, Dr. Carl, letter to Rupert Pratt, May 1996.

66. Now Marshall University. Located in Huntington, West Virginia, Marshall is an "up and coming" institution of higher learning.

67. That would turn out to be incorrect. In fact, a letter written by "Ronnie" to his wife revealed that he was held up a day because of fog in Seattle.

68. Col. West-Watson was buried at Fort Richardson with full military honors.

69. Montgomery, Chiquita, *The Mindspot Collective—An Anthology of Poems and Narratives*, Mindspot Press, Evansville, IN, 2005, p. 5.

Bibliography

Alaska Atlas and Gazetteer, DeLorme Mapping, Freeport, Maine, 1992.

Bowers, Don, *Back of the Pack*, Publication Consultants, Anchorage, Alaska, 1998.

Cloe, John Haile, with Michael F. Monaghan, *Top Cover for America*, Pictorial Histories Publishing Company, Missoula. Montana, 1984.

Connor, Cathy, and Daniel O'Haire, *Roadside Geology of Alaska*, Mountain Press Publishing Company, Missoula, Montana, 2001.

Elias, Scott A., *The Ice-Age History of Alaskan National Parks*, Smithsonian Institution Press, Washington, D.C., 1995.

Flynn, George Q., *The Draft, 1940–1973*, University Press of Kansas, Lawrence, Kansas, 1993.

Fort Wadsworth Website, http://anand2.home.att.net/sp/Fort.htm.

Greiner, James, *Wager with the Wind: The Don Sheldon Story*, Rand McNally & Co., New York, 1974.

Greiner, James, *Wager with the Wind: The Don Sheldon Story*, 2nd Ed., St. Martin's Press, New York, 1982.

HQ POC: AETC History Office Webmaster, http://www.aetc.randolph. af.mil/ho/atc50s.htm, Randolph AFB, TX.

Humphries, Nancy, Letter to Rupert Pratt, June 7, 1996.

Kavanagh, James, and Raymond Leung, *Alaska Trees and Wildflowers*, Waterford Press, 2001.

McDonnell-Douglass History Website, http://www.boeing.com/ history/mdc/skytrain.htm, April 2003.

Montgomery, Chiquita, *The Mindspot Collective—An Anthology of Poems and Narratives*, Mindspot Press, Evansville, IN, 2005.

Olson, Edward, *The C-47 Survivors' Sentinel*, A Newsletter, Elkader, Iowa, 1996–2004.

Pratt, Rupert, letters to Glenna Morrison, 1953–1957.

Prudential Alaska Relocation Website, http://www.move2alaska. com/alaska_communities/seward/history.asp.

Russell, Dr. Carl, letter to Rupert Pratt, May 1996.

Schofield, Janice J., *Alaska's Wild Plants—A Guide to Alaska's Edible Harvest*, Alaska Northwest Books, Anchorage, 2004.

Sheldon, Roberta, *The Heritage of Talkeetna*, Talkeetna Editions, Talkeetna, Alaska, 1995.

Sherwonit, Bill, *Alaska Ascents*, Alaska Northwest Books, Seattle, 1996.

Sherwonit, Bill, "Three Accessible Parks," *Alaska Magazine*, August 1997.

Switlik Parachute Company, Applications to join the Caterpillar Club, 1954.

United States Air Force Aircraft Accident Report #46975, USAF Historical Research Agency/RSQ, Maxwell AFB, Alabama, 1954.

Wetherbee, Kris, "One Man's Apples: Oregon Orchardist Tends 6,000 Trees," *Mother Earth News*, February–March 2004, Ogden Publications, Inc., Topeka, Kansas.

Printed in the United States
108778LV00006B/46-81/A

9 781587 365812